THE
UNHOLY
WAR

BYU VS. UTAH

THE UNHOLY WAR

BYU VS. UTAH

by

Phil Miller and
Dick Rosetta

Forewords by Paul James and Bill Marcroft

Salt Lake City

This is a Peregrine Smith Book, published by
Gibbs Smith, Publisher
P.O. Box 667
Layton, UT 84041

Design by Michael Overton
Cover art by Keith Larson
Edited by Paul VanDenBerghe

Printed and bound in the United States of America

Library of Congress Cataloging-in-Publication Data

Miller, Phil 1962-
        The unholy war : BYU vs. Utah / by Phil Miller and Dick Rosetta ;
foredwords by Paul James and Bill Marcroft.
        p. cm.
        ISBN 0-87905-560-X
        1. Brigham Young University—Football—History. 2. Brigham Young
Cougars (Football team)—History. 3. University of Utah—Football—History. 4. Utah
Utes (Football team)—History. I. Rosetta,
Dick, 1941- . II. Title.
GV958.B75M55 1997
796.332'63'0979224—dc21   97-13814
                                                                           CIP

ONTENTS

Foreword I

Having been a witness to the great BYU-Utah football rivalry in this state for forty-five years, I would like to offer a few verses of scripture from the "Gospel According to Paul."

And it came to pass during the time of the second millennium that Paul came down from his humble dwelling on top of Mount Gilead to a place known as Point of the Mountain. Looking to the Lands of the North, Paul saw only darkness, evil, and iniquity. Paul said, "Man, this is ugly." So he colored them Red—after brimstone and fire and he called it the Land of Ut (rhymes with Nut) or Utville (later to be known as Uteville).

And then Paul turned his gaze to the Lands of the South, and there he saw only goodness and light and purity. And Paul said, "Yeah, that's more like it!" And the color of Lands of the South was Blue, like unto the beauty of the sky, and he called it Happy Valley or the Land of Coog.

Now, in those days, the Land of Coog was ruled by the Great King Edward—Edward the Droop Mouth. Edward was called "The Droop Mouth" because never in his life had he smiled, never! For almost a quarter of a century, nothing but joy and happiness filled the Land of Coog. But Edward still could not smile. He only folded his arms and drooped at the mouth.

During that period of joy and harmony in Happy Valley there was at the same time nothing but gnashing of teeth, great wailing, and suffering in the Land of Ut and Gomorrah.

Well, it came to past that near the end of the second millennium that a new tyrannical dictator came to power in Utville. A red-haired, red-faced tyrant by the name of Ronnie-Mac, or Ronnie Mac the Red! Ronnie-Mac saw all the suffering and devastation in Ut. And at the same time, he saw all of the joy and harmony in the Land of Coog. And it made him mad. So Ronnie-Mac made plans for the total destruction of Happy Valley.

Ronnie-Mac and his evil sorcerers concocted a deadly virus, with the intent to spread a plague over the entire Land of Coog. This deadly virus was named simply U-34-31. For a period of two years, U-34-31 was inflicted upon the entire population of Happy Valley with devastating results. And as the people to the South suffered and grieved, Ronnie-Mac and his chief diabolical general Chad Kaa Ha Ha Ha Ha laughed at their misery!

Not satisfied with the devastating results from U-34-31, Ronnie-Mac and his warriors went for the jugular with an even more potent poison called U-34-17! The entire population of Happy Valley was on the brink of complete annihilation.

Still, a valiant few Coogs had faith that their great King Droop Mouth could save them. They prayed fervently in their temples; they increased their tithes and offerings; they fasted; they asked for a miracle. Despite all their efforts, the pestilence created by Ronnie-Mac threatened to get worse.

It came to pass in the ninety-sixth year of the second millennium that Ronnie-Mac, now consumed by visions of power, created a monstrous weapon of mass destruction. This biological monstrosity was called Alafa'am Utamauf.

Alafa'am Utamauf was a giant much larger than Goliath. The jubilant people of Utville worshipped the new monster, but with little or no education, they couldn't correctly pronounce his name. All the Ut's were dyslexic, so they called him Fuamatu-Ma'afala.

There was also in the Land of Ut at the time a certain simple-minded scribe who recorded all the deeds of Ronnie-Mac. This scribe, like Edward the Droop Mouth, also had an affliction. Not a droop of the mouth, but an over-running of the mouth. The nice but simple-minded fellow was named, appropriately, Mouth-Croft, and he always called Ronnie-Mac's warriors by their first names in battle—Rocky, Kevin, Keith, Brandon, and Billy. But Mouth-Croft never said Chris. He always said Chris Fuamatu-Ma'afala. Always.

To combat the monster, Good King Edward searched all parts of the world to find valiant warriors. Answering his call were Lewis of Chad, Itula of Mili, Shay of Muirbrook, and Henry of Bloomfield. From Armenia came Sarkisian, the greatest magician in all the world. And still others came to Good King Edward's aid: McKenzie the Swift and Jenkins the Swifter, and bombs of "K" not "A"—Kaipo and K.O., and "M" weapons, Morgan and McTyre. King Edward had assembled the greatest, most powerful arsenal in history as he prepared for the day of judgment!

It came to pass that on that fateful day of Armageddon that King Droop Mouth was totally prepared, while in the Land of Ut, Ronnie-Mac and his monstrous armies still laughed, drunken with memories of past victories and falsely deluded with glorious predictions from the unwitting town crier Mouth-Croft.

On the battlefield of Rice, the results were inevitable. Sarkisian the Magnificent became Sarkisian the Heisman with his deadly bombs to K.O. and Kaipo. Chad of Lewis, Shay of Muirbrook, and Henry of Bloomfield overwhelmed the giant Fuamatu-Ma'afala.

And, as all good tales have a happy ending, so does this one. On that fateful day in the ninety-sixth year of the second millennium, King Edward the Droop Mouth celebrated a huge victory over Ronnie-Mac and his evil forces of darkness.

The battle cry of Ut by five was banished forever from the land and a new battle cry was heard as predicted by Paul. The new cry was "Coogs by five, plus five, plus five and five more."

Yes, it was a glorious battle with many heroes and many wounded warriors, and even more wounded egos.

But when the battle was over, for the first time in history King Edward the Droop Mouth unfolded his arms . . . and he smiled!

P.S. Just moments after delivering this so-called Gospel According to Paul, I was stricken with severe chest pains that later necessitated six-bypass heart surgery.

Could someone be sending a message about tinkering with the Gospels?

PAUL JAMES

Foreword II

When I started covering sports in Utah (back when it all began), the Utah-BYU football game was anything but a rivalry. Back then, the state school was the University of Utah. The big rivalry game occurred on Thanksgiving Day between the Utes and Utah State. The Aggies were competitive. BYU was not.

Utah had won all the games with the Y with the only exceptions since 1922 coming in 1942 and 1958. It wasn't until Tommy Hudspeth brought in the Marines in 1965 and BYU started to win that the Utah fans turned from the north and started looking south for the big game.

Just after LaVell Edwards took over as head coach in 1972, I am told he had a special meeting with his coaching staff to discuss not what they could do, but rather what they couldn't do. Even though running back Pete VanValkenburg, a Hillcrest High School graduate, would lead the nation in rushing in LaVell's rookie season, there was a consensus that BYU had to go in another direction. They conceded they couldn't get the great running backs year after year. However, big homegrown Utah blockers were plentiful. They didn't have to be quick to pass-block . . . just big.

So LaVell looked to the airways. Enter California quarterback Gary Sheide and the passing game.

Then it was Utah, the traditional running school, that wasn't competitive. The outcome has to be in doubt each year to create a truly great rivalry. And for too long there was little doubt about the outcome.

Ron McBride's return to Utah as head coach added the necessary ingredient and the necessary respect to reestablish the rivalry. When he first arrived in Salt Lake City as an offensive line coach under Wayne Howard in 1977, McBride's dream was kindled. He wanted to be the Utes' head coach. He traveled to Wisconsin (1983–84) and Arizona (1987–89) as an assistant to prepare for the job, all the while endearing himself to the Utah faithful—players and fans alike. Because of his honest, straightforward, down-home approach to people, McBride made the word family mean more than any coach before him. McBride's extended family and his wife Vicki were a big part of the love affair, and it included all Utes past and present. McBride was so personable that boosters started standing in line to help him. He got their respect immediately.

The respect that McBride and Edwards have for each other, as shown by the series of commercials for Bank One, brought the rivalry to full maturity.

In spite of the attendant fanaticism of some fans (on both sides), I believe Utah versus BYU is the greatest rivalry in all of sports—because of its uniqueness.

Dick and Phil certainly picked the right title for their book. No rivalry in college athletics involves religion as much as Utah and BYU. That's what makes it so unique.

Religion never comes up when Notre Dame and Southern Cal fans go at it. SMU-Texas and Baylor-Texas A&M are just a couple of great games between in-state rivals rich in football tradition. When a Longhorn says he hates the Mustangs it doesn't mean he hates Methodists. An uninformed Aggie can question the parentage of a Bear and it doesn't demean the morality of Baptists.

But let a Utah coach say "I hate BYU!" like Wayne Howard did after his first Utah-BYU game, and it instantly translates into "I hate Mormons." At least that's what most of the Provo-based press assembled in Cougar Stadium that day in 1977 heard with a collective gasp.

Coach Howard went into that game thinking LaVell Edwards was a nice guy. But when quarterback Marc Wilson was reinserted in the game to throw one more pass completion for an NCAA record and score one more touchdown in the final seconds with the outcome already decided, Wayne felt LaVell had rubbed it in. It was Howard's contention LaVell had tried to humiliate the Utes.

When BYU assistant coach Doug Scovil yelled at the Utah bench, "Get your dogs off the field," Coach Howard got his first taste of the Utah-BYU rivalry, that this was not just another football game. When they met at midfield, Coach Howard told Coach Edwards what he thought of him. Howard later said to me that he told Edwards, "Bill Marcroft said you were a nice guy. I found out differently today." BYU starting defensive tackle Mekeli Ieremia was standing next to them. Ieremia started to cry and asked Howard to stop saying those things about his coach. Wayne turned from LaVell, faced the big defensive tackle and said, "You I love, him I hate." LaVell's recollection was that Wayne was fairly incoherent. He couldn't recall what Howard had said. But the word "hate" was on the table. You just don't say that word in Utah.

Politicians get into the act as well. Members of the predominantly LDS Utah State legislature have accused the U of being "anti-Mormon," or is that "anti-

BYU"?

Recruiting of athletes also cuts across religious lines. "If you are LDS, you go to BYU!" Sentiment in some circles goes so far as to suggest "the Almighty wants you to be a Cougar." That's what several players and their parents have told me—even after some of them signed with BYU.

I remember one I interviewed in particular; it was with a seven-foot-six basketball player after he announced he was signing with the Y. He lived in the arid Castledale area, so I facetiously asked, "Did you go out in the desert and pray about your choice?" He answered, seriously, "Yes." And? . . . "God told me to go to BYU." I never aired that sound bite.

Wayne Howard resigned as a winning coach at Utah, in part because of the ornery mail received after making that accepted-anywhere-else comment about hating his number-one rival. He said one letter in particular got to him. The writer (a self-confessed BYU fan) suggested he leave the state, but reminded Howard that no matter where he went, they'd get him—if not in this life, then in the hereafter.

This is indeed a rivalry that goes beyond.

BILL MARCROFT

INTRODUCTION

Every November, usually the next-to-last Saturday, time stands still in Utah. As in those football bastions like Palo Alto, Lawrence, Columbus, Seattle, or Tuscaloosa, the weekend is defined by The Game. You may have been for the Republican candidate for president of the United States or you may have been for the Democrat candidate in early November. But in late November, you are either for BYU coach LaVell Edwards or Utah coach Ron McBride. There is no Independent candidate here. It's either Edwards or McBride.

Mormon church wards, saintly haunts for fifty-one weeks of the year, become the pulpits of argument: Brigham Young University Latter-day Saints versus University of Utah Latter-day Saints, husband versus wife, brother versus brother, sister versus sister, uncle versus aunt—and heaven knows, cousin versus cousin. In cathedrals, synagogues, and sanctuaries of all religious persuasions, it is crimson and white versus royal blue and white. It is a late-autumn rite of passage—the BYU versus Utah football game on whose verdict rides fireside oneupsmanship fodder for the long winter months. It consumes Utah's sports constituency simply because with the advent of the 1990s and McBride's challenge to Edwards's two-decade rule, came the dawning of an honest-to-goodness rivalry.

It wasn't always so. Not until Bishop LaVell Edwards began his coaching mission in Provo in 1972 anyway. Prior to the arrival of the Utah State (bachelor's) and Ute (master's) graduate, BYU's claim to fame in sports dialogue with their Ute brethren was relegated to basketball. It was the Utah NCAA title of 1944 and NIT championship of 1947 against BYU's NIT championships. Coaches Vandal Peterson and Jack Gardner of Utah on one side, and Gardner's Naismith Hall of Fame colleague Stan Watts of BYU on the other. It was Utes Arnie Ferrin, Art Bunte, Billy "The Hill" McGill, and Jerry Chambers against Cougars Mel Hutchins, Joe Richey, John Fairchild and Dick Nemelka. BYU had won conference basketball titles—three in the Rocky Mountain Athletic Conference and five in the Western Athletic Conference. Utah had seven such crowns under Peterson and Gardner. But football? Utah State was Utah's most contentious rival. BYU was an afterthought, with just two victories (1942 and 1958) in the storied series that began in the 1890s and, with a brief interruption due to the school's concern with the violent nature of the sport, continued in 1922.

Then came 1972 and the elevation of Edwards from an assistant's post, which he had held since 1962, to the head coach's position. Seven coaches had preceded him since 1937, but only one, his immediate predecessor, Smilin' Tommy Hudspeth, had managed a conference championship. Hudspeth piloted an aggressive troupe of ex-Marines to the 1965 WAC title—even introducing a prolific passer named

Virgil "The Blue Darter" Carter to an ages-old, staid ground attack. But it would be the only title for the Cougars and after an eight-year run and a 39–42–1 record, Hudspeth went the way of beleaguered coaches Hal Mitchell (8–22), Tally Stevens (6–15), and Hal Kopp (13–14–3). There had been some excitement via a three-game winning streak over Utah (1965–67), but by 1971, the Utah County constituency and Y graduates witnessed their program's slide into ingratiating setbacks to the hated Utes, including a heartbreaking, last-second 17–15 loss at Provo in 1971. Saddled with a fourth straight losing season, Hudspeth was given his walking papers. And BYU turned to Edwards, the school's assistant line coach, who as head coach at Granite High School in Salt Lake City in the 1950s had failed to compile a winning record. But he did have a thorough knowledge of the single-wing rushing formation, and BYU had an up-and-coming runner named Eldon "The Phantom" Fortie on its roster.

Edwards catalogued some helpful hints through tours with Mitchell and Hudspeth. Most of them were rushing-oriented. Fortie's electrifying running in the 1962 season was a personal triumph for Edwards, but it was the quick-strike aerial pyrotechnics of Carter, who led the nation in passing and total offense in 1966, that tugged constantly at Edwards's psyche. Why, "The Blue Darter" even collected some Heisman Trophy votes. We'll throw the ball, Edwards instructed his staff during that first spring practice of 1972. So what happens? Running back Pete VanValkenburg led the nation in rushing. The next year, Edwards got himself a passer and the team went 5–6, which would be the only losing season in his career. By 1974, strong-armed quarterback Gary Sheide was at the controls. In the first two games, BYU was 0–2. Then the Cougars really went airborne. They won seven of their last eight games, trounced Utah 48–20, and received a Fiesta Bowl invitation, the school's first-ever postseason appearance.

The conveyor belt at Quarterback U had been fired up. Sheide begat Gifford Nielsen, who begat Marc Wilson, who begat Jim McMahon, who begat Steve Young, who begat Robbie Bosco, who begat Ty Detmer, who begat John Walsh, who begat Steve Sarkisian. With all-American honors, Davey O'Brien Award winners, and Detmer's Heisman Trophy—BYU has ruled the collegiate football passing world for the last quarter of the twentieth century.

But it took only one season for Edwards to launch a reign of terror over Utah. On November 18, 1972, in newly named Rice Stadium (Salt Lake businessman Robert L. Rice donated $1 million to renovate old Ute Stadium and install AstroTurf), the Cougars won 16–7. "I knew you wouldn't let me down," shouted a teary-eyed Edwards to his players from atop a bench in the visitors' locker room. His Cougs would let him down only two times in the next twenty meetings with the Utes, establishing one of the most dominant in-state runs of all time and igniting an unholy war between students and alumni of the two schools.

In the meantime, Utah was hiring and firing its way through five football coaches. It wasn't that the Utes couldn't beat BYU; they couldn't beat much of anybody. They got a guy, Wayne Howard, who did beat BYU once and posted two eight-win seasons, but they let him get away. They hired a defensive-minded coach in Chuck Stobart and fired him after three seasons: 6–5–1 in his last campaign, including a hard-fought 24–14 loss to the eventual national-champion Cougars in 1984. They got an offensive-minded coach in Jim Fassel—he even beat BYU once in 1988—and they fired him. Almost as if trying to repeat BYU's successful track record in rewarding the allegiance of Edwards, Utah signed two-term Ute assistant Ron McBride in 1989.

Steve Griffin/THE SALT LAKE TRIBUNE

Their fans may be bitter rivals, but Ron McBride and LaVell Edwards have long been good friends.

No one expected any miracles. Utah had been the nation's worst Division I defensive team under Fassel. Despite the fact his offenses captured national titles, including one led by prolific left-handed quarterback Scott Mitchell in 1988, Utah lost games 56–49 and 67–20. It was too much for new athletic director Chris Hill and his dwindling number of big-time supporters when Utah was skewered 70–31 by BYU in 1989, with an injured Mitchell on the sidelines and only weeks away from forfeiting his senior season and opting for the NFL draft. Fassel had to go. You could hear the snickering from Utah County—that's five coaches in and five coaches out at Futile U. It will be fun again in church today.

Enter McBride and the launching of Utah's New Deal. There were no quick-fix antidotes offered. Nor were any forthcoming, despite a two-game winning streak to start the 1989 season. There was, however, something infectious about McBride's tactics. Even losses of 45–22 and 48–17 to BYU his first two seasons were at least palatable. The Utes could at least steal a look now and then at their neighbors in Sunday morning sacrament meetings. After all, the Cougars weren't setting win-loss records, or national statistics, on fire despite winning WAC titles. Somehow, it seemed the McBride mystique was catching hold. By 1992, the Utes played the Cougars tough in a 31–22 loss in Salt Lake and managed to land the school's first bowl bid in twenty-eight years. And Edwards and McBride genuinely seemed to like each other, a friendship that was not reflected in the adversarial relationship of their schools' fanatical fans. For Cougar fans, any recognition of a Ute antagonist was surely patronizing. Like a sore thumb, Edwards's dominance of the Utes, nineteen wins and two losses, left Ute fans to their annual wait-till-next year moaning.

Until 1993. From the ashes of a season-opening 38–0 loss at Arizona State, the Utes rallied behind ironman defensive lineman Luther Elliss to forge a 6–5 record heading to Provo for the season finale. It had been twenty-two years since Utah had won in Cougar Stadium. It was a vulnerable BYU team, one that had lost four games in a row for the first time since 1973. Still, BYU was 5–4, and it was Utah, after all, that was coming to town. A late field goal by the Utes' Chris Yergensen lifted Utah to an inexplicable 34–31 win over the WAC's co-champion Cougars. A small band (Utah was limited to 750 fans) of euphoric Ute spectators tried to tear down the north goalposts through which Yergensen's kick had sailed. The main thing, however, was that Utah had ripped down an impenetrable curtain. The LDS brethren north of Point of the Mountain—not part of the 45,000 or so who migrate south from Salt Lake County every fall Saturday afternoon—could sit proudly in the front pew now, if, as many suspected, it were only for a year, as had been the case with 1978 and 1988 Utah victories.

There was no way anyone could have foreseen the abrupt turn this rivalry was to take. BYU finished 1993 with a 6–6 record, including a loss in the Holiday Bowl to Ohio State. That they won the WAC again—a three-way tie with Fresno State and Wyoming—was of little consolation. The Cougars had lost six games for the first time since 1973. A six-loss season was the kind of stuff Utah was made of, and sure enough, after a 28–21 loss to USC in the Freedom Bowl, the Utes finished 7–6, their second straight six-loss campaign. But the long-suffering Ute faithful were beginning to strut a little. In three years, the school had twenty wins and seventeen losses, the first such three-year success in forty years.

Lo and behold, the tides of change were indeed washing in. Buoyed by the victory over BYU the previous November, the Utes started 1994 with eight straight wins and by Halloween reached the nation's top ten—hallowed ground usually reserved in the Beehive State for the Cougars. Recovering from a two-game WAC skid in November, Utah edged BYU at Rice Stadium with another odds-defying 34–31 verdict. Although Ute buttons of pride were popping from Bountiful to Bluffdale, and despite an electrifying, last-second 16–13 victory in the Freedom Bowl over the University of Arizona, Utah had finished a season no better than BYU. Both were second in the WAC, both had won a bowl game, and both had won ten games. Old hat for the Cougars, the brethren preached. One difference: Utah had finished tenth in the Associated Press poll (eighth in the CNN/*USA Today*), while BYU was number eighteen in AP and tenth in CNN/*USA Today*. Don't think that ranking tidbit wasn't passed through the pews on Sundays.

Neither school, nor their fanatical fans, had much to brag about in 1995. BYU struggled to a 2–3 start and Ute fans were naturally crowing that their team had a lot to do with it. You know, those dual 34–31 losses to Utah were dogging the Cougs every step of the way. But the Cougars' Ute bashers were making hay out of the 3–4 start of that flash-in-the-pan bunch up north, too. No way, they were convinced, despite both schools rallying with four-game win streaks, would Utah be able to come to Provo on November 18 and interfere with the Cougars' WAC championship celebration.

Uh, check that. A swarming Ute defense forced BYU quarterback Steve Sarkisian into four interceptions, and the less-heralded Ute QB Mike Fouts hurling two touchdown passes, and 276-pound freshman running sensation Chris Fuamatu-Ma'afala chipping in with 108 yards and two TDs, Utah escaped Provo with a 34–17 victory. A third straight victory over the Cougars. Mount Timpanogos trembled. Normally bombastic Cougar faithful fell silent. Some say church attendance fell off in Utah County while reaching all-time highs in Salt Lake County. Membership in the Ute booster club, the Crimson Club, rose dramatically. For the first time in nearly thirty years, Utah had beaten BYU three straight years in football. And this time, there was a WAC championship—so what that it was a four-way tie—as a bonus for the Utes.

But was it a precursor of bad things to come when the co-WAC champion Utes were unable to secure a postseason bowl bid? Not that a bowl snub of BYU was any consolation. But cheez, no December football? Why, BYU had tied for the title before and ended up in San Diego's Holiday Bowl in 1993. What gives, moaned

Ute fans.

The answer came in 1996. Handed the WAC kingpin role always reserved for BYU, the Utes were christened WAC champs-to-be by the conference media and by many national sports publications. Utah immediately botched it. One week after BYU's Pigskin Classic victory over Texas A&M in Provo on August 24, a ver-

This is the rivalry—and for Utes, there's no better feeling than beating BYU, as Greg Smith and Joe Clausi remind Cougar John Hunter in 1988.

Steve Griffin/THE SALT LAKE TRIBUNE

dict that stunned the collegiate football world, Utah succumbed 20–17 at Utah State, stunning the whole of Utedom. All of King McBride's horses couldn't put the Utes back together again, although wins over non-conference foes Stanford and Kansas and a seven-game winning streak kept the Utes at least footnote-close to the Cougars. Meanwhile, BYU steam-rollered its way through an 11–1 season, rising steadily in the polls along the way. Almost on cue, Utah was blasted by Rice 51–10, while BYU drilled the same Owls 49–0 one week later. A Cougar feather merchant boasted that BYU (based on the schools' respective showings against Rice) should be favored by eighty-seven points over the Utes come November 23 in Salt Lake City.

It wasn't that bad. But BYU's 37–17 victory was thorough enough to convince veteran series observers that the pendulum had swung back the Cougars' way, that 1993 through 1995 had been an aberration. In fact, some felt the win was as insulting as the old days of 55–7 and 70–31 BYU triumphs. For heaven's sake, the Cougars had disdained their feared passing game and shoved their running game down Utah's throat with 376 yards on the ground and four rushing touchdowns. Translation: Edwards sent a message that, after twenty-five years, his scheme still included the run. And BYU sideline jesters were pointing out that, run or pass, the Cougars now owned a 4–3 record over Utah in the nineties.

On the Cougars went—where in July the Utes were projected to go—to the WAC championship game in Las Vegas. Handed a "gift" 28–25 overtime victory by Wyoming in Sam Boyd Stadium, BYU overcame a perceived snub by the national Bowl Alliance to land a New Year's Day Cotton Bowl game with Kansas State. As they had done in August with the Big Twelve's favored Texas A&M Aggies, the Cougars rode late-game heroics by Sarkisian to a 19–15 upset win over the Big Twelve's number fourteen-ranked Wildcats. Acclaim in the form of a number-five national ranking followed.

The more things had changed, the more they had stayed the same. BYU once again was king of the hill in the Cougar-Ute rivalry. Four days prior to BYU's supreme bowl moment, the Utes had been embarrassed by the University of Wisconsin, 38–10, in Tucson's Copper Bowl. Utah was left to assess the damage of a season gone awry. As was the norm for most of the previous twenty-five years, the mocking cries of BYU fans reverberated across the state . . . nyeh, nyeh, nyeh-nyeh, nyeh. And especially in the LDS wards, where the hymn "Come, Come, Ye Saints" might as well have been "Rise and Shout, the Cougars Are Out!" More accurately, "Rise and Shout, the Cougars Are Back!" Out or back, the Utes were still trying to catch them.

THIS IS A BYU FAN

A Brigham Young University football fan is first, a foaming-at-the-mouth, face-painted-blue-and-white, I-hate-Utah, I-love-Cosmo, and pour-on-the-touchdowns kind of person.

Second, a BYU fan goes to the ward house on Sunday to repent for his/her foaming-at-the-mouth, face-painted-blue-and-white, I-hate-Utah, I-love-Cosmo, and pour on-the-touchdowns demeanor. And to gloat over beating the Utes.

You see, we have a lot of years to make up for . . . like forty to forty-five of them. Like getting whipped by six or seven touchdowns every season by your Ike and Cactus Jack.

Say what you want about us running up the score against the Uteskis, the scoreboard lights blinking totals like forty-six and forty-eight and fifty-one and thirty-eight. And that was just in the seventies.

We remember. Oh, do we remember.

We remember the doofmiers demeaning our mothers and our church with language befitting a gutter derelict.

We remember the booze-breath sops exposing their naked chests to our beloved prophet with epithets that would make a death-row inmate blush. The letters painted over sweaty, stinky hair that covered a beer belly the size of the block "U" is the stuff of which some simpleton Uteski fans are made . . . "BYU Sucks!" Such ingenuity!

We remember the Rice Stadium snowballs raining down on our players, coaches, cheerleaders, and band members. The missiles were more accurate than most Uteski quarterbacks ever dreamed of being. And they certainly landed with more impact than most Uteski blockers. Or tacklers.

We remember the repugnant fans rocking the Cougar team bus back and forth as it halted in front of the Rice Stadium dressing quarters for a 1970s game. And we remember our coach LaVell Edwards turning toward his assistant and former Uteski player Norm Chow and quipping, "This figures—it's Chow's alma mater." All 2,000 of

those fans jammed into rickety Rice to watch our Cougs rock the Uteskis on the gridiron while dodging snowballs.

We remember the days of Ike Armstrong and Cactus Jack Curtice piling on the touchdowns late in the game and laughing that church missionaries couldn't do anything about it. Then the missionaries got stronger and quicker and older and they got all those touchdowns back in the seventies, eighties and most of the nineties. And then Uteski fans said, "Missionaries suck!" And we chuckled.

We remember the red paint on our blue fire plugs; the red paint on our white "Y" on the side of Mount Timpanogos; and the red paint at midfield in Cougar Stadium. And we remember the red faces of the Uteski players as our slow, white, mostly Utah-born returned missionaries ran past their sprinters imported from all corners of California.

Mark A. Philbrick

Seventeen times since LaVell Edwards became BYU's coach, the 65,000 fans at Cougar Stadium have celebrated being number one in the WAC, and occasionally, their aspirations run higher, as after this 1990 upset of the nation's number-one-ranked Miami.

We remember Uteskis fawning all over themselves when they went to a bowl game in 1964. And we remember how sweet it was when bowl games in December became as common for us as a visit from ol' St. Nick. All while the Uteskis stayed home and roasted their chestnuts and

sloshed down their buttered rums.

We remember when the Giffer passed the Uteskis dizzy in 1976, and Marco did the same in 1977, and Jimmy Mac in 1980 and 1981, and Stevearino in 1983, and Robbie B. in 1985, and oh, that delicious thrashing by Ty-One-On Detmer in 1989. Ah, the delicious, evil satisfaction we felt as Uteski fans slinked back to their pubs and potties. We remember that paybacks can be biting. For every bulls-eye snowball we sustained, we scored a touchdown in return. Who got the last laugh? The bigger the numbers of the scoreboard, the louder we laughed, and laughed, and . . .

We remember Uteski coach Wayne Howard spitting out those venomous words in 1977, insulting our prophet and throwing down the gauntlet for years to come. We remember that the aftermath didn't include many wins for the Uteskis. Turn the other cheek, we believe. Love thy neighbor. Wayne just didn't get it. Neither did the Uteski fans.

We remember how sweet it was when our coaching staff finally got an ornery gentile on board who fancied himself for pouring on the indignity. Doug "Light 'em Up" Scovil. We remember we scored a total of eighty-three points in 1979 and 1980 and the Uteskis got six. We wanted more, but our quarterbacks needed a rest in the final few minutes. And Scovil's phone lines got scrambled anyway.

We remember how the Uteskis wanted so badly to spoil our hard-earned national championship in 1984. The Uteski team did itself proud. The Uteski fans were at their odious, classless best. Can't beat 'em, castigate 'em. Uteski fans have become good at that. They've had tons of practice.

We remember 1985. Like Howard before him, your fair-haired Fassel didn't exactly say he hated us. But he did say the biased officiating was something he had been "warned" to expect at Provo. He didn't mention Robbie, our Heisman-challenging quarterback, or the six all-WAC players who beat him.

We remember the T-shirts of 1988 proclaiming the great Uteski win in Rice Stadium. We remember Utah scored fifty-seven. We also remember that the next November in Provo the Cougars scored almost that many in the first

half. We especially remember the figure seventy.

We remember the Uteskis' swagger when they squeaked out three wins in a row—by a total of twenty-three points—from 1993–95. We remember the Uteski fans trying to tear down our goalposts. We remember spanking them, changing their diapers, and sending them home to their mommies and daddies. And to the beer taverns.

And we remember in 1996, coming to Salt Lake City and meeting the predicted WAC champion Uteskis in Rice Stadium. Too bad, so sad. BYU 37, Utah 17. We remember that for years (decades), our Cougs beat you with the pass. This time, we pounded three years of frustration into the Uteski hide with a running game.

We remember the more things change, the more they stay the same.

We remember that in church on Sunday, November 24, 1996, we saw a lot of royal blue clothing and an awful lot of red faces.

And somewhere up there, we heard once more the words of our late, great university president Rex E. Lee, "We don't believe in revenge; but we do believe in paying our debts."

We remember someone saying on November 23, "The torch of WAC dominance has been passed."

We remember on November 24, someone saying "the torch of WAC dominance still burns brightly" in Cougar Stadium.

We remember on January 2, 1997, BYU was ranked number five in the whole U.S. of A. And the Uteskis were hoisting their Bloody Marys—to the advent of another basketball season.

We remember King Football is alive and quite well. In Happy Valley. For all 65,000 who rise and shout.

Ute Rules

Football is a complicated game. Being a University of Utah football fan is simple.

This isn't Big Ten country, where decades of losing have forced a lot of the lesser lights into pathetic attempts to generate some artificial excitement over "rivalry" games. Every year, for instance, Indiana pretends it cares about football while getting fired up to win the Old Brass Spittoon from Michigan State, the Old Oak Bucket from Purdue, and the Old Bourbon Barrel from Kentucky. Indiana and Kentucky playing football? No wonder they need so much bourbon.

Same thing at Iowa, which plays "rivalry" games with Minnesota, Illinois, and Wisconsin, and sometimes Iowa State, which isn't even in the same conference. Then there are the "big" games against the league's powers, Ohio State and Michigan, until basically every game except the one against North Dakota State is somehow supposed to be meaningful. It's a concept probably dreamed up by the marketing department that serves instead to drain all meaning out of those games.

It's so much easier in Salt Lake City. Here, true Utes believe that their favorite football team schedules ten or eleven practice games each fall in preparation for its one-game season. Beating New Mexico is fun, pummeling Utah State is good exercise, and visiting Colorado State is valuable training. And while winning as many of those games as possible is desirable, there is no sense getting worked up about it.

Because come the Saturday before Thanksgiving, nobody cares whether you whupped Wyoming or hammered Hawaii.

Don't believe it? Try asking a Ute fan what the team's record was back in 1988. He'll shrug, think a minute, then guess: "It was 6–5, wasn't it? Or maybe 5–6, or 7–4, something like that?" Then ask him the score of the BYU game, and faster than a Scott Mitchell laser screen, he'll exclaim "57–28!" before you can finish the question.

Not convinced? Chris Yergensen kicked forty-three field goals in his Utah career, but which one do you remember? (Most Ute fans can recall the fifty-five-yard distance, for that matter.) Curtis Marsh caught twelve touchdown passes in his two seasons, but one in particular sticks out, doesn't it? Of all the big plays in Luther Elliss's stellar college career, one fumble recovery in Rice Stadium cemented his place in school history.

And after last year's 37–17 disappointment, the other eight wins sure seemed awfully meaningless.

The Brigham Young game today completely defines the Utah football season, at least up in the Rice Stadium stands. It's the only game that combines the basic rules that we true-believers live for. Forget the WAC standings, forget the Beehive Boot (which only Utah State actually still cares about), forget rankings and bowls and national respect.

Tim Kelly/THE SALT LAKE TRIBUNE

No game is more emotional and no day is more draining for Ute fans than the annual matchup with BYU.

There are only three absolutes to remember about rooting for the Utes:

1) Utah must win.

2) BYU must lose.

3) Not necessarily in that order.

Few issues are as black and white, or rather as red and blue, as this one. To us Ute diehards there is no middle ground, no room for compromise, no mitigating

circumstances. And certainly no mercy.

It may not bring out the best in a person's human nature but sometimes being a devout Cougar hater is not pretty. For instance, the only time Utah fans could enjoy Ty Detmer's Heisman fraud was during the 1990 Holiday Bowl, when it got Texas A&M so inflamed they separated both of his shoulders.

When the Cougars play non-conference games against nationally ranked teams, some people will start to bray about how a BYU victory would "be good for the WAC." As if that matters. Utes would trade magazines full of national recognition for the WAC in exchange for one good UCLA 68, BYU 14 whipping.

And on those rare occasions when Utah's postseason hopes are riding on a BYU victory over someone else, well then, maybe next year. Ron McBride says differently, and God bless him, that's his job, but it's just plain impossible for a longtime Ute fan to bring himself to root for those blue-and-white helmets.

The Ute fans' hostility extends to other sports, of course, and lingers for years. The 49ers' victory over San Diego with Steve Young as MVP has to rank as the worst Super Bowl in history, narrowly edging that awful year Jim McMahon won it for the Bears.

Similarly, Jack Morris's career made it necessary to cheer against the Tigers, Twins, Blue Jays, and Indians in various years, and Wally Joyner has forever tainted the Angels, Royals, and Padres. But by contrast, one of the most memorable baseball games I've ever attended was the wonderful night in Cleveland's nearly empty Municipal Stadium in 1989, when Cory Snyder struck out four times.

I have enjoyed watching Danny Ainge (perhaps the worst third baseman in Toronto Blue Jays' history) build a reputation as pro basketball's biggest whiner, reveled in Duke recruit Chris Burgess "letting down nine million Mormons," and have even shouted at my TV in hopes of making Mike Reid miss a putt. (Reid, by the way, is the only guy on earth who could be nicknamed "Radar" and believe it's a compliment.)

Hell, when Rex Lee was solicitor general, I rooted against the U.S. government in Supreme Court cases.

And, of course, there could hardly have been a better basketball season than 1996–97, when the Utes rode Keith Van Horn nearly to the Final Four, while the Cougars went 1–25. Okay, 0–26 would have been better, but why quibble?

That single-minded focus is what defines Utah fans, to an extent that perhaps only Stanford and Cal fans could understand. Certainly, we want to be WAC champions. We want national recognition. We want to win bowl games.

But mostly, we want to beat BYU.

CHAPTER

• •

THE EMPIRE STRIKES BACK

That the University of Utah had left Provo on November 18, 1995, with an almost incomprehensible third straight victory over BYU was enough to make grown men and women cry. It was enough for elementary school students to learn that somewhere beyond Point of the Mountain there was a school older than Brigham Young University, closer to Temple Square and the alma mater of many of the church leaders. And in Salt Lake City, new travel pamphlets were hot off the presses proclaiming the reign of Sir Ron McBride: "Visit the University of Utah, Again the King of Intermountain Football." The Beehive State's centennial celebration, heralding its achieving statehood on January 4, 1896, would include the Utes at the head of the sports parade.

Alas, it was the winter that stood still in Utah County. No one remembers a January-February by the inches of snow or feet of smog that envelope the corridor between murky Utah Lake on the west and towering Mount Timpanogos on the east. Nor do denizens from Lehi and Alpine on the north and Springville, Spanish Fork, and Payson on the south occupy the hot-stove months embroiled in discussions about basketball.

Oh, make no mistake. There was a day some two or three decades or so ago when hoops was the talk of the county, when coach Stan Watts's BYU Cougars ran their twice-weekly track meets up and down the George Albert Smith Fieldhouse pine in the fifties and sixties, or briefly in the early eighties when Danny Ainge's frisky antics delivered to BYU its only NCAA Elite Eight reservation in history. From the booths down at Claire's in Provo to the Champions Café in Springville, old-timers would sip hot chocolate, Postum and caffeine-free coffee while reminiscing over Mel Hutchins's hook shot that helped win the 1951 National Invitational Tournament in Madison Square Garden or the yet-to-be surpassed guard tandem of bulls-eye shooter Dick Nemelka and magical passer Jeff Congdon, who led the Cougars to the 1966 NIT crown. Of course, Ainge's coast-to-coast drive past Orlando Woolridge to a game-winning layup over Notre Dame in 1981 in the

NCAA East Regionals is the standard by which all BYU basketball is measured.

But in the deep freeze of 1995–96, it was basketball-schmaz-ketball. Not much to chew over anyway with the Cougars whimpering their way through a 15–13 season and losing twice to Rick Majerus and his Runnin' Utes. Last thing in creation to spend a stitch of time on would be Utah, the state-supported school forty-five miles away. Would you believe it—Mormon brethren snorted—some of our tax money going toward Majerus's basketball program. There oughta be a law.

No, the topic on the front burner was football, the sport of kings, bishops, and high priests in Utah County. There was grumbling and grousing the likes of which no one could remember since Coach Smilin' Tommy Hudspeth's empire collapsed in the early seventies. What hath the demons loosed in our domain? the knights of the potbellied handwarmers asked. No bowl game in December? Why, it was like Mormon Pioneer Day without green Jell-O; October without a Santaquin pumpkin; Thanksgiving without a Sanpete County turkey. Must be that sixty-five-year-old coach LaVell Edwards. The game is passing him by after 214 victories. Why, the audacity of the guy! Losing to Utah again—and for the third time in a row. Then not delivering us a bowl game for the first time in eighteen years. Who's calling the plays? Where has our defense gone? Ah-ah, got another non-LDS kid at quarterback, some guy named Sarkisian. What's wrong with the Shoemaker kid, the returned missionary? Didn't we learn anything from that renegade Jim McMahon?

Lots of trouble brewing over there on University Avenue, all right. Even new school president Merrill Bateman is stirring the pot. Heard him say just the other day that he expects BYU to be in the top ten? Now, that's not just in football's top ten. That's every Cougar sport in the top ten. Now, that's our kind of guy. Never mind that there is not, nor ever has been, an athletic program in history that powerfully well-balanced. This is BYU and we've got that dad-burned Utah way ahead of us in basketball and beating us in football. Come on. It was even grating on Edwards. Reminded that the 1995 loss at—of all places—Cougar Stadium was the third loss in a row to the Utes, Edwards cut to the chase: "Yeah, we've got to start doing something about that." Fans wondered about his sincerity.

It was much more than November's loss to Utah that sent Utah County into a tizzy in 1995. By Labor Day, the Cougars were 0–1 in the conference—an eyesore-like 0–1 following a 38–12 ESPN-TV loss to Air Force at Colorado Springs. And it was worse than that with the Falcons leading 28–0 at one time, by 38–6. No Western Athletic Conference team had whipped the Cougars so badly since Ty Detmer's Heisman Trophy party was hit by a 59–28 Hawaii tsunami in 1990.

By the end of Edwards's Social Security-qualifying sixty-fifth birthday week (October 11), BYU was 2–3. Then came a five-week winning rally, so typical of BYU's two-decade history of recovering from early-season stumbles, and then the

34–17 setback to Utah before 65,829 fans. Not even a season-ending 45–28 victory at Fresno State that earned the Cougars a share of the WAC championship and a 7–4 record could dull the shock of another loss to Utah. And it was exacerbated when BYU was snubbed for the first time in eighteen years by the nation's nineteen bowls. The Cougars had lost to Utah five times in Edwards's tenure, but only in 1995 was the degrading setback compounded by a bowl-less December.

It was a wake-up call. Given an extra month—for the first time since 1977—to dissect the demolition, the Cougar coaching staff isolated two statistical culprits: The team was number 103 (out of 108) in the nation in rushing offense and was a dead-last number 10 in the WAC in penalties. In the middle of the season, starters tight end Itula Mili and defensive tackle Mike Ulufale were suspended for four games. Never mind that quarterback Sarkisian was *only* third in the nation in total offense and that BYU was number five overall. The team had lost national prestige with non-conference losses to UCLA and Arizona State. And there was no measuring cup big enough to gauge the destruction of the home-field loss to Utah. There were many endless nights when the lights blazed and film machines whirred in the war rooms of BYU football headquarters in the George Albert Smith Fieldhouse where, just to the north in the daylight hours, or on rare moonlit nights, the outline of cavernous 66,000-seat Cougar Stadium stands sentinel over the 631-acre BYU campus. From the night of November 25, 1995, in Fresno's Bulldog Stadium, when the Cougars rallied from a halftime deficit to pummel the Bulldogs with Sarkisian setting an NCAA record for passing efficiency in a game (thirty-one for thirty-four), a coaching brain trust that had remained pretty much in tact for twenty-five years picked, plotted, and programmed how, not if, the empire would strike back. And it was not just at Utah but at the national structure from which the Cougars were evicted in 1995 after a number ten CNN/*USA Today* ranking in 1994. Since 1984's national championship run, the faithful expected—nay, demanded—alongside BYU's name the phrase ". . . is ranked in the top twenty-five this week." That is a far piece from the top ten President Bateman coveted, but enough of a consolation for the brethren to throw in the face of the Utes who had been ranked only twice in the thirty-three-year history of the WAC.

It would take less shoring up than most people expected for the Cougars to set sail once again. WAC coaches said as much when their all-conference team listed four BYU juniors, including tight end Chad Lewis, offensive guard Larry Moore, and linebacker Shay Muirbrook. Then there was a Cougar rarity, in WAC special teams player-of-the-year James Dye, described by Edwards as the best return specialist he had ever seen. It was the coaches' second team that held the key to the reloading process when they punched in Sarkisian's name. The Coug QB had finished the season third in the nation in total offense at 297 yards per game. He was in the top ten in passing efficiency. *Football News* made him an honorable mention choice. Not bad for a guy who admittedly took the gas against Utah, throwing four of his season total of fourteen interceptions. Fans should have received a clue when Sarkisian rebounded the next week at Fresno to throw three touchdown passes—matching the number of his incompletions—in the season finale. The final 1995 tabulation listed Sarkisian passing for 3,437 yards and twenty touchdowns with fourteen interceptions. In 1982, a Cougar junior named Steve Young, the successor to McMahon, threw for only 3,100 yards with eighteen TDs and eighteen interceptions.

Other subtle reminders that a Cougar resurgence was imminent included WAC second-team cornerback Tim McTyer, plus top 1995 defensive point producer cornerback Eddie Sampson who had a team-leading five interceptions. By the time BYU's 1996 recruiting class was signed, sealed, and delivered, Cougar fans would learn of the enlistment of first-team junior college all-American cornerback Omarr Morgan. All the defensive forces BYU could muster would be called on to improve a porous outfit that had been ranked number sixty-two in the nation in 1995. All of the great teams under Edwards—among them the 1979, 1983, and 1984 clubs—were rugged defensive units. It would have to be that way again.

The first item of business was Texas A&M in the Pigskin Classic at Provo on August 24. It was the ideal showcase, however formidable, for the Cougars to begin their renaissance. The number-fourteen-ranked Aggies and national television. Why, BYU was in the la-la land of years-gone-by when high-profile opportunities had yielded gems such as a 21–14 win at Notre Dame and the 31–6 Copper Bowl victory over Oklahoma at Tucson in 1994. But not since that Camelot-like September evening of 1991 in Provo when the Ty Detmer-led Cougars stunned the nation with a 28–21 win over number-one Miami had BYU been presented such a fortuitous circumstance. Although no one except the coaching staff could remember, it was also a chance to get back at the Aggies for an awful 65–14 drubbing in the 1990 Holiday Bowl. Of overriding importance, however, was the necessity for BYU to show its constituency that 1995 was an aberration; that the Cougars intended to flaunt some dormant muscle; that they intended to fulfill the top ten quest outlined in their president's wintertime manifesto.

Meanwhile, in the Ute encampment forty-five miles north at the base of Red Butte, where the blinking block "U" on the side of the hill on November 18, 1995, had signaled a third-straight victory over the royal blue and white Edwards legions, the feeling was uproariously optimistic. The seemingly endless bridge to football parity with the despised Cougars had been crossed with a convincing 34–17 victory over the Cougars—in Provo no less—that delivered the Utes a tie for the WAC title.

For thirty years, the Utes had endured not only the indignity of losing to BYU on an almost perennial basis, but winters were spent by diehards living in the past, rehashing the glory days of Ike Armstrong, Jack Curtice, and Ray Nagel, when Utah actually did win a conference football crown and considered BYU no more than a prep school for missionary training. Young zealots, those thirty and under, couldn't remember. It had been 1964 when Utah last occupied the league throne room, and that was only a tie with Arizona. It was Nagel's 1957 club that won the old Skyline Conference outright. Yet, on that crisp, late-autumn 1995 afternoon in Cougar Stadium, junior quarterback Mike Fouts, overshadowed all year by the exploits of BYU signal caller Steve Sarkisian, threw for two touchdowns, while the Ute defense sacked Sark four times and forced the junior into four interceptions.

However, all the Ute euphoria was dulled by a bowl snub. For three straight years, even without a conference title as ammunition, Utah had spent December in the sun—1992 at the Copper Bowl and 1993 and 1994 at the Freedom Bowl, the last appearance producing a 16–13 victory over Arizona that was judged among the most exciting postseason games of all time. There they sat, like BYU for the first time in eighteen years, with their WAC trophy and no recognition. Beating the Cougars wasn't that big of a deal after all.

Well, yes it was. And winning a piece of the WAC title was. By midsummer, when all the preseason magazines began hitting the newsstands, it was obvious the nation had discovered coach Ron McBride's program. Why, for the long-suffering Utes it was genuine gloat time. Utah, not BYU, was getting the bulk of the ink in such notable publications as *Sports Illustrated, The Sporting News, Athlon,* and *Football News.* They all heralded Utah as the team to beat in 1996 in the expanded, sixteen-team WAC. And when conference journalists gathered in Las Vegas for the annual late-July Football Media Days, the final die was cast—Utah was picked to win the eight-team Mountain Division title and was projected to meet Pacific Division–winner San Diego State in the WAC championship game in Vegas on December 7.

Holy moly! Unable to make any significant WAC football headway in three decades and given one title season—a tie with BYU, Air Force, and Colorado State at that—the University of Utah was picked above BYU. In football no less. A year before, the Utes had been picked sixth by the media. When the votes were counted, McBride seemed outwardly mortified by the outcome: "I don't worry about the conference. Forecasting is politics and I'm no politician. I'm worried about our first game with Utah State." Edwards seemed . . . well, like the normal reticent Edwards. "Being picked second doesn't worry me. Utah has come up to a new level. After what they've done to us for three years it's to be expected. Utah deserves the accolades." Then came a disclaimer to the media: "Remember, you guys picked Hawaii eighth one year and they won the conference and the Holiday Bowl. That's how much you know." The WAC sage had spoken. Within a month, scribes and broadcasters wished they had paid more attention.

But why not Utah this time around? McBride's roster was rife with veterans—forty-five of fifty-eight lettermen returned from 1995—who had ranked number two in the WAC in total defense and scoring defense, and fifth in total offense—number twenty-three in the nation. Although not a serious statistical threat to the Y's Sarkisian—there was a seventy-five-yard-per-game gap between them in 1995—Fouts threw two fewer interceptions and had only two fewer touchdown passes than his more-decorated Cougar counterpart. Given the Ute QB reins a third of the way into the season, the nephew of NFL quarterbacking legend Dan Fouts was 7–2 as a starter.

Just as important was the corps of Ute receivers he would be feeding, led by second-team all-WAC choice Rocky Henry and junior Kevin Dyson, a pair of 4.35-second forty-yard-dash sprinters whose reception totals had landed them numbers six and seven, respectively, in a conference nationally known for receivers' prolific numbers. And as the Cougars knew full well, the Utes had a mountain

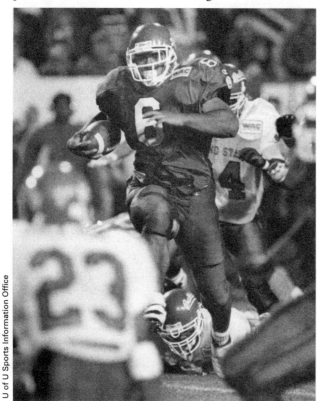

of a teenage rusher in six-foot-one, 276-pound Chris Fuamatu-Ma'afala, who burned BYU for 108 yards and two TDs in his rivalry debut. And junior Juan Johnson, who had 76 yards rushing against the Cougars in the same outing would also return.

Defensively, the Utes were making waves like the Cougars normally had in their greatest seasons. Defensive tackle Luther Elliss had followed linebacker Anthony Davis into the NFL to mark the nineties as the decade Utah's defense had returned to the stage occupied by coach Chuck Stobart's U teams of the early eighties. And there were seven defensive starters coming

Chris Fuamatu-Ma'afala, a 276-pound running back, established himself as Utah's most dangerous weapon during his impressive freshman and sophomore seasons.

back from the WAC title year—eight when end Henry Kaufusi was granted a medical hardship year. The defensive leader would be safety Harold Lusk, brother of 1994 Freedom Bowl MVP Henry Lusk and the WAC's interception leader. Speedy junior cornerbacks Clarence Lawson and Cal Beck—of the 1994 kickoff heroics against BYU and Arizona—were back. Plus, the Utes had kicker Dan Pulsipher returning as the WAC's leader in field goals per game and a finalist for the Lou Groza National Kicker-of-the-Year Award. "We don't have many question marks," said the traditionally pessimistic McBride. Fans were all lathered up. Rice Stadium's 32,500 seats were spoken for before August was complete. With an August 31 opener against upstate rival Utah State in Logan, and road games against Stanford and SMU, hometown fans would be in a frenzy for the first Rice Stadium encounter. A 3–0 and maybe top-twenty-ranked team coming back to Salt Lake City to open the home season against Fresno State on September 14? There was no question in the minds of ravenous Ute fans that this would be 1994 revisited: highlights weekly on ESPN, a weekly Sunday night date with Craig Bolerjack on KSL-TV's *SportsBeat* and headlines on KUTV's *Fox Den* to see just how high the Mac Attack had climbed in the national polls. Could it get any better than this?

Well, yes. For BYU. Naturally, as had happened almost annually since Richard Nixon was swept into a second term in the White House, the Cougars were dominating the football headlines almost before the Utes had completed two-a-day practices.

The annual Pigskin Classic, which had been switched from its permanent site in Anaheim, California, to selected collegiate locations around the country, just happened to be scheduled for Cougar Stadium on August 24. BYU versus Texas A&M of the powerful Big Twelve conference. Brent Musberger and ABC-TV would be showcasing the Cougars and the WAC to the nation, although in the minds of all but several thousand BYU bluebloods, this game would be no more than the Cougs' futile 44–28 losing Classic effort against Florida State in 1991. In fact, some railbirds were chortling that Edwards ought to hide Sarkisian in those bomb-proof, Mormon granite vaults in Little Cottonwood Canyon. The last time A&M got the scent of a BYU quarterback, Heisman Trophy–winner Ty Detmer ended up in surgery with two separated shoulders. That would be after the Ags skewered the Cougars 65–14 in the 1990 Holiday Bowl in San Diego. Now, here was coach R. C. Slocum—you know, the guy who rubbed it in the face of Edwards and whose Wrecking Crew relocated Detmer's clavicles four years previously—herding his Ags into the Beehive State for what was expected to be another romp. Bookmakers pegged A&M a ten-point favorite. Lombardi Award finalist Brandon Mitchell, A&M's six-foot-four, 275-pound defensive end, and his bookend mate Pat Williams—same size, same demeanor—would surely hunt down and . . . well, Sarkisian was wearing a flak jacket just as a precaution.

Provo does strange things to visitors, old and new. Many Ute fans, for instance, have been taken by the shakes for want of a cold beer, even a cold Coke. And if it's not the smog that hangs over the valley like a dusty quilt suffocating the soul and chasing any self-respecting environmentalist up into the spruces of the Wasatch Mountains for a respiratory reprieve, it's the pristine days and the sanitized BYU campus that capture and immobilize the senses. For A&M players in the sweltering pregame warmups, many of whom had probably never seen a mountain, it must have seemed those towering peaks east of sun-baked Cougar Stadium would surely tip over anytime, pushing everything in their path west into Utah Lake. Just looking at the everlasting hills seemed to leave the Aggies breathless. Or, was it the 4,400-foot elevation of Cougar Stadium? Or the ninety-five-degree, bone-dry heat that left the Aggies sucking for wind even before the made-for-TV 10:30 A.M. kickoff?

If it was bad at 10:30, imagine what the haughty Ags must have felt like by 2:30. Indeed, a mountain had hit them. At least a flood. Sarkisian, the quarterback who the win-at-all-costs fanatics had booed just nine months before for his debacle against Utah, threw for 536 yards and six touchdowns. It was the tenth-best one-game passing performance in school history—the stuff of which heroes like Nielsen, Wilson, Young, McMahon, Bosco, and Detmer are made. On a page of the annual BYU press guide of 1996, where eye-popping total offense and passing marks for a game, a season, and a career have been chronicled from Gary Sheide in 1973–74 to Detmer in 1988–91, the name Sarkisian was conspicuous by its absence, even if he had made the NCAA record book off his Fresno State passing efficiency in 1995. Sark assured his entry in the BYU QB Hall of Fame on a day when A&M yielded the most TD passes in a single game ever. Slocum's club had given up only eight passing TDs in all of 1995.

Although senior tight end all-American candidate Chad Lewis caught Sarkisian's first scoring toss, it was a day for wideouts K.O. Kealaluhi and Kaipo McGuire to provide Cougar fans a preview of coming attractions. McGuire hauled in seven passes for 146 yards and two touchdowns. The Cougars turned A&M's inexperienced, although speedy, secondary inside out all day. Sarkisian misfired on only eleven passes in forty-four attempts. The pass-and-catch flashed a zillion times the rest of the day on sports shows the nation over was a last-minute, forty-six-yard Sarkisian-to-Kealaluhi scoring missile that rescued BYU from a 37–34 deficit and delivered a 41–37 victory for 55,229 delirious, sun-baked fans. Said Sarkisian, a Californian doing a lot of basking himself after his greatest day ever as a Cougar, "When BYU gets rolling on offense, it's kind of hard to stop the train." If only the engineer had been whistling like that against those blasted Utes the previous November. "Yeah . . . if I had been on like that in the title game . . ." added a sarcastic Sark. Could it be he was on a Ute-seeking search-and-destroy mission—in

August?

The nation had watched. The writers, broadcasters, and coaches had noticed and responded by bumping the Cougars up to number nineteen in the polls. Sarkisian immediately jumped into the Heisman Trophy race, a fact *Sports Illustrated* illuminated by swooping into Provo for a story on the non-LDS quarterback who, to many, revived memories of the free-spirit McMahon days of the early eighties.

BYU hadn't exactly routed the Aggies, only its touted Wrecking Crew defense, which, after chasing Sarkisian all afternoon, was sucking for air at the end. Veteran BYU observers recalled another Aggie team wilting before a BYU onslaught in a season-opening game—1979 in Texas when QB Marc Wilson's underdog Cougs upset the Mike Mosely-Curtis Dickey-Jacob Greene clan 18–17 to set the foundation for an 11–0 regular season mark. The A&M offense was much more potent this time around and reminiscent of the Bucky Richardson-led crew that demolished BYU in the 1990 Holiday Bowl. The Ags had, after all, built a 20–6 second-quarter lead. Rookie quarterback Brandon Stewart ended up completing twenty of twenty-eight passes for 232 yards. Aggie running backs Sirr Parker and Eric Bernard combined for another 209 yards rushing. While linebacker Shay Muirbrook and his Cougar defensive colleagues had bent, they had not been broken, forcing A&M into three field goals by strong-legged Kyle Bryant, the returning Lou Groza Award winner.

But the die had been cast. Although nineteen spots from the top, and only four hours into the season, the Cougar faithful were already at work painting "We're No. 1" posters. They had history to work from. In 1984, BYU had marched into Pittsburgh and escaped with a 20–14 season-opening win over the Panthers. Immediately, comparisons were being made to that team that proceeded through a Jell-O-soft schedule, mowing down eleven regular-season opponents to reach the postseason with a 12–0 record—and a number one ranking that the Cougars preserved with a Holiday Bowl win over Michigan.

Voila! Right there for the taking in 1996 were twelve more beatable foes, chirped the faithful. Oh, the University of Washington in Seattle might pose a slight problem, but the Huskies were picked down the line in the Pac-10. This is a made-to-order 13–0 season. How about those Utes who were picked to win the WAC? You know, the guys who had whipped up on the Cougs three years in a row? The Utes, mocked the born-again, bellicose Cougar clan, are the Utes.

And so they were just the Utes. On August 31, having been unceremoniously shoved into the background by BYU's headline-hogging victory over A&M, and in a final insult, seeing the Cougars leapfrog over them in the national polls, McBride's troops responded with a 20–17 loss to Utah State. This was the same school Utah had beaten nine straight times, eleven of the twelve previous seasons and every year since McBride had taken over in 1990. In essence, the stunning three-hour episode in Logan in which USU outgained the Utes, 365–320, in total yardage, effectively erased all the glowing credentials Utah had accumulated: a third straight victory over BYU, a tie for the WAC championship, a preseason top twenty-five ranking, and in-state bragging rights.

The Ute football community was in mourning. It was of little consolation that the USU debacle was a non-conference game. Gone in a heartbeat were hopes for an unbeaten season. Those had been shipped forty-five miles south where Cougars were cackling from Highland to Holden. The immediate task for McBride and his staff was injecting some helium into a balloon that had been deflated by a mediocre USU team. Because Stanford of the Pac-10 was next up—again on the road.

There wasn't much to build on from the stumble in Logan. An offense that had closed with a rush in 1995—thirty-two points per game in a four-game winning streak—stumbled through a three-point second half, including a scoreless fourth quarter. Senior quarterback Mike Fouts barely matched the output of two far-less-heralded QBs, the Aggies' Patrick Mullins and Matt Sauk. The Aggie defense limited Utah's ballyhooed one-two rushing tandem of Fuamatu-Ma'afala and Johnson to forty-nine yards each, while USU's sixth-year senior Abu Wilson had 144 yards and two touchdowns. In the absence of the injured Henry, senior Terence Keehan had a career high 127 receiving yards plus a touchdown catch. Defensively, Lusk recorded his fourteenth career interception.

By Labor Day, it was obvious to even the most loyal Crimsons that 1996 could well be more of the same old "we're number two" story. BYU, following its 58–9 mismatch win over Arkansas State, was 2–0, ranked number fourteen in the country, and was scheduled for a bye week. Utah was scheduled for a biopsy. And with Stanford on tap at Palo Alto, there was serious speculation Utah could be 0–2, maybe 0–3 with an impending trip to Dallas to face new WAC opponent Southern Methodist on September 14.

The California sun was a healing influence on the Utes. Aided by a young Cardinal team that would eventually find its way to the Sun Bowl in December and a defense that shut out Stanford for over fifty-seven minutes, Utah rose up behind a 114-yard rushing performance from Johnson and another 64 yards from Fuamatu-Ma'afala to secure a 17–10 victory. In a scene witnessed so often a year earlier, the bullish Fuamatu-Ma'afala carried a host of would-be Cardinal tacklers into the end zone on a three-yard scoring run in the first quarter. Utah's superlative effort was dulled only by Stanford's ten-point burst in the closing three minutes. The Utes had righted their ship. As negative as a season-opening loss was to USU of the Big West Conference, a triumph over a Pac-10 team was chest-thumping stuff. Especially considering what transpired between the WAC and Pac-10 a week later.

The scenario was elementary. BYU's undefeated and fourteenth-ranked Cougars against the unranked Washington Huskies. Measured against all prior monumental BYU games, including the late-November game of 1984 against Utah that would preserve an undefeated season and ultimately the national title, this Seattle meeting was by far the most difficult matchup in the Cougars' march to an unbeaten 1996 season. That is until November 23 in Salt Lake City. It was not lost on the psyche of Edwards and his staff that the last visit to the shores of Puget Sound in 1986 had resulted in a 52–14 defeat. It was a loss that would ruin a season, one that ended 8–5 overall and interrupted a string of ten straight WAC championships.

On the surface, there seemed little to fear. The Cougars had ninety-nine points in their first two games highlighted by Sarkisian's ten TD passes, four of which came in a 58–9 romp past Arkansas State the week after the historical A&M conquest. The Cougars had a week off to savor the spoils and they were one-hundred percent healthy. The Huskies' Rose Bowl hopes had effectively been squelched in a season-opening loss to Arizona State in Tempe. Combined with the 38–18 thumping handed UW by Iowa in the 1995 Sun Bowl, it hardly seemed conceivable that coach Jim Lambright's Huskies would be a serious threat to the Provo juggernaut commanded by Sarkisian on offense and Muirbrook on defense.

With a national TV audience looking on for the second time in three games—a BYU TV-frequency record—the Cougars were made to look like any old WAC team. Husky running backs Rashaan Shaehee and Corey Dillon helped UW pile up 295 yards on the ground—two more yards than normally prolific BYU mustered in total offense. As brilliant as Sarkisian's offensive line had protected him through the first two games, it was eyesore-bad in its collapse before a ferocious Husky pass rush that produced eight sacks. Compounding the Cougars' woes was a pocketful of penalties. Sarkisian didn't throw an interception, but he was scrambling for his life most of the afternoon. Miraculously, he got off two touchdown passes—a thirty-two-yarder to McGuire and a one-yarder to tight end Mili. The coup de grace on this miserable afternoon came eighty seconds from the end when Sarkisian was tackled for a safety. As he went down, so did the Cougars—to number twenty-five in the polls. A national championship? By mid-September, the Cougs' fans were down in the mouth. Because up north in Salt Lake City, the Utes had turned their season around since the August 31 nightmare in Logan. Utah was all of a sudden 2–1 and leading the WAC's Mountain Division—as predicted.

All because the Utes had survived an attempted Cotton Bowl bushwhacking by SMU that saw the Mustangs blazing away for an upset in the final seconds. A fourteen-yard TD pass from Fouts to Henry lifted Utah from a 17–14 deficit to a 21–17 lead with 11:46 left in the game. As the clock wound into its final minute, the Ute defense thwarted Mustang quarterback Ramon Flanigan four times from the Utah sixteen yard line. As each Flanigan pass went up, anxious Ute fans in Salt

Lake watching the proceedings on TV in bars from Green Street to Iggy's to Port-o'-Call to Lumpy's held their collective breath. Senior cornerback Clarence Lawson broke up four passes in the game—two of them inside the final seventeen seconds, and linebacker Jason Hooks swatted away Flanigan's fourth attempt that was practically in a receiver's arms in the end zone. The Utes would enjoy the jet ride home with a 2–1 record—1–0 in the conference. But McBride would remind them they were averaging less than twenty points a game and were being out-gained in total offense through three games. However, the Utes were returning to Rice Stadium for five of their next six games, and the only road game was at perennial WAC cellar-dwelling UTEP. Even though the Utes faced a September 28 encounter with top twenty-five University of Kansas, it appeared, again as predicted, that both Utah and BYU could well proceed through cream-puff schedules to their appointed November 23 destiny in Salt Lake.

Proceed shakily as it turned out. BYU, still numb from its Northwest Passage stumble, returned to Cougar Stadium and promptly was embroiled in a save-its-skin skirmish with lightly regarded New Mexico. In fact, it required some last-second heroics to put down the Lobos 17–14. Trailing 14–10, the Cougars got a six-yard TD run from freshman Ronney Jenkins—his first Cougar score—with 6:11 left in the third quarter to assume a tenuous lead. It took a block of a Lobo field goal attempt by Omarr Morgan in the final quarter to preserve the win.

The Cougar offense sputtered again, mainly through two Sarkisian interceptions and a lost fumble. Saving the Cougars in their fifteenth straight win over UNM was a defense spearheaded by Muirbrook's three sacks of Lobo quarterback Donald Sellers in his sixteen-tackle afternoon. With Jenkins displaying breakaway tendencies, and Brian McKenzie and Mark Atuaia combining for 109 yards on the ground, the Cougars' rushing, almost nonexistent at Washington, got a much-needed shot in the arm. McTyer, who as a Cougar defender had time to assess the qualifications of Jenkins, said, "He has wheels. When he hits the corner with some daylight, man, he can go."

BYU, and its opponents, would find out just how much he could go. "He will play more as we go along," acknowledged Edwards. That was a major concession from the BYU coach. Freshmen rarely play in the Cougar system. One had, some nine years before. His name was Ty Detmer. He played sparingly as a backup to quarterback Sean Covey. By his junior season, he won the Heisman Trophy. Jenkins was showing promise and the Cougars needed him. There was still a neighboring team to catch and plenty of time to do it.

That night, in Salt Lake, the Utes spotted Fresno State a 14–0 lead in the first six minutes and then embarrassed the Bulldogs with a crushing ground and air attack highlighted by Johnson's school-record four rushing TDs and another 169 yards by Fuamatu-Ma'afala. As in Provo, Utah's defense sparkled, forcing FSU into six turnovers. As September 22 dawned, the 2–0 Utes still had the WAC Mountain lead over 1–0 BYU. But the next two weeks would produce telltale signs that would eventually define the arch rivals' seasons.

On September 28 in sold-out Rice Stadium, Utah racked up one of the school's all-time great victories, a 45–42 come-from-behind victory viewed by an ESPN2 audience. Fouts threw for 476 yards and four touchdowns in Utah's fourth straight win. But sensational Jayhawk running back June Henley shredded the Ute defense for 216 yards on forty-one carries. The following Saturday night, Utah was pushed to the limit by UTEP with only a monumental, seventeen-point fourth-quarter rally at El Paso's Sun Bowl rescuing the Utes in a 34–27 win. It took the second-best rushing performance in school history—236 yards—and three touchdowns by Fuamatu-Ma'afala to save the Utes from succumbing to the WAC's ultimate last-place Miners. The twenty-four–ranked Utes were 3–0 in the WAC and 5–1 over-all, but three road wins had come by a total of eighteen points.

As the Utes searched, their I-15 rivals were destroying. First SMU, which Utah had barely beaten, was drilled by the Cougars 31–3 in Provo behind Sarkisian's 375 yards passing. One week later, BYU traveled to Logan where Utah had been humil-iated and easily dismantled the Aggies 45–17. Kicker Ethan Pochman hit two field goals, and a forty-five-yard TD return of a fumble by Muirbrook sent the Cougars on their way early and Sarkisian passed for 310 yards in a 24-for-37 effort. A glimpse of the future was provided by freshman QB Kevin Feterik in the final quar-ter when he hooked up with Ben Cahoon for a five-yard TD pass. It was the first aerial TD by a BYU freshman since Jim McMahon had turned the trick in 1977. In a nutshell, BYU on consecutive weekends had drubbed SMU and USU by a combined 76–20. Utah had lost to one of them (USU) and beaten the other (SMU) by four points.

It would be November before the true meaning of those point comparisons was driven home. Suffice it to say, the Utes were living on the edge while BYU was . . . being the BYU of old living high on the hog with a number-twenty national rank-ing. The Utes—if you were counting "others receiving votes"—were number twenty-six. BYU would score 205 points in October—100 in back-to-back road games at Tulsa and TCU. And the nation's pollsters noticed. By Halloween, the Cougars were number fourteen. By the time of Clinton's landslide election win on November 4, they were number twelve. Moving up rapidly in the rankings playing pushovers Utah State, UNLV, Tulsa, and TCU was not in the cards, not when Penn State, Virginia, Northwestern, and Notre Dame continued to win. Voters were not going to make the same mistake they committed in 1984. Were they? Real photo-graphic memories could even recall 1990 when the 11–1 Cougars headed to Hawaii, where Detmer would be announced as the Heisman winner, hours before the Rainbows shellacked BYU 59–28. As for the 1996 bunch, it was obvious

Sarkisian had become a masterful button pusher.

Following the narrow win over New Mexico, Sark's frustration at the Cougs' inability to score clearly showed. "When we get down inside the twenty yard line, we need to stop calling it the red zone and start calling it the green zone." BYU began making opponents see red in the red zone. Through nine games the Cougars had scored forty-six touchdowns. Sarkisian played only three quarters in a 63–28 thrashing of UNLV, but his 400-yard, four-TD afternoon netted him WAC player-of-the-week honors. A 329-yard, five-touchdown outing in a 55–30 rout of Tulsa kept him on a roll, and on October 26 he had 313 yards and three touchdowns as the Cougars swamped TCU's Horned Frogs. BYU was 8–1 overall, 4–0 in the WAC, and Sarkisian was the first quarterback to throw for over 3,000 yards in the 1996 season. The Cougars, only 7–4 in 1995, were the Cougars of old.

There was little reason to think Utah wasn't just as good—not compared to the prolific BYU numbers by any means. But except for 1988 and quarterback Scott Mitchell, Utah rarely achieved the mega-thousand-yard plateau. The Utes had 362 yards versus UTEP and, in a Salt Lake snowstorm, slogged their way past TCU 21–7 with 357 yards offense, 182 of it from Fuamatu-Ma'afala on the ground.

With six wins in a row and a 4–0 WAC mark, Utah had given little indication of what was to come on October 19 when Tulsa visited Rice Stadium. After groundskeepers shoveled nine inches of snow off the turf, the Utes buried the Golden Hurricane with an avalanche of yards and points in a 45–19 romp, even without injured Fuamatu-Ma'afala. Johnson rushed for 197 yards, scoring three touchdowns and catching a Fouts pass for another score. Junior receiver Kevin Dyson hauled in four passes for a career-high 176 yards and two touchdowns. Fouts had 327 yards passing and three TDs. Defensively, the Utes stifled a Tulsa offense that had been averaging 380 yards per game. The Hurricane managed only 302 yards and coughed up two interceptions, one of them Lusk's fifth of the season and a school-record eighteen overall. McBride's assessment: "This was a pretty good measure of how successful we can be." Utah had won seven in a row. With a bye week and another off-week prior to the titanic season-ender versus BYU, Utah only had to protect its WAC unbeaten mark in road games at Rice and New Mexico. By November 2 in Houston, when the twentieth-ranked Utes lined up against Rice, it would be two months since the night of horror in Logan.

This time horror came calling in the daytime, on the ground. Five Owls gained sixty or more yards, led by senior fullback Spencer George's 108 and wending through quarterback Chad Nelson's 99, Michael Perry's 87, freshman backup quarterback Chad Richardson's 66, and Benji Woods's 60—a bulbous 496 in all. Utah was powerless against the Owls' wishbone offense. In sifting through the rubble of a 51–10 Rice victory, the Utes found—in the school's worst loss in six years—an early second-half injury to Fouts, a shoulder injury to Henry, an ankle injury to

Johnson, and a shoulder injury to defensive end Nate Kia. The Utes managed only 278 yards total offense and were shut out in the second half 28–0. Utah converted just one third down in thirteen tries. One three-hour afternoon and Utah was dumped from the rankings and from their season-long perch atop the WAC Mountain Division standings.

Taking the Utes' place, naturally, was BYU. Because on the same afternoon in Provo, the Cougars wouldn't make the mistake of overlooking a team they had annually feasted on . . . well, since 1985 anyway, and the infamous 23–16 loss to the UTEP Miners in El Paso. Highlighted by James Dye's school-record-tying 100-yard kickoff return to open the second half, BYU breezed past the Miners 40–18. It wasn't a typical brilliant game for Sarkisian, who was twenty-two of thirty for 235 yards and two touchdowns. He had two interceptions along the way, including one at the Miner goal line that UTEP's Michael Hicks returned a stadium-record 100 yards. However, the Cougar rushing game continued to impress, with Jenkins picking up sixty-six yards and McKenzie adding fifty-one and two touchdowns. The overall mission had been met. The Cougars had been scoreboard-watching. When the Rice conquest of the Utes was complete in Houston, BYU players were doing an awfully lot of internal celebrating. Their two-month pursuit of the Mountain Division lead was complete with a 5–0 record and 9–1 overall. Now ranked number twelve, they needed only to run the table with wins over Rice at home and Hawaii and Utah on the road to qualify for the WAC title game in Las Vegas.

Any questions about the relative strengths and weaknesses between BYU and Utah—if strengths hadn't already been established in the comparative scores against Utah State, SMU, and UTEP just to name three common opponents—were settled on November 9 in Provo. The Cougars buried Rice 49–0. On consecutive weekends, Utah had been pelted 51–10 by the Owls and the Cougars won by forty-nine—a ninety-point swing. Inside BYU's numbers this day was a precursor of things to come. The Cougs rolled up 354 yards rushing, topped by 109 from Jenkins and 97 from McKenzie, who added two touchdowns. The normally reticent Edwards was moved enough to say, "We may never throw another pass, now that we've got it going running the ball." The outburst would be the beginning of a three-week run during which BYU's rush total would exceed its pass yardage. And of the 219 passing yards, sixty-seven came on a second-quarter TD strike to Dustin Johnson, who had 105 receiving yards overall. BYU's defense literally suffocated the Owls in the Cougars' first shutout since a 35–0 blanking of New Mexico in 1992. Rice had 119 rushing yards and zero passing yards. It was the first time BYU had ever held a team without a yard through the air. Of course, Rice threw just five times. The overwhelming victory catapulted the 10–1 Cougars to number ten in the nation and put more rankings distance between themselves and the Utes, because in Albuquerque, the Utes could muster only a 31–24 win over New Mexico. That was adequate in view of the pasting at Rice a week earlier. But it was hardly the authoritative decision McBride was looking for in the final combat before meeting BYU. With Fuamatu-Ma'afala still sidelined, Johnson was the workhorse, carrying thirty-four times for 111 yards and a touchdown. Fouts had recovered sufficiently from his hip pointer at Rice to throw for 240 yards and two touchdowns. Utah's defense was under a microscope after the annihilation by the Owls and it responded, holding the Lobos to 218 yards on the ground—forty yards under the average of the nation's number-eight-ranked rushing team. Lusk intercepted his sixth pass of the season. Utah was 8–2 overall and 6–1 in the WAC and had a week off to prepare for BYU's invasion.

The Cougars used their week prior to The Game by taking a sunny "vacation" on Waikiki. On a trip where they had lost three out of the last four games, it seemed ominous again with unusually rainy and cool weather. BYU, unable to get any beach time, unloaded its frustration on the Rainbow Warriors in a 45–14 contest that was closer than the final score. The Cougars scored three touchdowns in eighty-three seconds to break a 24–14 game wide open early in the fourth quarter. Again, BYU's rushing game, led by McKenzie's 129 yards and 91 by Jenkins, overshadowed the passing-game yardage 285–206. Defensive tackle Henry Bloomfield returned a fumble—one of five Hawaii turnovers—for a twelve-yard TD, and Cougar kicker Pochman became the school's top season scorer with ninety-six points off his six PATs and a twenty-five-yard field goal.

At 11–1 and 7–0 in the conference and ranked number seven in the country, the Cougars had reached their appointed date with destiny: a meeting with the well-rested Utes in Salt Lake City with the WAC Mountain Division title and a trip to Vegas on the line. There was no doubt about the Cougar momentum. And just in time, the bonfire of anticipation for The Game was whipped up when BYU's Sampson threw down the gauntlet: "We have some business to settle with the boys up in Salt Lake City."

November 23, 1996 . . . not the first time a game of this magnitude between Utah and BYU had been played in Rice Stadium. Oh, of recent vintage, Ute fans would unkindly refer to 1994 when their 9–2 heartthrobs denied the Cougars a WAC title with a 34–31 victory. The only other Ute home victories in the prior twenty-two years had come in 1978 and 1988, and neither time did Utah have a shot at the WAC title. BYU fans might point to the 1984 match in which their guys needed a victory to preserve an unbeaten season and a number three national ranking. Indeed, in a tenacious battle during which Utah was within a field goal, 17–14, in the fourth quarter, BYU's 24–14 victory clinched an unbeaten 12–0 regular season, and on the following Monday, the Cougars ascended to the number-one spot in the country. Five weeks later, BYU rallied behind quarterback Robbie Bosco in the Holiday Bowl to subdue coach Bo Schembechler's Michigan Wolverines 24–17. When the final polls were released on January 2, the Cougars were proclaimed national champions.

There were ramifications of near-equal import this time around in The Game. At 11–1, the Cougars needed not only to win the game for the division title, but to preserve—or advance—its national ranking. Given a victory in the WAC title game and a 12–1 record, surely the Bowl Alliance would consider them for one of three major bowls—the Fiesta in Tempe being BYU's dream. Unless, of course, the moon, sun, and planets lined up just right and gave the Cougars a shot at the national title in the Sugar Bowl.

For the Utes, a victory over their despised rival would earn a trip to Vegas, where optimistic and zealous Utah fans had made reservations months earlier, shortly after the media anointed Utah the WAC champion. There was no Cotton Bowl or any Alliance Bowl in Utah's future, but its first Holiday Bowl would be just peachy, thank you. Fuamatu-Ma'afala would be back after missing three games. He had rushed for 108 yards and two touchdowns in the 34–31 win in Provo in 1995. And the six-foot, 276-pound sophomore had four straight 100-yard-plus games to his credit. Defensively, Utah would send free safety Lusk into action with a school-record nineteen interceptions in his portfolio. He could be seen licking his lips in remembering 1995 when one of his picks helped Utah post a total of four against Sarkisian in Provo. And Utah pass defenders as a whole were confident since they led the WAC and were twentieth in the nation in pass defense. The most powerful trump card for Utah were those three wins in a row over the Cougars.

But this was a different Cougar team than the previous three who had succumbed to the Utes. Sarkisian had hurled twenty TD passes in all of 1995. By the time he lined up against the Utes, he had thrown thirty-two. He stood seventh in yardage on the all-time BYU quarterback list in only twenty-three games. Since a TD-less game against Utah State, the California slinger had hurled eighteen aerial scores in six games. A reasonable 343-yard day would send him past 4,000 yards total offense for the season—gaining him membership in a BYU fraternity with Detmer, McMahon, Young, and Bosco. In addition, Sarkisian was on a mission: He had been plagued for twelve months by the recurring vision of that botched 1995 afternoon in Provo against the Utes.

Defensively, it was hard to ignore the Cougars' last four games. They had allowed only thirteen points per game, and the shutout of Rice and the Owls' powerful running game kept tugging at the psyche. Tackle Henry Bloomfield, linebacker Shay Muirbrook, and cornerbacks McTyer and Morgan seemed to be cinch all-WAC players. To longtime observers, those who had watched the Cougars finish with a flourish during so much of the glorious Edwards reign, BYU showed many of the same old attributes for success, not that an 11–1 record left much to the imagination, regardless of the caliber of competition. And in November 23 games under Edwards, BYU was 3–0—all against Utah. Plus, that huge point swing between the two schools against Rice earlier in the month . . . it just wouldn't go away. Nor would a haunting comment made earlier in The Game week by Hawaii offensive coordinator Guy Benjamin: "BYU plays like it has confidence. That is what separates them from the other WAC schools."

It was an almost idyllic—forty-five degrees, a slight wind and broken clouds that allowed for an occasional burst of sunshine—autumn Utah morning when the two combatants came eyeball to eyeball and facemask to facemask before 35,378 Rice Stadium fans. It was only about half of what there would have been in Provo, but it was nonetheless the Utes' fourth-largest crowd of all time. Never mind that the kickoff had been moved to 10:30 A.M. for an ESPN telecast. Ute fans had ingested their own version of antifreeze at sunrise-early tailgating parties. Utah students were a bit chagrined they would be denied their second-most favorite activity—hurling snowballs at any Cougar target—since the Thanksgiving-Week blizzards had not yet unleashed their fury on the Wasatch Front. But they were fully charged for priority number one—screaming uncensored insults.

They never got a chance to hurl their epithets. The Cougars mounted an awesome storm of their own: a ground-pounding assault that, when complete 192 minutes later, left Ute players, coaches, and boosters in its numbing lurch. Say it isn't so. The passing offense by which the nation judges the prevailing winds effectively junked in favor of the run? The nation's fourth-leading passing quarterback handing off to the right? And then to the left? A Cougar team that once saw quarterback Marc Wilson throw for 571 yards against the Utes (1977) and Jim McMahon for 565 (1981); one that had Young heaving six TD passes over Utah's beleaguered secondary in 1983 now playing the Woody Hayes-Bo Schembechler bull-in-a-china-closet style?

It was a Cougar game plan to be remembered for the ages; one to be enshrined in Mormon ward archives from Nephi to Nantucket, from Alpine to Albany. It was a running backs day, a throwback to Cougar plow horses like Eldon Fortie of the sixties, Pete VanValkenburg of the seventies, and Lakei Heimuli of the eighties. Edwards was typically grim-faced throughout, but the Wizard of the Wasatch had to be smiling inside. He had come to BYU thirty-five years before, armed with a technical knowledge of the running game, albeit the soon-to-be antiquated single wing. So what that he was quickly ordained Potentate of the Pass.

On this day, the pages of the foot-thick Cougar passing manual were virtually undisturbed. Running-back coach Lance Reynolds distributed to his troops a one-page leaflet on straight-ahead plowing. McKenzie and Jenkins, hardly unknowns by this time, took the reins and burrowed in behind 300-pound blocking behemoths Larry Moore, James Johnson, Matt Cox, Eric Bateman, and John Tait. They carved a furrow on Utah's SportGras turf and imprinted one on the collective foreheads of Utah defenders. Anyone who couldn't see this master planning stroke coming was blind in one eye and couldn't see well out of the other. Utah was ranked tenth in the WAC and eighty-sixth in the nation in rushing defense. And hadn't Edwards tipped his hand a month before following the 323-yard rushing rout of Tulsa with his "we may never pass again" aside?

By the time it was BYU 10–Utah 0 with 8:41 left in the first quarter, Sarkisian

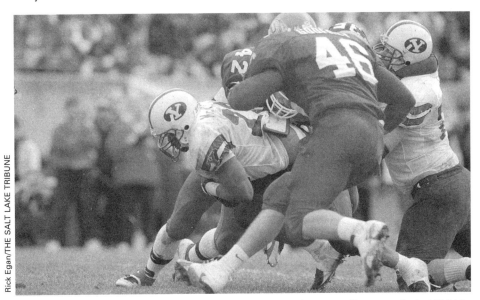

Rick Egan/THE SALT LAKE TRIBUNE

Brian McKenzie spearheaded a relentless running game for normally pass-oriented BYU in the 1996 game with Utah. He and Ronney Jenkins combined for 332 rushing yards.

knew he need not worry about a repeat of his ghastly 1995 Provo experience. "Utah knew by that time we were smash-mouth," said Sark. Oh, the Utes knew before that. BYU's first play sent McKenzie off left tackle and into Ute-less territory for twenty-nine yards. Six more running plays later, the Cougars settled for a twenty-two-yard Pochman field goal. BYU had kept the ball for nearly four minutes, setting the tone for what ultimately would be a lopsided advantage in time of possession: thirty-eight minutes to twenty-two minutes. That the Utes had prevented a touchdown when the Cougars had a first and goal was a moral victory, the only type of victory Utah would muster this day.

Seeds of a massive Ute failure to come were sown on Utah's first possession. Pochman's kickoff nearly sailed through the uprights seventy-five yards away. On first down from the Utah twenty yard line—amazingly, the Utes' ten possessions of the day started at their own twenty-four or deeper—Fuamatu-Ma'afala gained three yards over the right side where he was stood up by BYU defensive end Ed Kehl and tackle Harland Ah You. On second down, an unpressured Fouts overshot by ten yards his wide-open tight end Jeff Jex. On third down, out of the shotgun formation, Fouts zeroed in on Henry right over the middle. He found senior BYU linebacker Muirbrook. "Usually, you have to break one way or the other for an interception. But whoa! This one came right to me," said Muirbrook, who two weeks later would be named WAC Mountain Division defensive player of the year.

From the Ute twenty, Sarkisian, unable to find a receiver, rolled right for five yards. McKenzie was stopped for no gain by Ute Chris Godfrey. More Ute frustration surfaced on the next play—a short pass from Sarkisian to his tight end Mili, who fumbled at the Utah five yard line with Ute Clarence Lawson recovering. However, Utah was flagged for an offside infraction, giving BYU a first down at the Ute ten yard line. Utah's defense again rose up—for one play—when Sarkisian's swing pass to running back Mark Atuaia was stopped for a two-yard loss. On second down, McKenzie took a delayed handoff and zipped over left tackle for a twelve-yard TD run. With Pochman's PAT, who with the earlier field goal had become BYU's all-time single-season point producer, it was an almost unbelievable 10–0 BYU lead. Sarkisian was one-for-two in passing for a minus two yards. BYU's running game showed seventy-one yards. There would be more, much more.

Utah's second possession was essentially as futile as its first. Johnson brought Ute fans to their feet with a nine-yard dash over the left side. But any semblance of momentum was squashed on second down when Fouts' pass into the left flat was hauled in by Fuamatu-Ma'afala, who was immediately hauled down by Bloomfield for a two-yard loss. Then Bloomfield got the first of his two sacks of the day, swarming over Fouts for a seven-yard loss. Three downs and out. Down and out as it turned out for the Utes.

On their third possession, BYU continued its relentless running game—Jenkins right for a yard, McKenzie left for eleven, McKenzie on a right-end sweep for twenty-one, Jenkins up the middle for two, Jenkins right for seven, and then, as if right on schedule, conjuring up other visions of this heated rivalry's ill-timed Ute transgressions, a personal foul on the Utes moved the ball to the Utah eight yard line. Another courageous Ute defensive stand limited BYU to Pochman's twenty-two-yard field goal and a 13–0 Cougar lead.

Where, oh where, was the Ute offense that was ranked thirty-fourth in the nation at 409 yards a game? It again failed to surface on Utah's third possession. Two Fouts incompletions and a feeble, one-yard plunge by Fuamatu-Ma'afala led to Hunter's forty-four-yard punt that mercifully was not fielded by Cougar return ace James Dye. The punt rolled dead at the BYU thirty-four yard line. Dead, a concise analysis of Utah's offense and its capacity crowd, which had witnessed a first quarter that in 4:19 had produced four yards of offense while in the other 10:41, BYU had 124 yards in a penalty-free, mistake-free quarter. Not to mention a 13–0 lead. And a picturesque BYU march to open the second quarter would send Utah's players deeper into oblivion and drive many of their fans to the halftime tailgate spirits trough.

Taking more than half the quarter—8:07 to be precise—the Cougars showed the Utes how a seventh-ranked team plays the game. Sarkisian teased his back-pedaling foes with his first successful pass—an eleven-yard hit to McGuire. Then, he simplified his attack, even lugging the ball himself four times, once on a successful fourth-down carry. Mostly, it was McKenzie and Jenkins, hunkering down behind their boxcar-sized linemen, chewing up the yardage—five for McKenzie, four for Jenkins . . . five, four, four, and on it went. Excruciatingly slow but surgically precise, the Cougars pressed the dagger deeper and deeper into the Ute subconscious. With a third-and-eight at the Ute thirty-eight, Sarkisian spotted Kealaluhi at the first-down marker. Sensing the coup de grace, BYU disdained another Pochman field goal from the twenty-one yard line with Sarkisian trying not once, but twice, for one yard. He got two on fourth down, and five plays later, Jenkins ended Utah's twisting-in-the-wind misery, spinning to his left and into the end zone for a four-yard TD run. With Pochman's PAT, it was 20–0 after twenty-three minutes.

A sixteen-play drive, consuming over eight minutes. It sent Cougar statisticians scurrying for the record book to determine if, indeed, the normally quick-striking Cougs had set a school record for time of possession on a TD drive. They had. Oh, just great, seemed to be Utah's reaction. BYU sets another record against us. Forget the time of possession. The Cougars were about to record their first opening-half shutout over the Utes in four years, which had come, not so surprisingly, in 1992, the last time BYU won.

In twenty-three minutes, Utah had four yards total offense—a minus two yards passing. Fuamatu-Ma'afala finally brought the Ute crowd into the game with a thirty-nine-yard run to the BYU thirty-seven yard line, but it was on his next first-down attempt from the BYU twenty-four that his end sweep was turned into a six-yard loss by BYU freshman end Bryon Frisch (one of nine rookies on the Cougars' two-deep). Three plays later, facing a fourth-and-one at the Cougar twenty-one, the Utes opted for a thirty-eight-yard field goal from Dan Pulsipher. While getting only three points, at least the Utes had held the ball for almost five minutes. As a bonus, the Ute defense held on the ensuing Cougar possession, its only stop of the first half. Having given up 222 yards and gaining only 69 themselves, and with Fouts only two-of-seven in passing, a 20–3 halftime deficit was maybe not all that bad. After all, seven years ago, some Ute fans remembered, BYU had led at the half in Provo 49–7. And as recently as 1992, the Cougars had led 24–0 at halftime in Rice Stadium. Plus the Utes would receive the second-half kickoff.

For Ute fans, the proceedings turned uglier in a hurry. Again pinned against their own goal line by Pochman's booming second-half kickoff, the Utes moved to mid-field, largely through a fifteen-yard personal foul against the Y. Bloomfield's second sack of Fouts forced a Ute punt and on a Murphy's Law day—if something can go wrong, it will—Hunter got off only a thirty-one-yard punt. McKenzie and Jenkins again took control. It was the quick-strike Cougars of old. McKenzie swept left end for thirty-nine yards; Jenkins swept the other end for nineteen, and for good measure, Jenkins sliced up the middle for a sixteen-yard TD run. It was vintage BYU—three plays, seventy-four yards, twenty-one seconds. The glaring difference? No passes. Pochman's PAT ballooned the BYU lead to 27–3. It would take one of those Vegas-like, one-pull-of-the-handle jackpots to extricate the Utes from this morass. Twenty-four quick points would help, too.

Utah got eight of them, but not quickly. Still, the five minutes it took to go seventy-six yards and get a one-yard TD run from Fuamatu-Ma'afala and a two-point conversion pass from Fouts to Henry at least kept the Cougar offense off the field. For optimists, it would take only two more touchdowns and a couple of two-point conversions to tie it. Fouts had displayed some heretofore absent aerial verve on the TD drive with passes of eleven yards to Kevin Dyson, twenty-nine to Terence Keehan, and ten to Henry. Shoot, the Ute coaching staff even helped stoke up the crowd, when on the two-point conversion, they employed the Daffy Duck formation, made popular by the struggling Utah offense of 1986. However daffy it might seem, if the defense could just contain the Cougars, an assignment the Utes had completed just once in the first six BYU possessions . . . well, do you believe in miracles?

Utah would break again, or bend if you consider BYU would get only a field goal on its next possession. The Cougars continued to stay on the ground. Sarkisian hadn't thrown a touchdown pass yet, but who among the BYU faithful was counting? The clock was winding inexorably toward the end of the third period and at twenty-five seconds at a pop, either the junior from Sarasota, Florida (McKenzie), or the freshman from Port Hueneme, California (Jenkins), would punish the weary Ute defense. Eleven plays, fifty-seven yards, and 3:18 later, Pochman connected again, a forty-one-yard field goal that spread the Cougar advantage to 30–11 with 1:51 to play in the third quarter. Now the Utes were three scores down and it was clear Utah had to go airborne to be any threat.

Fouts brought the crowd back into the game one more time. Starting at his own twenty, he found Dyson on a middle screen for thirteen yards, then connected with Keehan for twenty-two. On a fourth down gamble at the BYU twenty-nine, Dyson hauled in a Fouts pass just before stepping out of bounds at the first-down marker. It was the Utes of old, and when Fouts came back to Dyson with a nineteen-yard TD strike over the outstretched hands of BYU defender Ben Cahoon, there was an obvious lift in the hometown spirit, from the capacity crowd to the Ute sideline. The two-point conversion attempt was denied by Cougar cornerback Chris Ellison. Still, the Utes were within two scores and their crowd was worked into a frenzy. Hey, two touchdowns and two extra points and it would be 31–30. Not exactly 34–31, but it had a nice ring to it.

It was BYU that rang the bell again. Not that Utah didn't have a chance after holding the Cougars on the next possession. But Utah couldn't move either as the Cougar M&M troops, McTyer and Muirbrook, made key plays that forced a punt. With 6:42 left, BYU—make that Jenkins—sealed Utah's fate. Sweeping, slanting, slicing, and dicing, Jenkins carried seven consecutive times with the payoff his two-yard plunge with 3:24 to play. Pochman's PAT spread the margin to 37–17, and the Ute crowd, as it had done for nine of the previous twelve Salt Lake games, threw up the white towel in front of the Edwards brigade.

Harold Lusk lost to BYU only once during his four-year Utah career, but the senior safety took that loss hard, even when BYU players consoled him.

It was as convincing a BYU victory as the Utes' 34–17 conquest one year earlier. The Cougars monopolized the ball with a sixteen-minute time of possession advantage. They amassed 436 yards offense to Utah's 261. The Cougar defense had three sacks to Utah's none. "We didn't just beat them, we dominated them," said Sarkisian. Edwards, who had endured three straight losses to a team his troops had once beaten as regularly as UTEP and New Mexico, was like a gorged kid who had just exited a candy shop: "I didn't lose any sleep over losing three straight to them, but it's great to win again."

Tait, just a rookie, was sounding the BYU arrogance McMahon exuded nineteen years earlier: "If we run the ball, we can beat anybody. Running is new here, and it's going to stay this way." Then he went one step farther: "Hey, we've still got our best game to play."

And even if the first-ever WAC championship game in Las Vegas against once-beaten Pacific Division champion Wyoming wasn't their best game, it was the top-rated game of three ABC-TV conference title games that day. The Cougars, ranked number six in the nation after their victory over Utah, prevailed in overtime over the Cowboys 28–25 to match their NCAA-record thirteen-win season of 1984. Two of Pochman's four field goals in the game came with no time left in regulation and in overtime, to rescue the Cougars from what seemed like sure defeat after Wyoming staged a fifteen-point fourth-quarter rally.

In fact, like BYU's national championship of 1984, the Vegas verdict, witnessed by an overflow crowd of 41,238 fans in Sam Boyd Stadium, will be argued for years. Call it the Great Safety Caper. Did the best team win? Had Cowboys' lame-duck coach Joe Tiller (who had accepted the Purdue University head coaching spot several days before the game) gift-wrapped the Cougar victory with a regulation-time decision to have his team take a safety with 2:05 left? Cougar detractors from Las Vegas to Long Island to Lumpy's would have you believe the Halo Theory had worked again. They failed to take into account that BYU had been there and done that on numerous occasions. As evidence, did anyone remember the 1980 Holiday Bowl when McMahon rallied the Cougars from 21 points down in the last four and a half minutes to a 46–45 win over SMU?

BYU had gotten the big head with a 13–0 halftime lead over the Cowboys. Intercepting Wyoming quarterback Josh Wallwork twice and eating up the clock with a running game spearheaded by McKenzie, BYU had called on a pair of Pochman field goals, sandwiched around an eleven-yard TD run by McKenzie to manufacture its lead. Wyoming penetrated the BYU thirty yard line just once in the half. At intermission, the press box was abuzz about the Cougars being so dominant that even a January 2 date in the Sugar Bowl and a shot at the national title were within the realm of possibility. Not even a season-ending knee injury to Mili early in the first quarter could detract from the BYU euphoria.

That is, until Wyoming laid seventeen unanswered points on the Cougars' reeling defense. A twenty-five-yard TD run, a fumble recovery by Jay Jenkins, Corey Wedel's twenty-yard field goal, and Wallwork's seven-yard pass to David Saraf transformed the press box conversation from BYU's entry into the Bowl Alliance picture to just what bowl game Wyoming might be headed for with a victory. After all, BYU's nationally renowned offense had generated a grand total of fourteen yards in the third quarter. Even 420 miles away, you could hear Ute fans chortling their approval. Had there been a game at Rice Stadium, surely the roar for the 17–13 Cowboys' lead would have been deafening. However, the proceedings in sunny Las Vegas were just beginning to get interesting.

Given a late-afternoon wake-up call, the Cougars responded. With Morgan's interception of Wallwork giving BYU the ball at the Cowboy forty-four, the Y gave a three-play offensive clinic—Sarkisian's thirty-yard strike to tight end Chad Lewis, a one-yard teaser completion to Atuaia followed by another thirteen-yard rifle shot from Sarkisian to Lewis for the touchdown. Three plays, forty-four yards in 1:08—the script for so many Cougar drives during the season. Pochman's PAT made it 20–17 and Alliance chatter began anew. For twenty seconds.

On Wyoming's first play after BYU kicked off, an undaunted Wallwork hooked up with Richard Peace for a sixty-six-yard pass-run to the Cougar fourteen yard line. Four plays later, Wallwork teamed with Saraf again for a fourteen-yard TD strike. Wyoming knew quickie stuff of its own—eighty yards on four plays in 2:12. Wallwork's two-point conversion pass upped Wyoming's lead to 25–20 with 9:24 left. Glorious WAC football was in full bloom. The flower would open wider and the pulse of the national TV audience would quicken.

Over the next six minutes, Sarkisian, Atuaia, fullback Dustin Johnson, McKenzie, and a punishing BYU offensive line would slice up the Pokes' defense for seventy yards—all the way to the Wyoming two yard line. A field goal was of no use. On three consecutive plays, BYU got zilch as McKenzie was stopped for no gain by Cowboy linebacker Jim Talich and Sarkisian threw two incompletions. A clock-consuming drive, one that gave every indication of depositing BYU in the end zone with little time left on the clock, had worked against the Cougars. They were staring at 177 ticks of the clock until the end of their miracle run of ten straight wins had elevated them to the nation's number-six ranking.

Dame fortune—the traditional "halo" as Ute fans have come to know it—was on BYU's roster as Wyoming started from its own two yard line. Bloomfield made consecutive stops on senior Cowboy running back Len Sexton and before third down at their own five yard line, Wyoming called time-out. There was 2:09 left. On third down, Wallwork threw incomplete to Saraf. There was 2:05 left. Another Wyoming time-out. Then, came the play that will be debated in Laramie for years. Tiller ordered punter Aron Langley to step back out of the end zone and take an automatic two-point safety. Momentarily, a hush fell over the stadium. But just as quickly the BYU sideline erupted in delirium. They had been handed two points. In forty-eight minutes, since taking a 13–0 first-quarter lead, they had fought and scratched for seven points and now two freebies? And a Pochman field goal could tie it. Shoot, with nearly two minutes left, BYU's potent offense had several options. But almost to a person, the conjecture was Pochman can tie this baby with a field goal and send it into overtime.

And he did. Not without an intervening water bucket full of anxious moments. For instance, Langley's free kick from his own twenty yard line sailed to the BYU forty where Cougar up-man Jeff Ellis promptly fumbled. Final regulation drive lucky break number one: Cougar freshman Nate Foreman pounced on the ball. Six plays later, following three Sarkisian pass completions and a Steve Young–like twelve-yard scamper of his own, up popped lucky Cougar break number two: From the Wyoming seven yard line with eight seconds left, Sarkisian hit Atuaia for a four-yard gain to the Pokes' three yard line. Now, here's where confusion reigned supreme. Wyoming's Tiller argued the game was over, that time had elapsed. BYU and Atuaia knew better. The Coug senior was on the ground frantically signaling for a time-out, which the officials acknowledged by putting one second back on the clock. It was Pochman time. A field goal try from twenty yards away. Good! Overtime at 25–25.

Now the odds were with BYU. Not that Wyoming wouldn't emerge with something in overtime, which allows for each team to have four downs from the twenty-five yard line. The Cowboys did, after all, have all-American kicker Wedel in their arsenal. But up stepped BYU's Bloomfield again. On first down, he sacked Wallwork for a five-yard loss. Two Wallwork pass incompletions later, it was up to Wedel to get Wyoming three points—from forty-seven yards away. Inexplicably, his kick was wide left.

Pochman's thirty-two-yard field goal seconds later, after a couple of safe ducks into the line by McKenzie, was not. "The kick was basically a PAT," said Pochman, a former Washington High soccer player. "I prayed really hard and kicked it through. I wasn't really nervous. I was more calm than at any time this season. I've dreamed about winning a game with a last-second field goal."

This time, some Ute fans—and most assuredly McBride—could accept the prayer angle. Not only had Pochman booted BYU into a New Year's Day—maybe even January 2—appearance, but probably had elevated Utah into the front-runner's position for the December 27 Copper Bowl.

The answer to both schools' postseason hopes came within twenty-four hours. No amount of lobbying by WAC commissioner Karl Benson, or even testimonials by football-savvy national spokespersons, or even BYU's number-five national ranking could sway the Bowl Alliance into allotting the Cougars one of its six precious January 1-2 slots and an accompanying $8.5 million payday and a possible national championship. Snubbed by the Sugar, Orange, and Fiesta Bowls, BYU accepted a bid to the Cotton Bowl in Dallas to meet fourteenth-ranked Kansas State. Utah indeed was a beneficiary of BYU's victory, landing a Copper Bowl berth in Tucson to meet the Big Ten's University of Wisconsin Badgers.

Everybody, it seems, was crying foul. Except the Utes. BYU felt chagrined that the Alliance would go against every one of its nationally publicized precepts for qualification and place lower-ranked Texas and Nebraska in the Fiesta and Orange Bowls, respectively. Wyoming's 10–2 Cowboys did everything but appeal to the

U.S. Supreme Court to plead its bowl case. But from the beginning, the WAC knew it would have slim bowl pickings. If it hadn't been for the Cougars' lofty standing, they would have been Holiday Bowl bound. The WAC had just two bowl possibilities, and this time around, after both were snubbed as conference champions a year before, it would be BYU off picking Cotton and Utah mining Copper.

Incredibly, especially for the 13–1 Cougars against the 9–2 Wildcats, both Beehive State schools were underdogs. Utah would have the first shot at proving the oddsmakers wrong. They failed miserably against a Badger team that had finished strong in a 7–5 season, but nonetheless was the Big Ten seventh-place finisher at 3–5. Billed as a game between 270-pound running backs Ron "Great Dane" Dayne of Wisconsin and the Utes' Chris "Locomotive" Fuamatu-Ma'afala, the Copper Bowl quickly turned into a rusty bucket for the Utes. Fuamatu-Ma'afala's year was finished when he went down with an ankle injury in the first quarter. Dayne, taking a cue from what Rice and BYU had done to Utah's mushy run defense, ripped off 246 yards and scored three touchdowns in a 38–10 Badger rout. Although amassing 430 yards offense behind Fouts—who threw four interceptions—the Utes muffed chance after chance and were a mere shell of the team that captured a dramatic 16–13 win in the 1994 Freedom Bowl. The Utes finished 8–4 and faced a winter of discontent in sorting through the wreckage.

The Cougars swung to the other end of the pendulum in Dallas, where K-State fans would outnumber the BYU faithful three to one. The Cougars started, however, with no respect, being cast as a three-and-a-half-point underdog. Hadn't anyone paid any attention to the Y's August 24 victory over that other, more-heralded Big Twelve team? By halftime, the oddsmakers looked like geniuses. BYU scored the game's first five points . . . the Wildcats scored the next fifteen, in the process borrowing a page out of the Cougars' Hail Mary playbook. K-State quarterback Brian Kavanaugh hurled a dying quail pass into the end zone as the first-half clock expired, where Wildcat receiver Andre Anderson emerged from a pack of players to catch the ricocheting TD pass as he lay prone on the turf. With Mike Lawrence's run tacking on two points after the touchdown, KSU—having been outplayed nearly the entire half—led 8–5 at intermission.

Having already established themselves as comeback kids against A&M and against Wyoming, the Cougars were just sort of teasing their fans by allowing K-State to go up in the third quarter 15–5 when Kevin Lockett latched onto Kavanaugh's pass and loped seventy-two yards to score. It was then fourth-quarter time—Cougar time.

Sarkisian turned the Wildcats every which way but loose in the fourth quarter, throwing for 139 yards, just under half of his 291 game total. His thirty-two-yard scoring toss to kick-returner-turned-receiver Dye with 10:55 left, plus Pochman's PAT, narrowed the deficit to 15–12. Sarkisian and Kealaluhi finished the season in

January the same way they polished off A&M in August. K.O. ran a post-corner route and was wide open in the end zone to pull in a twenty-eight-yard TD pass. It was the same corner he went to for the game winner against A&M. And with Pochman's PAT, it was 19–15, same margin as in the A&M triumph.

When the numbers were broken down, the Wildcats were just another team to these Cougars. K-State had 278 yards offense, less than most WAC teams collected during the season. The Wildcats did most of the talking during Cotton Bowl week and during the game, a diatribe led by all-American cornerback Chris Canty. When it was over, Sarkisian, his BYU eligibility complete, tested the school's honor code for good sportsmanship by six-gunning the Wildcat bench. His aim was directly at Canty. Added Muirbrook, the defensive player of the game, "K-State gave us trash all day. We heard stuff like 'this ain't the WAC anymore.' I wanted to run up to some of those guys after the game and tell 'em 'it's the WAC Champions to you. What do you think of us now'?"

K.O. Kealaluhi was fired up even before he caught the game-winning touchdown at the Cotton Bowl.

In fact, at 14–1, with the most victories ever amassed by an NCAA Division I team and the most games ever played by a Division I team, and a well-earned number-five national ranking, the Cougars didn't have to ask what anyone thought of them, not even the milquetoast Bowl Alliance stoolies. BYU had returned to the mountaintop from where Edwards could once again look out over the empire his program had ruled—still ruled—for two-and-a-half decades. That a New Year's

Day Cotton Bowl trophy was his and that he had conquered the "new WAC" with his fifth perfect conference record (8–0) were bonuses. His biggest trophy had come on November 23—the day the Utes were brought to their knees in Salt Lake City.

Old WAC, New WAC—Same Champ

One hundred years after BYU and Utah first played football, and almost a century to the day the Cougars first beat the Uteskis on the gridiron—December 5, 1896—the school that was launched as BY Academy was still explaining to its northern brethren how the game is played.

Oh, Utah got the message loud and clear on November 23, 1996.

Deluded by newspaper-, radio- and TV-types in a Las Vegas crapshoot vote in July that their heartthrobs would win the WAC championship—don't they know nobody should be picked to win the WAC title other than BYU—Uteski fans were dumbfounded, or just plain dumb to the real facts.

Those football fundamentals were delivered via the flying feet of running backs Brian McKenzie and Ronney Jenkins and through a punishing defense spearheaded by Shay Muirbrook. A final score of 37–17 was not an accurate barometer of the devastation BYU wreaked on the hapless Uteskis, who accumulated just 261 yards offense. At 12–1, the Cougars displayed to a sold-out throng in Rice Stadium that there is a price to pay for BYU losing three straight games to the Uteskis.

How sweet it was for coach LaVell Edwards to have his club respond to taunts from Utah fans that the sixty-six-year-old legend was over the hill, that he should retire to the golf course or to his backyard garden and orchard in Provo to raise daffodils and peaches the rest of his life. There the Uteski boosters were, most of them in their dark, dank, and despicable watering holes with their glasses raised on high, singing the praises of a new generation of football players—the gladiators in crimson and white. Until the Cougars launched their Salt Lake City November assault that settled the best-of-seven series to open the 1990s—four wins to three in favor of the Cougs.

BYU's glee extended beyond the late-November Rice

Stadium atonement. Imagine the delight of the blue-and-white faithful when legions of Uteski fans joined up to root for a Cougar victory over Wyoming in the WAC championship game in Las Vegas on December 7. In barrooms from Sugarhouse to downtown Salt Lake City, Utah boosters were hanging on every Steve Sarkisian pass, every Ethan Pochman kick, every Muirbrook tackle, every McKenzie rush, praying for Cougar success.

Without a BYU victory, the Uteskis wouldn't be going

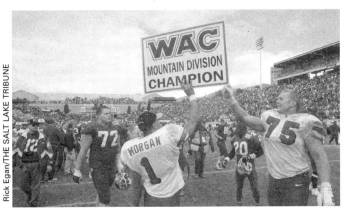

To Omarr Morgan (1) and John Tait (75) a Division Championship is still a championship, and it's even sweeter to win it on Utah's home field.

bowling in late December. Jack-Mormons the state over were hinting at repentance. If only BYU can win! They tell me that the loudest cheer—*for* BYU—ever heard at Lumpy's private club in Sugarhouse came when Pochman's thirty-two-yard field goal beat Wyoming in overtime. Bowl games do make for strange bedfellows.

After earning Utah a Copper Bowl invitation by virtue of the victory over Wyoming, the Cougars left the Uteskis on their own the rest of the month. And Utah, without their Happy Valley partners to negotiate the deal, botched the arrangement. The Utes got in over their heads against Wisconsin in the Copper Bowl and lost 38–10. McKenzie and Jenkins softened up the Uteskis in November. Badgers' steamroller Ron Dayne buried them in December.

BYU could baby-sit their second-rate cousins only so

long. The Cougars had other, much more profound goals to achieve than beating the Uteskis for the twentieth time in twenty-five years.

For a team ranked number five in the country, it was time to get a call from the Bowl Alliance "white house." You know, that spoiled-brat fraternity of six that controls the postseason football destiny of 103 other schools? Given guidelines that would allow for a number-five-ranked team from the WAC to join the snobs from the Big Twelve, ACC, SEC, and Big East in the major New Year's Day games, BYU spent the day after the WAC title win savoring its 13–1 record and waiting for the phone call from the Alliance.

Well, the Alliance, aided and abetted by their television cronies in New York, gave BYU the bowl shaft. Opting for marquee matchups like Virginia Tech-Nebraska (Orange Bowl) and Penn State-Texas (Fiesta Bowl), the Alliance got rich ($8.5 million per team), but NBC got stiffed in the ratings. The most exciting game of New Year's Day, naturally, came in the Cotton Bowl where the Cougars rallied to beat Kansas State 19–15. We could have predicted such an outcome for the TV folks based on the Cougars' marvelous and dramatic bowl history—remember 1980, 1981, 1983, 1988, 1989, 1991, and 1992? BYU is the most exciting bowl team of the last quarter century. But nooooooooooo, said the Alliance. We can't be surrendering $8.5 million to a team outside our little consortium.

Thus began the lawsuits and Congressional hearings into the hooliganism of the Alliance, repercussions that spilled into the 1997 season and likely will create a push for an all-inclusive NCAA championship playoff. Perhaps someone somewhere will realize the money-grubbing antics a few bully schools pulled off at the expense of schools that had the geographic misfortune of being born in the Mountain time zone. Even anybody-but-BYU die-hards—a few of them anyway, including University of Utah athletic brass—were siding with BYU on this argument, although there were still a gaggle of Uteski fans who had sadness hangovers on January 2 following BYU's magnificent Cotton Bowl conquest and a final number-five national ranking. Some things never change. Never.

But the WAC did change in 1996. Not that BYU's football title was a drastic modification. It was the WAC landscape and number of colleagues the Cougars would run roughshod over that underwent a transformation. From the charter membership of six in 1962—Arizona, Arizona State, BYU, New Mexico, Utah, and Wyoming—to the inclusion of Colorado State and UTEP in 1968, Hawaii in 1979, and The Air Force Academy in 1982, the WAC grew to sixteen schools in Utah's centennial year. Rice, TCU, and SMU of the old Southwest Conference, along with Tulsa, San Jose State, and UNLV joined the league.

BYU said nice to meet you and then proceeded to mow down SMU, UNLV, Tulsa, TCU, and Rice as if they had been WAC members all along—by a combined 243–82, or an average of 48–16. The kind of score you would expect from a BYU-Utah matchup. In an accurate comparison of strengths between the Cougars and Uteskis in 1996, try the scores of the two schools' games with Rice on consecutive weekends. Utah lost to the Owls 51–10 on November 2; BYU beat the Owls 49–0 on November 9. There weren't a whole lot of Utah men, sir, after that seven-day turnaround.

Is this a great conference or what? Okay, so the Cougars shouldn't be in the WAC. It's those Saturday afternoons in the Rose Bowl or the L.A. Coliseum, or in Nebraska's stadium, or at the University of Texas where the Cougs belong. Hasn't the case been made and reinforced over the past twenty-five years that the WAC is just not the caliber by which BYU football is measured?

Yet, the years come and the years go and the Cougars continue to dominate a league where once in a while a school sprouts up for a season or two only to wilt in the face of a BYU resurgence. Wyoming won a couple of WAC crowns in 1987–88 and could only beat the Cougars by a total of twelve points over two years. San Diego State won the championship in 1986 and overwhelmed BYU 10–3. CSU won in 1994 and beat the Cougs by a touchdown. So, in the four years since BYU's WAC title dominance began

in 1976, the Cougars lost out on the championship by a combined twenty-six points.

And out of the five seasons Utah beat the Cougars since 1972, the best the Uteskis could do was a share of the WAC crown in 1995. Five Utah victories by a combined fifty-five points. The Uteskis are just another woebegone WAC opponent.

Just goes to show you how much pent-up anger and frustration the Cougars felt in 1996. The fact that Utah tied them for the conference title in 1995 worked on the Cougar psyche for a full season. Oh, did they remember when it came time to fish or cut bait. In fact, the Uteskis acted like fish out of water in Rice Stadium.

And the Cougars, like ol' man river, keep rolling along. They brought on Texas A&M to open 1996, many figuring the he-men from College Station, Texas, would thrash the Provo crew much as they did in the 1990 Holiday Bowl. But lessons well learned are lessons well taught a second time. The TexAgs succumbed 41–37. Only a first-class bilking by the officials—119 yards in penalties!—at the University of Washington kept BYU from an undefeated season.

But as the Mormon hymn tells us, all is well, all is well. And on January 1 in Dallas, all was well. The Cougars reigned supreme over K-State. Everything was right with the world again. BYU was football king with the longest winning streak in NCAA Division I (12). Utah knew it. The WAC knew it. And most of the nation, the myopic Alliance notwithstanding, knew it. Make no mistake about that snub by the Tostitos Fiesta Bowl. So nachos are out and cotton candy is in. There are nine million Mormons out there who just switched snack foods.

Winners and Whiners

It didn't seem like it at the time, not with all those cheese-heads celebrating in Tucson and Cosmo's boys winning on New Year's Day, but 1996 may be the most hopeful sign yet of how far the Utah football program has come.

That sounds a little funny, considering how painful November and December turned out to be, and how badly the Utes missed fulfilling their preseason promise. But the mere fact that the football season seemed so unsatisfying shows just how much better life is at Rice Stadium in the McBride Era.

The Utes had an 8–4 record, a seven-game winning streak, a national ranking for a while, a one-game show-down for the division championship, and a bowl invitation. Face it, a season like that was as unfathomable as a Don King haircut in the sorry seventies or awful eighties. So why is everybody so unhappy?

Okay, the Cougars beat us, and did it in the most insult-ing way possible. Sure, the Copper Bowl got a little embar-rassing when the Utes showed up with their retro-Jim Fassel defense. So there's a little room for improvement at Utah. Big deal. Before Ron McBride arrived, that little room was about the size of the Astrodome.

No doubt, it's a little disappointing that the Utes were unable to capture the championship that so many were conceding them. And even when the Utes were running off their seven-game streak and climbing into the top twenty-five, they never seemed especially dominating or deserving.

"These guys will make you crazy," McBride said—after winning six straight games.

All of this is hard to figure, too, since Chris Fuamatu-Ma'afala was performing as advertised, with four straight 100-yard games, Juan Johnson was chipping in, Kevin Dyson and Rocky Henry were alternating big games (until Henry got hurt), and Mike Fouts was having an even bet-ter season than expected. In fact, he was sensational; he did-n't throw an interception until the fifth game, finally learn-ing not to panic under pressure.

Then came the crash.

Fouts got hurt in the Rice game, and was never the same. Neither were the Utes, who lost three of four. Maybe we could see it coming, but nobody expected the losses to be so awful. The defensive line finally paid for all its injuries, and opponents just started running right over Utah.

Rice had five backs run for more than sixty yards, BYU had a pair with more than 150, and Dayne picked up 246 yards and several Heisman votes.

It wasn't all as bad as it sounds. The Rice game (51–10) just sort of made you numb it got out of hand so fast. And anyway, we still had a shot at the WAC title.

The Copper Bowl wasn't horrible either, because it was nice just to be in a bowl after that maddening season. Besides, who could dislike the Badgers and their fans—so earnest and exuberant and inebriated?

The BYU game was different, of course. It's one thing to lose to the Cougars, not that we'd done that lately. Or to be beaten at home. Or to watch them celebrate another title.

What really hurt, though, was the way they beat us. The Cougars threw twelve passes all day. Instead, they kept running the ball, like big brothers showing off how they can beat up their kid brothers with one hand.

It was insulting. I left Rice Stadium more enraged than disappointed, furious at the disdainful game-plan BYU used. That may sound a little illogical, that I wish the Cougars had gone to their strength more, but at least we knew what that's like. You couldn't escape the arrogance that each rushing first down brought (and there were, what, three hundred or so?).

But then, arrogance was really plentiful in Provo all season, wasn't it? (Surprise.) From the first week of the season—a week earlier, actually—when BYU beat the startlingly mediocre and overrated Texas A&M Aggies, talk started about such ludicrous concepts as undefeated seasons and national championships.

Their weak schedule was always cited as a plus—how's that for twisted logic? "We've got a shot at being the best because we'll never have to prove it." Then again, it worked

Tim Kelly/THE SALT LAKE TRIBUNE

Mike Fout's senior year was spectacular for two months, but that was little consolation after a below-par performance at the Copper Bowl.

once before.

Still, doubt their football ability if you like (and I do), but let's give the Cougars credit for truly excelling at one thing in 1996: whining.

Only in Provo could a football team reach its most prestigious postseason destination ever and go out of its way to proclaim how unhappy it was to be there. It's like going to Las Vegas and complaining there's nothing good on TV.

But BYU and its fans managed it. Instead of being grateful that its bogus 13–1 record and inflated ranking had somehow fooled the Cotton Bowl into offering the

Cougars their first New Year's Day berth—and, by the way, their biggest payout ever—all anyone could talk about was how the Bowl Alliance had somehow cheated BYU. They "owe" us this and we've "earned" that. On one hand, Cougar fans moaned about how terrible it was that the Bowl Alliance thought only about money. In the next breath, they ranted about how unfair it was that BYU couldn't get one of the Alliance's big-money payouts. Interesting logic. Of course, these are the same people who bought up bags of Tostitos and burned them just to show how mad they were at the Fiesta Bowl's sponsor. Ouch, punish me some more—at $2.79 a bag.

What nobody seemed to grasp was that the Bowl Alliance was designed to match, if possible, the top two teams in college football. Beyond that, the bowls wanted—as they all do, every year—the teams that would deliver the most fans to the stadium and the most viewers to the TV sets. BYU had that silly ranking, but little national credibility. C'mon, they got blown out by Washington, then fattened up on the UTEPs and UNLVs.

So the Bowl Alliance used its two at-large berths on Nebraska and Penn State, though you'd have thought it was Delaware and North Dakota State, the way people huffed about it. Who would you rather invite, the two-time defending national champs who still had a shot at a third as late as December, or a team that was still thanking Wyoming for the gift-wrapped WAC crown? A Penn State team that beat Michigan, Northwestern, and Southern Cal, or the Provo squad that trounced New Mexico by three points at home? Bowl committees figured it's their $8 million; how exactly is it their "obligation" to give it to a bunch of overrated whiners that most of the country has never heard of?

Instead, the Cougars got to play on New Year's Day for the first time, but they reacted as if they had to sweep up the stadium. When the WAC signed on with the Cotton Bowl a few years back, everyone agreed it was a coup for such a little-known conference. Now BYU was mentioning Dallas and conspiracy more often than Oliver Stone.

The game itself wasn't much better, since Kansas State surprised everyone by leaving their playbooks at home. Was it just me, or did the Wildcats never seem to have any idea what play they were running? After about the third delay-of-game penalty, somebody should have gotten his head knocked in. And still the Cougars had to rally in the last five minutes to win.

Funny how phony fourteen wins can seem. But even funnier was the debate after the Cotton Bowl, to wit: Is this the best BYU team ever?

You mean, there's never been a better BYU club than the one that Washington dismissed without mussing its hair? That Provo's proudest season includes an impressive three-point win over New Mexico? At home? That no Cougar squad has ever been as talented as the one that got pushed around by Wyoming? (Believe it, nobody in Laramie was saying this was their best team ever.) That the greatest team that LaVell Edwards has ever coached was quarterbacked not by Jim McMahon, not by Steve Young, not by Ty Detmer or John Walsh or Robbie Bosco—but by Steve Sarkisian?

If you say so.

Granted, BYU was better than Utah this year. It wasn't close. But it wasn't hopeless, either. If that's the Cougars' best shot, and if those tired, hurt, and plummeting Utes could keep the game reasonably competitive—hey, we've seen a lot worse, haven't we, Jim Fassel?—there's reason to feel a whole lot better about the 1996 season. And giddy about the future.

Mac is capable of building a better team than those Cougars. His 1994 and 1995 Utes were arguably better than the 1996 Cougars, and nobody's claiming he can't improve on those teams.

If I were a Cougar fan, I would be embarrassed by the notion that these are BYU's greatest days. Because if it's true, there are going to be a lot more of them at Utah.

CHAPTER

A STATE DIVIDED

Generally, it is a figment of the imagination that BYU versus Utah (we use the schools in alphabetical order for diplomacy purposes) is a rivalry between the Church of Jesus Christ of Latter-day Saints and the Catholic Church. Nor is it the LDS versus (a) Baptists, (b) Methodists, (c) Presbyterians, (d) Unitarians, (e) Episcopalians, (f) Lutherans, (g) Greek Orthodox, (h) Unitarians, (i) Hare Krishna, or (j) atheists, et al.

LDS versus LDS? Now we're getting closer to the heart of the matter.

Still, there is no documentation that prayer on Temple Square in Salt Lake City, or in the Manti Temple, or in the Provo Temple, or in the St. George Temple has ever impacted on a Cougar-Ute football game. If so, then the big guy wasn't listening from 1922 to 1941, or from 1945 to 1957, or from 1959 to 1964, or from 1968 to 1971, dark days during which BYU won a grand total of five games from the U.

By the same token, Utah fans were finding little consolation at their football altars from 1972 to 1992, winning only twice against the Cougars. So for the righteous or unrighteous—and fans are quick to tell you on which side of the aisle they take residence—supplication provides precious little nourishment in the documented history of football between the Cougars and Utes.

Make no mistake. There is a rivalry, bitter at times, even competitive at times, but in the annals of collegiate football, the Ute-Cougar showdown hardly compares with Notre Dame-USC, Ohio State-Michigan, Harvard-Yale, Texas-Texas A&M, or Alabama-Auburn. Not yet. Anyone remotely connected to those O.K. Corral–type duels can only scoff at the infancy of the BYU-Utah game-week feuding. Because, in reality, the serious ramifications of the annual Beehive State shootout have been felt only since 1979.

Until then, when the pendulum swung heavily BYU's way, Utah had been king of the football hill. The Utes' attention was focused on the traditional Thanksgiving Day skirmish with upstate rival Utah State, and the almost-annual attendant prize of a Rocky Mountain Athletic Conference, Big Seven, or Skyline Conference championship. Utah claimed the title eighteen times, ironically starting with 1922, the year the Utes and Cougars resumed their annual matchup after BYU dropped the sport in 1898 because of in-state gridiron-related fatalities. The score of that "first" game on October 14, 1922, was Utah 49, BYU 0.

It took fifty years for BYU to inject some pizzazz into its program with nine wins in thirteen seasons over the Utes from 1965–78. But no one knew with any certainty the sleeping giant of the Wasatch was taking permanent, Sasquatch-type steps that would squash not only Utah, but the Western Athletic Conference and often other national powers for nearly two decades.

Utah had dominated the Cougars, as had most every BYU opponent, since the Cougars resumed an intercollegiate schedule in 1922. From coach Alvin Twitchell's three-year record of 5–13–1 up through 1971, BYU employed nine coaches over forty-seven years. Only one, Eddie Kimball, posted a winning record (34–32–8 in eight seasons). The rest of them—Twitchell, C. J. Hart, G. Ott Romney, Floyd Millet, Chick Atkinson, Hal Kopp, Tally Stevens, Hal Mitchell, and Tommy Hudspeth—were 97–172–10.

Utah and BYU had paired off in football as early as 1896. No one is certain whether the rivalry began as some sort of observance of Utah's first year of statehood. It was probably just a coincidence. Known as Brigham Young Academy, the Cougars played the sport for three seasons with Utah posting a 3–2 record. For those keeping score, Utah won the opener 12–4 in the days of the four-point touchdown. The first-ever touchdown in the series was scored by a Utah end, Charles Albert Peak, on April 6, 1896, at Utah. The Utes followed with a 6–0 victory on November 14, 1896, with captain Fred Odell scoring a four-point TD and adding the two-point conversion. After BYU posted three wins in a row, 8–6, 14–0, and 22–0 behind the scoring of Heber Larson, David V. Hyde, John Peterson, and Orville Larson, the Utes ended the BYU experience with a 5–0 win on November 24, 1898, on the strength of Albert Margetts's five-point touchdown. Running the ball would be the Ute forte for most of 100 years. Sending the ball airborne would be introduced later in the Midwest and eventually patented in the West by BYU.

Since 1896, the two schools have been arguing about the all-time record, and even that quarrel is of recent vintage. The Cougars didn't have any grounds for quarreling for so many years. The Cougars scored just two touchdowns in the first six years after resumption of the rivalry. A tie with the Utes was a moral victory and even in the tie, BYU didn't score. It was 0–0 in 1928. The Cougars scored four more touchdowns in the next nine seasons until the next tie, 7–7, in 1938. Two more Ute wins and a 6–6 tie in 1941 left Utah with seventeen victories and three ties in the first twenty years.

It was the first "glory" era of Utah football. Seven Utes had gained all-American recognition by 1941. They included tackle Alton Carman; center Marvin Jonas; fullback Earl "Powerhouse" Pomeroy from the unbeaten teams of 1928, '30, and '31; fullback Frank Christensen (1931–32); tackle Jack Johnson (1932); tackle Bernard McGarry (1938), and tackle Floyd Spendlove (1941). From 1928 through 1932, Utah posted an overall record of 33–3–3, and had outscored BYU in five games 161–20. There was a reason.

Isaac J. "Ike" Armstrong, a no-nonsense Iowan, entered the Ute coaching scene in 1925. A newspaper story heralded his University of Utah arrival by claiming "the Mormon school's new coach will succeed Thomas Fitzpatrick who has resigned." Mormon school? Try that one on 1990s Ute fans.

Contemporary, fire-breathing Utah fans would appreciate Ike. He just happened to come along in an age when schools kept coaches for more than three or four years. Of course, Ike won. Not that there wasn't a fair amount of pressure on his twenty-nine-year-old shoulders. Wrote R. L. Olson of the *Salt Lake Telegram*: "The University of Utah is a big school, with a wealth of athletic material. Can Armstrong utilize this to a greater extent than did Fitzpatrick?" The coach Ute patrons knew as "Fitz" had gone 23–14–3 and had never lost to BYU.

In his first year, Armstrong posted a 6–2 record. In his second year, the Utes went 7–0, allowed only twenty-three points, and beat BYU 40–7. Amazingly, Armstrong would have a team that was better defensively than the 1926 crew. In 1930, his 8–0 team yielded just twenty points while scoring 340. BYU went down 34–7, and USU succumbed 41–0. Ike was the area's first genuine coaching icon. His teams would win thirteen conference championships during his 141–55–17 run over twenty-five seasons.

Ike discovered early on some of the little nuances of coaching at the "Mormon" school. His wife, Pearl, writing of her Ute recollections in 1985, recalled this experience:

> Ike began his job at Utah in the spring of 1925. He and Ben Lingenfelter held practice in the spring and returned in August with high hopes for a good season. When the squad reported, one of the players they were depending on failed to show up. Ike asked where he was and was told the young man had gone on a mission for the Mormon Church.
>
> Ike, who knew nothing about the church, panicked. He contacted Gus Backman, the president of the Salt Lake City Chamber of Commerce, and demanded an explanation. "Who sends these boys away? They just can't do that! How do they expect me to have a football team?" Gus patiently explained that the young men are sent on a mission by the president of the LDS Church. They spend two years at their own expense in this country or in foreign countries converting people to the Mormon religion.
>
> Ike was unwilling to give up. He yelled, "Where's this guy's office? I'm going up there." Gus politely told him the office was in the LDS Church building situated next to the Mormon Temple. Gus also told Ike in a very fatherly voice, "If I were you, I wouldn't go up

there." When LDS President Heber J. Grant heard the story several years later, he laughed and said, "I really wish that young man they call Ike had come up to see me."

Armstrong, like his defensive-minded teams, was seemingly bullet-proof. Pearl was reminded of that in relating a 1929 New Year's Eve experience when she and Ike were in Los Angeles for the Rose Bowl between Cal and Georgia Tech:

We had decided to get in our Model A Ford sedan with our friends Marge and Herb Dana. We were cruising down Hope Street, Herb and I in the front seat, Ike and Marge in the back. There were so many people. We were barely moving down the street. Everyone had horns and noisemakers.

It was almost midnight when Ike yelled, "Hey Marge, why did you hit me with that horn?" Marge laughed and said, "You must be crazy, I didn't hit you with any horn!" About that time, Ike looked out the window and reached back on the ledge of the rear window and picked up a .32 lead bullet and in his trademark loud voice shouted, "I've been shot!" We thought he was kidding. We didn't believe him until he took off his felt hat, which had grease on the rim. The bullet had gone through the top of the car, through the rim of his hat and glanced off his neck. He was uninjured. We knew him from that moment on as Ike the Roughneck.

There was little soft about Ike's persona. But he won the hearts of Utahns forever during the depression. Ike's $6,000 salary had him making more than the governor of the state. The story goes that one day Ike confronted the chairman of the board of regents, Dr. Clarence Snow, to tell him that he didn't like the stories circulating that he made more than the governor. To which Snow reportedly replied, "Hell, you are worth more than the governor." As Pearl tells it, "During the depression, the university had to retrench by cutting faculty salaries. Ike's $6,000 annual salary was unaffected because of his three-year contract. Ike went to university president Dr. Thomas and asked to have his salary reduced commensurate with the faculty reduction. This decision took Dr. Thomas off the hook with the faculty, who no longer resented the football coach or his salary."

Ike remained about as invincible against the Cougars as he had against that L.A. bullet in 1929. But he was the eternal skeptic. "Ike lived in mortal fear of being the first coach to lose to BYU," says John Mooney, who was sports editor of the old *Salt Lake Telegram* and later the *Salt Lake Tribune* for a period covering 1939 to 1990. "There might not have been a rivalry with BYU in 1942 in the eyes of the Ute boosters, but for Ike, there wasn't a lot in his football life more important than beating BYU," says Mooney. Armstrong would scrimmage his troops until 7 P.M.— the night before the game. Mooney says he can still hear the Armstrong refrain resonating through the dim twilight, "Let's do that situation one more time!"

October 10, 1942, was a day that would live in infamy for Ike. BYU was coming to town. The Utes had lost two games and were scoreless after being blanked by Santa Clara 12–0 in Salt Lake and 14–0 at Arizona. In addition, Ike was losing players nearly every week to World War II duty. But so was BYU. The Cougars had even lost their coach, Eddie Kimball, to a U.S. Navy commitment. Stepping in for a season to take Kimball's place was Floyd Millet, a former Davis High School coach. A rookie coach to face the Utes? Millet's four predecessors had been beaten by a cumulative 142–21 in their debuts against the Utes.

Millet recalls using every psychological ploy known to man to prepare his Cougars, starting with the fact that in 1941 BYU had emerged with a 6–6 tie versus the Utes. He knew the disadvantages.

> *Utah normally had about 100 players and we had about 30. We used to drive around a three- or four-state area trying to recruit players. We used to get a few guys, mostly the ones Utah didn't want. We got some LDS kids and some non-LDS kids. But we didn't get very many. I figured the only way we had a chance against Utah was to compile as much information about each of their players as I could. I would tell the team stories about how each of them could beat the man on the other side of the line. I had coached Ute center Burt Davis and their end LeGrande Gregory at Davis. Any little scrap of information we had on them we imparted to each of our players.*

It looked like most any other year at Ute Stadium. By the start of the fourth quarter Utah had a 7–6 lead on fullback Wood Peterson's two-yard TD run. Utah had overcome a 6–0 BYU lead provided by Fred Whitney's four-yard TD run. But late in the fourth quarter, the Cougars struck. "One of our tackles, Dee Call, who later became a prominent doctor in Salt Lake City, blocked a punt," Millet recalled. It only took us a couple of plays before Herman Longhurst plunged in for a one-yard TD."

The twenty-year drought was over. BYU fans stormed the field and mobbed Longhurst, quarterback Mark Weed and Coach Millet, among others. The Cougars' entourage claimed, among other souvenirs, the Ute goalposts. A distraught Armstrong stood on the north hill overlooking the field and was so irate that he ordered Chet Evans, superintendent of grounds and buildings, to turn on the sprinklers. Still, all Millet remembers is the drenched BYU fans hollering, "We'll get them again next year."

BYU didn't get much of anything or anybody for quite some time. The Cougars never won another game the rest of that year. Utah didn't lose another game all year, and won the Big Seven Conference championship. BYU's misfortune ran deeper than a four-game losing streak to end 1942. Because of the war, BYU suspended football for three seasons. When they resumed, Ike hadn't forgotten, nor had some of his Ute players who had returned from military duty.

From 1946 through 1949, Armstrong's last season before departing for the athletic director's post at the University of Minnesota, Utah buried BYU four straight years by a margin of 142–12. One Ute war veteran who had to absorb the indignity of the first BYU win in 1942, but who reveled in the 35–6 revenge victory in Provo in 1946, was gangly end Tally Stevens. Thirteen years later, he would become

BYU's head coach.

Another Ute stalwart was Stevens's colleague on the other end of the line, Grant Martin, who later coached three state champions at Salt Lake City's East High School. "I know this is hard to believe when you consider BYU's dominance of the series under LaVell Edwards, but really, I don't remember BYU crossing the fifty yard line against us very many times in my playing days."

The Utes were riding tall in the saddle after the war. It involved much more than beating up on BYU. The reward for a 7–2 regular season in 1946 was a trip to Honolulu where Armstrong's troops beat a Honolulu all-star team 40–6, before engaging the University of Hawaii in the Pineapple Bowl. This was big stuff considering BYU had never been in a bowl game. And this was Utah's second postseason game under Ike. In 1939, the Utes had shut out New Mexico 23–0 in the Sun Bowl on January 2—the first Intermountain football team to play in a January showcase game. Utah, the nation's leading rushing team in 1946, lost to Hawaii 19–16. But two bowl games and five conference titles in nine years was the stuff state bragging rights are made of. This was a fact the state would find out three decades later, at a different venue.

There were always high hopes for BYU football. Millet recalls every year after he joined the staff in 1937 the cry would be "We'll get the Utes next year." Millet contends that Kimball had BYU pointed in the right direction before the war. "We were starting to get some good football talent—not the numbers that Utah had, but we had enough." Kimball was 21–15–7 in the five years prior to his military service. Against Utah, his teams played competitively, including scores of 14–0, 35–13, 12–6, and 6–6. The group he had in 1941 and the one that Millet fashioned into the Cougars' first victory over Utah, went 3–1–1 down the stretch for a second place finish in the Big Seven. Future award-winning *Deseret News* sports journalist Dee Chipman was the Cougar quarterback. But by 1946 when football was resumed after a three-year hiatus, BYU was back at square one. And Kimball, after losing to Utah for the third year in a row and the sixth time overall, was gone. He was replaced by Chick Atkinson in 1949.

Armstrong's career was coming to a close also. The University of Minnesota came calling with an attractive offer for Ike to become athletic director. Utah had been a heckuva run for the "roughneck." And it was a grand learning experience for Pearl, whose words nearly four decades later could probably be echoed by any coach's wife who served before or after at Utah:

> When Ike took the Utah job, I was unaware of the tension, stress, criticism, and responsibilities as the wife of "the coach." I had to learn to keep quiet when there were rumors that he wasn't doing a good job, that he might be fired or not rehired when his contract expired. To maintain my poise, I gave up reading a newspaper or the sports pages after Wednesday. I learned about dual personalities. I learned that some of the sweetest, most amenable,

docile individuals could—and often did—turn into savage, second-guessing, raving mani-acs at football games. Although it became tough at times, I tried to be tolerant of fans who yelled obscenities and became verbally violent. They paid to get in; I didn't! It was especially important to be nice to members of the press. Why? Because they wrote the last story.

I learned to smile and close my ears when a pass was intercepted, or when a seventeen-year-old quarterback called the wrong play and raucous fans screamed for his scalp. I was caught in the middle between love and loyalty for my husband and resentment and bitter-ness toward those who were critical.

But in the end, there were so many wonderful people, so many enduring friendships. Those were my rewards. And my husband? He made the National Football Hall of Fame. What better legacy? A wonderful husband, a wonderful father, a wonderful coach.

And a Utah man, sir, until he died at eighty-eight.

So, you see, fans have never really changed much; nor have sportswriters.

Nor did the BYU-Utah football rivalry. It raged on. With Ike gone it was up to

Ray Nagel (left) and Jack Curtice were among early dominating coaches for Utah.

Jack Curtice—Cactus Jack as he would come to be known—to perpetuate Utah's bully-boy image over the Cougars. And he did. A tie in his first venture into Provo in 1950 was followed by seven straight victories. But in the minds of many Utes—and some Cougars—the only game in the rivalry that will stand for all time was the 1953 showdown on November 26.

For the first time in history, the final game of the season was between the Utes and Cougars on Thanksgiving Day. But this was different in a far more profound way—it would be on national TV. Famed broadcasters Mel Allen and Lindsay

Nelson were on top of the press box, calling the game for the entire country. No regional stuff. Everybody got this one.

Cactus Jack was in rare form the night before in a meeting with TV officials, BYU brass, and the Ute athletic hierarchy. Recalls Utah athletic director James R. "Bud" Jack of the Hotel Utah strategy session:

> *I see Cactus Jack over in the corner with his pencil and paper drawing something for Chick. I wander on over and what do I see? Curtice is diagramming all the Ute formations. For the opposing coach! Chick seemed to be taking it all in. He was no dummy. I drove Jack home later. I asked him why in the world would he want to give his plays away. Cactus Jack just threw his head back and laughed. "No problem . . . they can't defend us anyway."*

Problem was, Curtice's troops had a devil of a time defending against the Cougars. Because he was defending against his own offense. Atkinson had remembered everything Curtice had told him. He had installed the Ute offense. It was a game for the ages. The game was tied at 7 and 13. Utah led in the fourth quarter 33–26 on the strength of a two-yard TD plunge by Don Peterson. But the Cougars roared back with a thirty-two-yard TD pass from LaVon Satterfield to Phil Oyler. But the extra point snap was bobbled and Utah survived 33–32, even though its coach had given the game plan away. "Cactus Jack did that more than once," says Mooney. And he didn't win every time. But it was BYU in 1953 and perhaps Curtice was just trying to provide a level playing field considering the Ute dominance of three decades.

Someone else was worrying about gridiron topography, at least the BYU-Utah rivalry field that showed one Cougar victory for as long as he could remember. And the imbalance galled BYU president Dr. Ernest L. Wilkinson, who had taken control of the school in 1950.

It was a year after Atkinson had become head football coach. The 1949 season had been a disaster. As bad as it had been in some years, BYU had never gone winless in a season. But Atkinson, a Mormon, was at the helm for an 0–11 season and most of the defeats were embarrassing—47–6 to Texas Mines, 35–7 to Denver, 25–6 to Montana, and most deflating, a 38–0 loss to Utah in Salt Lake City. Adding insult to injury, was the fact no college team to that time had ever lost eleven games in a season. BYU was allowed an extra game because of playing Pacific Fleet in Hawaii. It was just enough for a dubious record.

At least the Cougars were respectable the following three seasons, posting a 14–14–2 record. There was even a 28–28 tie in 1950 against Utah, and a 7–6 loss to the Utes in 1951. It was the 1950 game that defined the rivalry's church versus state leanings in no uncertain terms. The Utah quarterback was Mitt Smith, son of Joseph Fielding Smith, a member of the LDS Church's governing body, the Quorum of the Twelve Apostles. Benny Mortensen quarterbacked the Cougars. Both signal callers had served their church missions in Argentina. President Smith and his wife were in the stands long before the kickoff in Provo. Whether it was because of their son in action or because of Cactus Jack's pregame pronouncement is a matter for conjecture for the early arrival of Smith and his wife. Curtice, just in from the head coach's job at Texas Western, said, "If we lose to BYU I'll ride all the way back to Texas on a jackass!" For a school that had lost just one time in all of history to BYU, Curtice got into the spirit of the rivalry quickly.

What disturbed Wilkinson more than anything was the fact BYU was competitive in nearly every other sport except football. Take basketball for instance. The Cougars had been playing intercollegiate hoops since 1905 and had experienced just five losing seasons. Three of them came from 1944–45 to 1946–47 as the school was rebuilding at the end of, and immediately following, World War II.

When Wilkinson took the BYU helm, the Cougars had just come through the rookie season of coach Stan Watts. Following on the heels of the football futility, Watts guided BYU's basketball team to a 22–12 season and into the NCAA tournament. Hoops hysteria gripped Provo. And it escalated into a real frenzy in 1950–51, President Wilkinson's first full year on the job.

Long before BYU won a national football championship, thirty-three years to be precise, the school had a national championship basketball trophy in its possession. And not long after, the school had a gleaming new hoops facility that could seat 10,500 fans—the George Albert Smith Fieldhouse. Prior to that time, the team played in the women's campus gymnasium, and before that, in the Springville High School gymnasium.

Watts was to Cougar basketball, starting in 1949 and continuing through 1972, what LaVell Edwards has been to football since 1972. Watts's basketball teams provided a rejuvenation of sorts for what annually was a colossal misadventure on the football field.

In 1950–51, Watts's second full season on the job, Roland Minson, Mel Hutchins, and their teammates stormed to the National Invitational Tournament (NIT) title with wins over St. Louis, Seton Hall, and Dayton in Madison Square Garden. National attention was overwhelming. "In those days, the NIT was just as prestigious as the NCAA," says Watts, who was enshrined in the Naismith Hall of Fame in 1986. Adds Pete Witbeck, longtime assistant to Watts, "Back then, the NIT champ was the big champ. Playing basketball in Madison Square Garden was like playing football at Notre Dame."

The Cougars' 1950–51 basketball team put BYU on the map. Because of athletics, the Mormon Church received more national press attention in one week than it had in 100 years—at least since the 1880s, when abolition of polygamy was at the forefront of the nation's psyche. BYU followers were devouring the athletics adulation. And Ernie Wilkinson was taking notes.

If there was one sport in which the Cougars could match talent with Utah, it was basketball. And with the NIT title, they had snatched away one of the Utes' hole cards in the boasting game. In 1944, coach Vadal Peterson's Utah club, led by upstart freshman Arnie Ferrin, came from nowhere—sixteen war-year games had kept the program afloat—to capture the NCAA championship. Having been unceremoniously dumped from the NIT in New York by the University of Kentucky, Utah peeled off consecutive victories over Missouri, Iowa State, and Dartmouth for the title. Just for good measure, the Utes then polished off NIT champion St. John's in a benefit game in Madison Square Garden.

To further cement its standing as the Wasatch king of the hardwood, Utah returned to New York in 1947 and behind Ferrin, Leon Watson, and Vern Gardner, mowed down Duquesne, West Virginia, and Kentucky for the NIT championship.

Utah had been the pacesetter in basketball facilities, too. The sprawling Einar Nielsen Fieldhouse, named for the longtime Ute trainer, had been christened on January 9, 1940. Seating nearly 6,000, it was a sister facility to Utah State University's George Nelson Fieldhouse. At Provo, there was still the cracker-box campus facility that seated about 700 and Springville High's gym, which could handle maybe 1,400 fans all scrunched together with the legs of front-row spectators protruding out on the playing floor. As Mooney recalls, "Some of those well-placed knees and feet often caused havoc with the players—especially visiting players." The gym was so small that doors had to be opened at each end so that a player driving to the basket would have room to roam rather than crash into the cement wall.

Wilkinson had seen enough of poverty-like basketball conditions. Basketball was the Cougars' strength. In fact, it was the athletic focal point of the church. Period. Every ward house had a basketball floor. The early spring M-Men tournament, capped by a "state championship" in Salt Lake City, was a marquee event, surpassing even the state high school championships in popularity. At Wilkinson's urging, the church authorized the construction of the 10,500 George Albert Smith Fieldhouse on campus. For the first time—but not the last—BYU had assumed the lead in on-campus athletic facility construction. It didn't matter that the Cougars had to play every one of their Skyline Conference games at the University of Utah in 1950–51. Watts's fast-breaking Cougars won the league title and the NIT. Imagine Wilkinson's delight strutting his stuff in front of the Ute faithful.

It didn't take a genius to figure out the paradox. A Cougar football team had gone winless in eleven games and finished last in the Rocky Mountain Conference, while in the same season the basketball team—playing at Springville High, which was just big enough for two baskets and the center jump circle, and at Utah through the graciousness of the Utes because of the Smith Fieldhouse construction—won the conference title. And Wilkinson was considered a genius, especially in America's courtrooms. When it came to arguing, Ernie had no peer. And that included coaches.

Atkinson was a nice guy, an innovative coach, and an upstanding member of the LDS church. But his football teams were losing. The Cougars lost thirteen of the last fourteen games he coached. Nearly everyone in Utah County, and especially those on the BYU campus intimately involved with football, knew the sport was on the ropes. "We played constantly under a cloud of uncertainty," says Dick Felt, who was a Cougar letterman from 1952–54. Later a pro with the Boston Patriots and for twenty-six years a loyal assistant to BYU head coaches Tommy Hudspeth and Edwards, Felt says other than beating Utah, the most common theme heard around football was that the sport could be abolished. "Wilkinson fought any improvements. There was little scholarship help, no recruiting money, and we rarely had more than thirty players on the team. Playing was for a love of the school and a love of our church."

Not even the season-ending TV thriller at Utah in 1953 could stem the tide of misfortune. Nor could a narrow 12–7 defeat the next season in which the Cougars stalled on the Utah eight yard line in the final minute. "We were doing some pretty innovative things, especially in passing, like throwing to the halfbacks out of the T-formation," says Felt. "We even used Curtice's Utah shovel pass some." But innovation or not, the Cougars were still doing the same stale stuff—losing. They were seventh and last in the Mountain States Conference. BYU languished in the cellar two more seasons, going 2–17 from 1954–55.

The school was growing by leaps and bounds in enrollment and the basketball team was a national player. But Wilkinson, writing in the four-volume *History of BYU* that he co-authored with Utah historian Leonard Arrington in the 1960s, said, "The prolonged struggle to establish a football program was a source of frustration and embarrassment for students, faculty and alumni for so many years." Felt contends it was President Wilkinson's sons, Ernie Jr. and David—athletes in their own right—who had a profound influence on their father's change of heart toward football. "They always told me they were after their dad to make BYU the Notre Dame of the West."

Felt contends BYU's president made an abrupt turn in 1956 and "altered the course" of the Cougars' football history. Wilkinson turned east, way east, and hired a non-Mormon coach whose Rhode Island team had won the Yankee Conference championship. One BYU insider said it was Wilkinson's dream, not necessarily to make BYU the Notre Dame of the West, but the Harvard of the West. And they had played some pretty successful football over the years at Harvard while at the same time maintaining a high-profile academic standard.

Hal Kopp was an Ike Armstrong clone, although Crimsons at the U would cringe at the thought that there could ever be another Ike. Ute followers couldn't know that the real Ike look-alike was sitting in their own stands taking notes for future reference. Edwards was twenty-six when Wilkinson ordained Kopp as the Y's seventh head coach in 1956. But Edwards was a struggling coach at Salt Lake's Granite High School, rarely winning more games than he lost. But his football appetite was insatiable. He liked what Utah was doing under Curtice, and he admired BYU's revived interest in football with the acquisition of a proven college coach.

There was one big difference readily discernible between Kopp and his BYU coaching predecessors: Kopp was not a member of the church and frequently, in private, would make fun of the brethren. Of course, nothing was private in Ernest Wilkinson's world. Sometimes, Kopp went public with his barbs. Recalls Dave Schulthess, longtime BYU sports information director, "Hal loved to say he had one team on the field, one team in the hospital, and one team on missions."

Kopp, affectionately dubbed "The Mad Dutchman," had changed the normal retinue at BYU by bringing in a number of players from out of state. And his offense was more pass-oriented with quarterback Carroll Johnston passing for more yards than BYU amassed on the ground in 1957–58. Kopp also surrounded himself with capable assistants like Al Davis, Max Tolbert, and former Utah great Tally Stevens. "He let the assistants do most of the coaching," says Raynor Pearce, a halfback under Kopp. But everyone knew he was the general. Everyone toed the line." One incident that happened in 1957 separated Kopp's BYU's teams from any of their forerunners. "Utah State was playing at our place and a bench-clearing brawl broke out. The next day the papers reported Kopp crowing, 'Who says missionaries can't fight?' He got a lot of static over that one," says Pearce. Some of it was from Wilkinson.

The new coach received more flak over his first-year record of 2–7–1 in 1956. It was barely better than in the Atkinson years. But in 1957, the Cougars nearly matched Utah's win total (6–4) with a 5–3–2 mark. Unfortunately for Kopp's troops, the 41–6 loss to Utah in 1956 didn't get much better in 1957 (27–0). Still, there wasn't a lot of pressure. "Basketball was king. We took it in the shorts fanswise," says Pearce. Matter of fact, the most competitive game was the paper airplane contest. Since not much else was going on, it was real competitive to sit in the stands to see who could make the best airplane and get it to sail the furthest onto the field. "It was silly and it was sad," recalls Pearce. And the same old moan went up from Utah County: "Why can't we beat Utah?"

Curtice, beloved by Utes far and wide, was gone after the 1957 season, headed for the head coaching job at Stanford. His 45–34–4 record and four conference championships represented the end of an era. Utah would share a WAC title in 1964, but that was the only gold hardware the Ute football program would earn from 1957 through 1994. It was a glorious departure year for Curtice—the 27–0 victory over BYU to mix in with four wins in the last five games. The only loss was to Army 39–33, with quarterback Lee Grosscup at the controls—a game still regarded in Ute annals as the "victory" over Army.

When BYU made its near-annual foray into Salt Lake City on September 27, 1958, there was no reason to believe the Utes wouldn't put the hammer down on the Cougars—again. Even though new Ute coach Ray Nagel was on board, veterans like Grosscup, Pete Haun, and Don McGivney were ready to send the Cougars scurrying for cover. One thing haunted Ute followers, recalls Mooney. "Kopp's team had won four of their last five games in 1957 and they beat up on Fresno State in the 1958 opener. BYU hadn't had many stretches of success like that." If handicappers had dug deeper, they would have noticed that BYU had allowed only sixty-four points in their last seven games since the 27–0 loss to the Utes in 1957—a paltry nine points per game. And BYU's defense had forced a national-best thirty-two fumbles the previous year.

Regardless of what was happening on the football field, Wilkinson had a habit of sauntering into the public address booth on game day and simply taking over the microphone. This day was no exception. Anyway, he was good friends with Ute president A. Ray Olpin. Nothing to worry about in the way of recriminations. The game was tied 7–7 at half, adding fuel to Ernie's flair. "Come on down to BYU to go to school," he would intone. Like in Logan for the USU game, he would get on the public address system and openly proselyte Aggie students and faculty to make the switch to Provo. "Ernie wasn't bashful. It was his way to help the school grow and prosper," says Schulthess.

One example of Wilkinson's preaching is related by longtime BYU play-by-play broadcaster Paul James in his 1984 book *Cougar Tales*. James was mikeside doing BYU's NIT semifinal game against Army in 1957 for KSL radio in Salt Lake City and was expecting legendary Boston Celtics coach Red Auerbach to be his halftime guest. "Suddenly, President Wilkinson slipped into the seat beside me and took the microphone," relates James. "Before I knew it, he was launching into a dissertation on how the U.S. government had dispatched Johnson's Army west to keep the Mormon settlers in line in the 1850s and that now the Mormons had come east to get back at the army. Before I knew it, he was gone and Auerbach had taken the seat I had held for him."

It was really too bad that Ernie couldn't have taken the microphone that 1958 night in Ute Stadium after the game. Cougar quarterback Wayne Startin hit R. K. Brown with a thirty-six-yard touchdown pass in the fourth quarter, and George Kinder booted the extra point and BYU had secured a 14–7 win.

Think the Cougars' second win of all-time over Utah and the first since 1942 didn't send Cougar fans into never-never land? "I got so excited that I determined right then and there if I ever had a son, I would name him R. K.," says Cougar booster Gary Dayton, who became the campus barber in the Wilkinson Center.

And he did. R. K. Dayton lives in Provo. There were other interested Cougar spectators that day. West High School baseball coach Glen Tuckett, who would become head baseball coach and later the athletic director who spearheaded BYU's 1982 stadium expansion to 65,000 seats, was on a date with his eventual wife, Jo. Granite High School's head football coach was in a $1 seat in the coaches' section. The Farmers' coach, LaVell Edwards, approved of the way Startin was throwing the ball.

This had to be it, Cougar fans figured. We've turned the corner. Kopp would see Weldon Jackson lead the conference in rushing, and the Cougars finished with a 6–4 record, good for third in the conference. His teams had won eleven games and lost just seven and tied two in two years.

Mysteriously, to some, Kopp was back in Rhode Island by the fall of 1959. No details were ever released, but Kopp's generosity led to his dismissal. A Cougar player had become homesick and Kopp bought the youngster a TV set. The NCAA was alerted—of course BYU officials pointed straight to the U as the reporting culprit—and when it was determined the purchase was a violation, Wilkinson, ever the plea-bargaining attorney, threw himself at the mercy of the collegiate watchdogs in Kansas City. For self-reporting the incident and probably assuring the NCAA, Kopp would be dismissed; BYU escaped NCAA sanctions.

That meant the Cougars would have their fourth coach in twelve years. Tally Stevens, who had achieved stardom in crimson and white and who had led East High School to three football championships in 1952–53 and 1955, was elevated from his assistant's post into the head chair by Wilkinson.

By this time, the school president had visions of grandeur. He was purchasing large parcels of land around the school. "He had the foresight to provide for expansion," says Schulthess. "No one, to this day, can think of anyone else who could have handled it. Ernie just burrowed right in." The win over Utah had done wonders for his outlook on football. "It occurred to him, based on the attention the school had received from Watts's basketball teams, that public relations and athletics went hand-in-hand. There was much more public support when you won," said Schulthess. Plus, it quieted those blasted Ute fans for a few months.

Stevens was the antithesis of Kopp. A more reserved, almost distinguished sideline coach, Stevens had a record of losing a lot of close games—five by less than thirteen points his first season in 1959, including a 20–8 decision to the Utes in Salt Lake City. But his Cougars, however stout on defense, didn't score much either. In the twenty-one games he coached, BYU exceeded nineteen points only once—a 34–14 win over Cal Poly to open the 1960 campaign. When the Cougars lost to Utah 17–0 in Salt Lake City, and when the Cougars lost four of their last five games, Wilkinson had seen enough.

He had plans in the works for a new 30,000-seat stadium on the northwest edge of the campus. Losing to Utah—losing to anybody—would not help the fund-raising campaign. Utah had found success again with Nagel, who had won twelve games in two years and finished second in 1960 in the Skyline Conference. Stevens had the shortest tenure of any permanent coach in school history. After two seasons, Wilkinson's coaching revolving door swung open for Cougar assistant Hal Mitchell.

Utah had gone fifteen seasons without an all-American, but Grosscup's performance—326 yards passing for two TDs and another score by rushing—in front of the eastern press in the 39–33 loss to Army in 1957 gained him first-team honors from the Football Writers Association of America. Then in 1959, Larry Wilson was anointed an all-American as a halfback/defensive back. Finally, in 1961, BYU broke into the "all" fraternity with tailback Eldon Fortie's rushing exploits landing the honor despite the fact that BYU finished only 2–8. Fortie's two touchdowns had helped BYU mount a serious challenge to the Utes who actually had to come from 20–14 down to win 21–20 in Salt Lake City. An interested spectator at Ute Stadium was—again—Edwards, who had coached Fortie the nuances of the single-wing offense at nearby Granite High.

By the next fall, Mitchell had invited Edwards to join his staff. Reunited with Fortie, the Cougars' rookie assistant not only perked up his former student to a league-leading 1,149 yards rushing, but helped mold a defense that scored two shutouts—the school's first in three seasons and two of only three whitewashes in five seasons. Mitchell was a respected coach, devoted to his church and with deep feelings about the destiny of the school's football program. A 4–6 season in 1962 and a third-place finish—ahead of the Utes—in the inaugural season of the Western Athletic Conference helped him win the league's coach-of-the-year award. But he lost a 35–20 decision to Utah in a game in which the Cougars trailed in the fourth quarter 35–7.

Mitchell could have been a "great scientist," says Schulthess. In fact, he was often referred to as the "mad scientist." One innovation he tried was removing the front bar on the helmet and putting more padding inside the helmet. There were fewer concussions but more broken noses. And by 1963, with Fortie gone, opponents were breaking the Cougars apart. The record plummeted to 2–8 overall and 0–4 in the WAC. Worse, BYU had lost to the Utes 15–6, extending the latest Y losing streak to Utah to five games. Wilkinson couldn't tolerate the gridiron shortcomings. Work was underway on a brand-new stadium. It would seat nearly 30,000—perhaps as many as 35,000 could be crammed in with the right combination of circumstances.

No one was surprised by Wilkinson's charge to the forefront of area football. "He was a strong-willed person," says Schulthess. A successful attorney who had won a $32-million settlement from the U.S. government for the Ute Indian tribe,

Wilkinson was fond of saying he was running the school on a salary of $1 per year. Others figure it took prodding from higher authorities for him to get kick started toward concessions to football. LDS President David O. McKay, who had played football at Utah in the early 1890s, may have been one of them, says Mooney. Church spokesman Adam S. Bennion was the messenger from the LDS offices on South Temple in Salt Lake City. "Bennion told Wilkinson in the early 1960s that a football winner at BYU would open more doors to the missionary program," Mooney claims. Given that green-light blessing, Wilkinson plunged full speed ahead.

Well, sort of. Says Millet who took over as athletic director in 1964, "Dr. Wilkinson told me I could not use any school funds or any church funds to recruit athletes. To Ernie, it was as if all the good football players would just come to BYU no matter what." A search for funding led Millet to form the Cougar Club in 1964. "Things really started clicking for us. Of course, we had Tommy Hudspeth winning the conference title in 1965 for the first time in school history. And we beat Utah. I went into California and Arizona and signed up new members. It helped us in so many ways. We got a bigger coaching staff and that staff could go out and recruit."

After having been the fat cat on the block for so many years, it was Utah's turn to play catch-up. The Ute athletic hierarchy knew it had kept BYU at bay for two reasons. One, Armstrong and Curtice had been successful coaches, and by winning, the area's top football players flocked to the U.

Plus, BYU simply would not spend any money on football. But as Utah athletic director Bud Jack said, "Getting money out of our leadership was like pulling teeth. I could negotiate some with President Olpin. We had a $25,000 deficit one year and he called me on the carpet and said, 'We just can't reconcile losing money in football. I can cover this [deficit], but work hard on getting us even.' And I did. But when James E. Fletcher came, we had a budget and it wasn't much. And he didn't waver . . . until near the end of his tenure. When he turned things over to Alfred Emery, he said, 'You screw up Bud's athletic budget and you'll have to answer to me.' See, no university president likes losing money, especially in athletics."

What "screwed up" Utah and the WAC was the awakening of the "sleeping giant" in Provo. "We had so many conference meetings in the early years of the league where athletic directors would ask when BYU would wake up. Once they started spending money, we were all in trouble. Because as a private school, they would be able to spend whatever it took to be successful, and they wouldn't have to reveal their budget to anybody," recalls Jack. A shortage of money would haunt Utah for three decades. "When I first took over, we had to pay rent to use Ute Stadium. Little ridiculous things like that really stymied our growth."

Before BYU started winning there were moments of humor. As Jack recalls, "For a long time we played all the Utah-BYU football games in Salt Lake. One year, BYU athletic director Eddie Kimball called me and said since it was their designated home game at our place, he would prefer we didn't serve coffee. I said fine, then when we come to your place and we are the home team, I would prefer you serve coffee. Eddie said, 'Bud, I think you should do things your way, and we'll do things our way down here.'"

Once their hand was forced by BYU, especially with Hudspeth bringing in the Marine recruits who helped him roll up three wins in a row in the rivalry from 1965–67, the Utes swung into action themselves. At Jack's urging, Utah formed the Bleacher booster organization. Plans were drawn up to renovate the football stadium, and local entrepreneur Robert L. Rice donated $1 million toward a scholarship box, AstroTurf, and a new lighting system.

The facility, now capable of seating 32,500, became Rice Stadium in 1972. "The scholarship box helped fund financial aid for out-of-state recruits," says Jack. John W. Gallivan, publisher of the *Salt Lake Tribune*, was named chairman of the Scholarship Box Fundraising Committee, and through his efforts the box had a waiting list of contributors after only three years. "We started out with $500 seats and it mushroomed to $1,500 per seat by the 1990s." The Ute booster club became known as the Crimson Club in the 1980s, a fund-raising entity whose annual haul now competes favorably with the Cougar Club.

With its new stadium in place in 1964 and a new coach, Hudspeth, who, more by chance than anything, launched the passing revolution with Virgil Carter, BYU began making rumbling sounds. One season after Utah's triumphant 9–2 campaign that resulted in a Liberty Bowl invitation and subsequent 32–6 romp over West Virginia at Atlantic City, the Cougars captured a WAC title in 1965. Suddenly, BYU had established itself as a major WAC player. Even though the program vacillated between good and average, punctuated by seasons of 2–8 in 1968 and 3–8 in 1970, there was enough excitement generated by close games with Utah to keep Cougar fans coming to the stadium—in droves compared with the crowds of 5,000 to 8,000 in the late fifties.

Utah was existing primarily on its victories over BYU—30–21 in 1968, 16–6 in 1969, 14–13 in 1970, and 17–15 in 1971. There was one exception. In 1969, the best of Utah coach Bill Meek's six seasons, a defense spearheaded by Larry Stone and Norm Thompson joined with an offense directed by quarterback Ray Groth and complemented by receiver Fred Graves to forge an 8–2 mark. Utah had the WAC title in the palm of its hand, but in the next to last game of the season, a 2–7 University of Arizona team stunned the Utes 17–16 at Tucson, delivering the championship to Arizona State. It was a defeat from which Meek would never recover. For the next four seasons, the Utes would do no better than third place in the WAC, and by 1972, a rookie head coach named LaVell Edwards had guided his BYU club past Meek and the Utes 16–7 in Salt Lake City and a second place WAC finish.

No one could have fathomed the significance at the time. Even though Edwards was the first BYU newcomer to treat the Utes so irreverently, there had been another time—under Hudspeth—the Cougars had made overtures at breaking free of the in-state shackles. Surely a nine-point loss was not the end of a Ute dynasty, or the beginning of a Cougar reign.

Mark A. Philbrick

LaVell Edwards holds trophy from 1980 Holiday Bowl while Kyle Whittingham whoops it up. Kyle later joined the Ute coaching staff.

But a 46–22 Cougar win the next season was the signal BYU faithful had been waiting for. Never before had BYU scored that many points, or won by that margin. And in Salt Lake at that. Could it be, even though the Utes (7–5) managed to finish ahead of the Cougars (5–6) in the WAC, that this upstart coach Edwards, who had earned his master's degree from Utah and rarely achieved a .500 record at a Salt Lake County high school, would be the messiah BYU had been seeking all those years?

For nearly 150 years, a basic tenet for nineteen-year-old male members of the Church of Jesus Christ of Latter-day Saints has been to serve a two-year mission, spreading the Mormon gospel and proselytizing new members worldwide. This fact was brought to light for Ike Armstrong in 1925, but Armstrong wasn't a member of the church. Missions had been served long before 1925 and remain a sustaining, burgeoning function of the church as the twentieth century comes to a close. All members of the church, be they men or women (who must be twenty-one to serve a mission), learn very early on that a church mission is a special calling, ordained by the president (prophet) of the church. A mission is not mandatory and is an extraordinarily personal decision.

Aspiring mechanical engineering students serve missions; future law school students serve missions; medical school prospects serve LDS missions; and home economics majors serve missions. And athletes serve missions. They go to Argentina, Indonesia, England, Australia, Malaysia, Japan, Mexico, and all corners of the United States. As a male Mormon approaches nineteen, the introspection begins—to serve or not to serve. Same for a female Mormon approaching her twenty-first birthday.

For many Mormon athletes, the mission call has been an excruciatingly tough decision. Future NFL Hall of Fame quarterback Steve Young opted not to serve and interrupt his budding collegiate career in 1980. The decision weighs on his mind, even thirteen years into his pro career that by 1997 had included a Super Bowl title and a pair of MVP honors with the San Francisco 49ers. Young insists he'll serve a church mission eventually. Shawn Bradley, the seven-foot-six high school basketball phenom from Castle Dale, Utah, accepted a scholarship from BYU, played one season in 1990–91 and then served a mission. Upon completion of his mission, he signed a mega-million-dollar deal to play in the NBA.

Hundreds of other Cougar athletes have committed to play for BYU and opted to go on missions either before they entered school, or often, after a freshman season of eligibility. Bart Oates, who went on to win three Super Bowl rings as a center with the New York Giants and 49ers; running back and return specialist Vai Sikahema, and lineman Tim Hanshaw are other examples of returned missionaries (RMs) who excelled after an absence of two years from their collegiate careers.

Since Edwards took the BYU reins, it has been a rarity that a Cougar athlete started his career, left on a mission, and didn't return to play. Edwards changed a long-standing policy that a player might not have the availability of a scholarship when he returned from a mission. That is further validation of how strongly the Cougar coaching legend feels about his church and about his players. "A mission broadens a person's outlook on life. Certainly, they may not return in great athletic shape. But mentally and spiritually, I've seen most of them grow way beyond their years," says Edwards.

Ute fans cynically contend the missionaries are off somewhere on a far different calling. "Malaysia? The guy isn't in Malaysia, he's in Miami, at a Dolphins' football training camp," chides one Ute. "You kidding me? BYU sends their missionaries off into the Waimea Falls weight room," carps another. Even retired Fresno State University football coach Jim Sweeney, a near-lifelong friend of Edwards, felt the Cougars had an "unfair advantage" with RMs. "If you put a twenty-year-old kid against a twenty-four-year-old kid, there's a tremendous difference at that age."

Sweeney's troops didn't have much of a problem with the age difference in the 1992 and 1993 seasons when his Bulldogs were winning two WAC titles and rolling up seventeen wins against BYU's fourteen victories, including a 48–45 win at Provo in 1993.

In fact, Edwards accurately points out that "when we weren't winning in the 1960s, nobody said anything about the missions. But once we started winning championships, people came out of the woodwork pointing to our 'older guys' as the reasons." No one could point to quarterbacks getting older, bigger, and wiser through missions. None of them—Virgil Carter, Gifford Nielsen, Marc Wilson, Jim McMahon, Steve Young, Robbie Bosco, Ty Detmer, John Walsh, or Steve Sarkisian went on one. McMahon, Detmer, Walsh, and Sarkisian were not LDS, although Detmer converted while in school.

Concessions for religious missions are not indigenous to BYU. An NCAA rule allows exceptions for two-year religious and military interruptions of a college career. Instead of the normal five-year window in which athletes must complete their eligibility, returned missionaries are allowed seven. So, many BYU athletes are twenty-four or twenty-five years old by the time their careers are complete. One well-traveled route is to play one year at nineteen, serve a two-year mission, return for a redshirt year to get back in shape and resume playing at twenty-two.

Utah, whose athletic programs rarely included RMs even though the school is forty-five miles closer to the nerve center of the LDS church, began horning in on BYU's near monopoly of landing blue-chip Mormon players when Ron McBride took the Ute head coaching reins in 1990. He had been a keen observer of what was happening in Provo. Two previous tours of duty as a Ute assistant (1977–82, 1985–86) had educated him to a system where BYU often, if not always, locked up an LDS athlete simply because the mission avenue was made available.

There had been rare occasions when Utah athletes served missions. In the mid-1950s, running back Gordon Oborn played two years, went on a mission and decided not to continue his football career when he returned. Other early athletes-turned-RMs included Phil Moody, Jeff Jonas, and Lane Walsh. "Most guys back then just couldn't get interested again after their missions," said Dr. Ned Alger, an assistant football coach at the time who later became Utah's assistant athletic director. Basketball players Josh Grant, Craig Rydalch, M'Kay McGrath, Keith Chapman, and Jon Hansen returned to productive athletic careers after missions in the late 1980s and early 1990s. Utah's most outstanding defensive player, Alex Jensen, left what would become Utah's best back-to-back basketball teams in history (1996 and 1997) to serve his church.

McBride says he simply addressed a facet of the program that had been neglected, or at least conceded to BYU. If the Cougars wanted a top-flight Mormon athlete, they got him. "Parents felt their sons' spiritual needs could best be fulfilled at BYU, where the missionary program had been in place for decades," McBride explained. So he put his own plan in place. "A better one than at BYU," says twenty-year Ute assistant Sean McNabb. "Mac beat BYU at its own game by telling a recruit he could have a scholarship, serve his mission, and come back and have five years to complete his eligibility. In essence, Mac says 'we want you, your future is established.' The recruit has a piece of paper that promises him a scholarship when he starts his career."

So, Utah, already a school with a student body population comprised of 60 to 65 percent LDS, was becoming another Mormon football school. Maybe that newspaper in 1925 knew something after all in citing Armstrong taking over at the Mormon school. McBride says people can call it what they want, but where there wasn't a system in place to lure prospective missionaries, there is one now. "BYU has enjoyed a lot of success and RMs have been a big part of it. They had a corner on the market. Now we can go into the home of an LDS kid and tell the parents their son can attend Utah, go on a mission, and have his scholarship and five years to complete his athletic eligibility when he gets back."

Veteran Ute trainer Bill Bean says there is no question that RMs, while physically softer at the outset, are more mature in handling the long road back to top playing condition, regaining what he calls "physical aggression." He sees a big difference in personality. "They are more task-oriented. They spent two years following a rigorous schedule in the mission field and now, combining athletics with academics, they know precisely how to allocate their time." The maturity factor is measured by the minimal dropout rate of RMs from the program compared with the general student population loss.

Edwards says he always encourages players to serve their missions. "It's so ingrained in our faith that you don't even think twice about it. I think missions, in some cases, have helped guys, and in some cases they haven't. It's an individual thing, just as it is with the different commitments you'll find on the football field." In any event, the two schools located some forty-five miles apart will now have, on a yearly average, some sixty to sixty-five players either on missions or returned from them.

Parity in the "bigger, faster, more mature" mission sector achieved, the Utes continue, in the waning years of the millennium, to close the dollar gap. Required by the Federal Equity in Athletics Disclosure Act to reveal budgets, even by private institutions, BYU showed expenditures of just over $14 million for the 1995–96 school year, $5.4 million of which was earmarked for football. That compared with Utah's budget of around $12 million, $3.3 million of which went toward football.

Naturally, eyebrows twitched when the Cougars' budget was disclosed. No one had ever known before, for sure, just what kind of money BYU threw around or where it came from. Antagonists like to claim it only took a bump in church tithing to jump-start, or infuse new enthusiasm, into a lethargic Cougar program. At the root of all outside speculation was that the LDS church's financial well had no bottom.

BYU tells another story and it reflects what Dr. Wilkinson told Millet in 1964—no church funds are included in the budget. And only a portion of student fees charged through tuition are used. The Cougar Club, directed by Dale McCann since 1975, continues to raise millions of dollars earmarked for recruiting, athlete tutorial assistance, and other athletic endeavors. "We have approximately 4,000 members," said McCann. That number fluctuates by about 750 according to BYU's won-loss athletic record. It hasn't hurt that the school had a 1984 national football champion and a passel of conference titles to use as fund-raising enticements. "But in down years, such as when we lost three straight football games to Utah (1993–95) or when we've undergone a controversial coaching change, we've lost members. But with success, we continue to grow."

The Utes' Crimson Club, launched in 1984, has mushroomed to nearly 4,000 members from Bleacher Ute days of the 1960s and 1970s when forty or fifty people was a big crowd at Monday rehash sessions. While Ute athletics receive a token portion of their budget from the state, less than 10 percent, the bulk is from private donations. In 1996, for instance, the Crimson Club generated $2.3 million. There are no tax dollars used for facilities, either new or upgrades. Other than the football stadium, which will be almost completely redone by 1998 and in plenty of time for the 2002 Olympics' opening and closing ceremonies, Utah's athletic plant compares favorably with BYU's. But Utah has done a considerable amount of catching up. The Eccles Tennis Center, the Dee Glen Smith football complex, the McCarthey practice football facility, and an on-campus softball field are luxuries of which even BYU can't boast. It's probably just a matter of time, though, before BYU acquires similar accommodations. Utah's ten-time national champion women's gymnastics program played second fiddle, facility-wise, to BYU until fund-raising efforts resulted in a state-of-the-art building for Utah expected to be completed for the 1998 season. Utah built the Special Events Center for basketball in 1969, which became the Huntsman Center. By 1970, BYU retaliated with the 22,500-seat Marriott Center. By 1998, the Utes' football stadium, although smaller capacity-wise by 15,000 seats, will be second to none in luxury accommodations.

Up through the 1996–97 school year, BYU and Utah continued their all-sports comparisons, a race normally won by the Cougars. But measured by national titles over all sports, Utah was clearly the runaway winner. The Utes won the NCAA basketball title in 1944, one Association for Intercollegiate Athletics for Women (AIAW) gymnastics title (1981), nine NCAA women's gymnastics titles (1982–86, '90, '92, '94, '95) two AIAW skiing titles (1978 for women and 1981 for men), and eight NCAA skiing championships (1983–84, '86–88, '93, '96–97). The

Cougars won NIT basketball titles in 1951 and 1966, and the NCAA golf championship in 1981.

But the debate rages on because Cougar fans figure the 1984 grid title supersedes any and all Beehive State athletic achievements. Ute fans counter by saying the football championship is mythical, voted on by sports writers and broadcasters, while basketball, gymnastics, and skiing competitions are head-to-head against the nation's best at the same venue. Utah followers could only snicker in 1997 when BYU compiled a 14–1 football record, won a New Year's Day verdict over Kansas State, and still finished only number five in the country. Utah finished with a 10–2 football record in 1994 and was ranked number ten in the country, its first-ever top ten appearance.

No one will ever get at the core of the deep-seated animosities of the two institutions, which, connected by a major thoroughfare (I-15), are only forty minutes apart. If it's a church-driven issue, then Ute fans must explain why many LDS general authorities graduated from the U and still, however deep and hidden, harbor crimson feelings. David O. McKay, president of the church from 1951–1970, was a Ute grad and played on the varsity football team in 1894. Gordon B. Hinckley, president of the church in the 1990s when Utah won three straight games, was a Ute graduate. Joseph B. Wirthlin, a member of the church's Quorum of the Twelve Apostles, was a Utah football letterman in 1936 and earned his degree there. In 1997, of the Twelve Apostles, only one, former BYU President Jeffrey R. Holland, graduated from BYU. Now, ask those church general authorities who they cheer for from the general authorities suite in Cougar Stadium and you'll hear a lot of "Rise and Shout" responses.

Holier than thou? The Notre Dame of the Wasatch? Just as the Irish are the team to beat on everyone's wish list, so too are the Cougars, for any team from the Rockies on west and at several stops to the east. "Anybody but BYU" chant the Ute fans. The most cherished license plate holder is "I root for anybody playing BYU." Whenever a BYU football score is announced in Rice Stadium it is met with derision if BYU is leading. BYU's band, cheerleaders, songleaders, athletes, and school officials are routinely booed at athletic contests.

As *Sports Illustrated* reported in 1992, "Clean, Sober and Insufferable," or as the front cover stated "BYU is Hated." The reply of Edwards when the publication hit the newsstands prior to the 1992 season: "We haven't been winning long enough to get that kind of reputation. When I got here in 1962, there was no animosity or respect. We just kind of existed."

It was Edwards's way of turning the other cheek. Because there had been animosity and very little respect as the BYU athletic program made a wide, sweeping turn toward success. Edwards was a football assistant in the 1960s as the Cougars gained a football foothold with their first WAC title in 1965. And in basketball,

BYU had the NIT championship in 1966 and three WAC titles (1965, '67 and '69) to boast about. However, the road to success in the late 1960s was fraught with peril. What happened to Cougar athletic teams from 1968 to 1971 made any disrespect by Utah fans—past and present—seem pale by comparison.

Racial overtones permeated the athletic scene at almost every road stop the Cougars made. At issue was the stance of the Church of Jesus Christ of Latter-day Saints on African-Americans holding the priesthood. To many, including Dr. Harry Edwards, a one-time sociology professor at San Jose State University and himself an African-American, the church doctrine prohibiting blacks from the priesthood was a racist stance. Dr. Edwards claimed there wasn't any doubt that the LDS policy conflicted with language of the Civil Rights Act of 1964, which assured equality to all and prohibited any form of discrimination on the basis of race, creed, or national origin.

Open hostility pervaded the scene at San Jose State in 1968 for the Cougars' final football game of the season. Black members of the Spartan football team boycotted the game and urged fans to do the same. There were few fans in the stands and there were no incidents. Amazingly, the Spartans, playing without many of their starters who were black, beat BYU 25–21, ending a 2–8 Cougar season, the worst since Tommy Hudspeth took the BYU reins in 1964. Racial tensions between BYU and its opponents would get worse.

In 1969, the Cougars traveled to Laramie, Wyoming, to meet the Cowboys. There, passions had been inflamed by an article in the student newspaper in which the campus organization Black Students Alliance vowed to stage a demonstration outside War Memorial Stadium prior to the BYU-Wyoming game protesting the "racist practices" of the Church of Jesus Christ of Latter-day Saints. The letter further stated a demand that the University of Wyoming, as well as other WAC schools, stop using student fees and university facilities to "play host to, and thereby, in part, sanction inhuman racist policies of the [LDS Church]. We invite all white people of good will—athletes included—to protest with their Black fellows a policy clearly inhuman and racist. The symbols of protest will be the black arm band worn throughout any contest involving BYU."

Fourteen black members of the Wyoming team approached head coach Lloyd Eaton informing him of their desire to wear the armbands. Eaton, whose teams had won three straight WAC titles, denied the request on the grounds that the football field was no place to decide theological differences and that no players of his would be involved in any sort of spectacle. Undeterred, the players met for a second time in Eaton's office on Friday afternoon, this time wearing the armbands. Eaton summarily dismissed all of them from the team. Wyoming beat BYU that day 40–7, but the "Black 14" incident caused reverberations in the Cowboy program that would last fifteen years.

BYU's problems with the black-athlete dilemma persisted into the new decade. A basketball-court disturbance at Colorado State University on February 5, 1970, again spawned by a request in the student newspaper by the Black Students Alliance that there be a "peaceful protest," ended up with riot police dispersing a band of protesters. Two people were hurt and seven were arrested in a melee in which fights broke out and Molotov cocktails were hurled. Fans were removed from the arena in handcuffs. The game was played and Colorado State won, but the thought persisted, "How long might these types of situations go on?"

As it turns out, at almost every stop BYU's teams made, there were disturbances, some mild, some downright scary. At the University of New Mexico's "Pit" and at the University of Arizona, fans hurled debris and threatened recriminations against the school they felt practiced discrimination. Still in the 1969 football season, BYU regained its composure to win four games in a row. Only a 16–6 loss in Salt Lake City interrupted the late-season rush. BYU seemed at "home," even if Ute Stadium could hardly be construed as home for the Cougars. From a crowd comprised of probably 80 percent Mormons, there were no visible or audible signs of racial protest.

By 1972, whether through the fallout from the protest years or just plain bad recruiting years, BYU was the laughingstock of college football. Three consecutive losses to end 1971—to Arizona State, Arizona, and Utah—created a furor. Attendance was down. Utah again had the upper hand. Again, rumors were making the rounds in hotstove conversations that BYU football was indeed expendable. One guy already jettisoned was Hudspeth.

Then came BYU's coach selection decision of the ages. Recalls Watts, then the athletic director who chaired the search committee: "I told President Dallin Oaks that we had a great candidate right on our campus. I told him the guy was LaVell Edwards." Watts, who received the school's Presidential Medallion on April 24, 1997, says the reason for the most prestigious honor the school accords "was my brilliant suggestion to hire LaVell—my sole claim to fame, I guess." Not really. Basketball had carried BYU athletics, financially, since the war, and Watts was the catalyst. No wonder when the hoops coach spoke on football topics, the church's general authorities listened.

By the end of the 1970s, Watts, with the endorsement of the BYU hierarchy, was being hailed as a genius. Under Edwards, Cougar football stock was soaring. Conference championships (five), all-American honors (seven), Heisman candidates (Gary Sheide, Gifford Nielsen, Marc Wilson), national statistical leaders, national rankings, NFL draftees, and weekly sellouts at Cougar Stadium elevated the Cougars into the elite of college football. Glen Tuckett, who had taken the athletic director's reins from Watts in 1976, was at the controls of a stadium expansion fund-raiser with the full support of the Cougar Club. The Cougars would have

65,000 seats by 1982, all paid for through private donations.

As BYU was mushrooming into a national player, its former bully-boy neighbor to the north was stagnating. By 1982, the Utes were employing their fourth different coach in eleven years in an effort to dent the mystique of Edwards. Bill Meek (0–2), Tom Lovat (0–3), and Wayne Howard (1–4), were a combined 1–9, and their teams had been outscored 394–146 by the Cougars. Utah had five seasons of three or fewer wins in the seventies. The Ute constituency began to pin its hopes on beating BYU in November. But Bud Jack's worst fear, much like those of coach Ike Armstrong's thirty years earlier, had been realized. The "sleeping giant" nestled in Utah County, or "Happy Valley," as curmudgeons preferred, had not only awakened but was crushing anything in its path, especially in the WAC. In the first decade under Edwards, his teams lost only fourteen conference games and nine of those came in the first four seasons. And only one of his setbacks was at the hands of the Utes.

BYU wasn't strictly a Utah problem. "Everybody in the conference felt the pressure," says Jack. "When the Cougars made a commitment to their facilities, the gap between them and the other league members widened. It was some turnaround. In my younger days, nearly every Utah-BYU game was played in Salt Lake because they couldn't draw enough fans to meet expenses in Provo. Before you know it, they were playing to crowds of 65,000 in their expanded stadium."

BYU changed the face of WAC football when it expanded Cougar Stadium by 35,000 seats for the 1982 season. By the end of the 1980s, Tuckett's nationwide lobbying had attracted Baylor, UCLA, Washington, Pitt, Texas, and Washington State to Provo. In the nineties, national powers Miami, Notre Dame, and Penn State visited Utah County. The Cougars had made their commitment. Most other WAC members sat on their hands.

As Salt Lake County grew, Rice Stadium remained essentially the same capacity-wise. In 1982, a facelift included the Spence Clark Football Center in the south end zone, new locker rooms, and lowering the field by nine and a half feet, which added new seating along each sideline. Still, a capacity of 32,500 was hardly any answer to the mammoth edifice on BYU's campus.

And the Utes had struck too late. "By the time BYU's expansion was completed, and with the success of its program, they had sucked some 30,000 season-ticket holders out of Salt Lake County," says Arnie Ferrin, the all-American basketball player who served as Ute athletic director from 1976–85. "They were selling season tickets in Cougar Stadium for the price of one of our best seats for one game. As BYU won, those fans stayed in their seats. We had spent $5 million on renovation and they had spent $30 million." Those figures alone speak to the difference in football commitments. In fact, Ferrin took the athletic director's job in 1976 only after a pledge of athletic support from school president David Gardner. Says

Ferrin, who watched the athletic program grow by leaps and bounds in the 1990s from a foundation he helped lay during his tenure, "There is much truth in the axiom 'you are only as good as the president wants you to be.' Even in getting President Gardner's support, it was three years before we got the go-ahead for stadium remodeling."

The one big advantage Utah gained from an extra 5,000 seats was better funding for coaches' salaries and a better recruiting budget. Recalls Ferrin, "When we hired Howard in 1977, the first thing he said was, 'We'll beat BYU.' And he did. But once he saw BYU go to that bigger stadium and when he measured it against our commitment, he decided to retire. He told me and others we would never be able to compete if we didn't match their support of the football program."

Howard was a clairvoyant. Utah would march through two more coaches—Chuck Stobart (1982–84) and Jim Fassel (1985–89)—and eight more years with just a single victory over the Cougars. The best Utah could do in the WAC was a third place finish in 1985 in Fassel's rookie season. But in 1986, the Utes, picked to win the conference by some publications, were dead last in the league at 1–7. Utah had hit rock bottom. Utah had never been last in the WAC. The basement had been BYU's residence in 1963 and 1964. Now, the pendulum had made a complete swing. In a two-year span, BYU had won a national championship (1984) and Utah had finished last in the nine-school WAC. The last time the Utes could boast of anything remotely close was in 1964 when coach Ray Nagel's club tied for the WAC crown with New Mexico and went on to a Liberty Bowl victory over West Virginia. Things sure had changed in twenty-two years.

The one thing Cougar fans have been famous for is gloating over getting even, even if the brethren have to flaunt it among themselves in a state made up of 60 percent LDS. But, to hear the Ute faithful tell it, BYU has been insufferable since the Cougars launched their great turnaround in 1972. BYU fans like to think of it as jealousy. The fact is, BYU hasn't had to rely solely on football for bragging rights. In basketball, where the Utes like to say they have employed a get-even tactic, BYU and Utah have each won eight championships in the 1972–1997 era. Since the WAC began in 1962, BYU has won twelve hoop crowns and Utah nine.

But nothing inflames the passions of the two schools like football in November. It is convenient to date the deep-seated passions from Howard's 1977 "I hate BYU" speech. *Sports Illustrated's* 1992 article cut more accurately to the core, tracing the anti-BYU sentiments to 1830 when church founder Joseph Smith declared his the "true church." Taken in its literal sense, and since the church owns and operates BYU, it naturally follows opponents are meeting the "true football team" on Saturday afternoon. It is that pious attitude that irritates Ute fans. That, plus the fact the "true" team has been beating the bejesus out of their football team—twenty-one times in twenty-six seasons under Edwards.

Some believe sanctimonious Cougar fans are those who have known only success—the Edwards years for instance, with those rare blips in 1978, 1988 and 1993–95. And many contend it is the current generation—both blue and red—who perpetuate the enmity. They work together, live side-by-side, and many attend church together. BYU wins and Cougar fans look down on Ute followers as liberal gentiles. Or, if they happen to be sitting in the same ward house, they view their crimson-and-white brethren as WAC wanna-bes. Basically, Ute patrons respond, BYU is just spoiled rotten by all their success, however recent it might be, and that what goes around, comes around. That sector is obviously rhapsodizing over a return to the late 1960s, or a continuation of 1993–95.

Rick Egan/THE SALT LAKE TRIBUNE

Scott Mitchell grew up just ten miles from Cougar Stadium, but the left-hander forsook BYU in favor of a career as Utah's best-ever quarterback.

Utah followers fan the controversy by striking out at the holier-than-thou BYU persona, even if the U perpetrators are themselves LDS. "Most members of the church, students, or alums, do not hate BYU," says Laury Livsey, a Ute graduate and a member of the LDS Church. "They don't wear the rivalry on their sleeves like non-Mormon Utah fans," he adds. Could it be that BYU fans are so used to winning The Game, they just don't care?

There was no great anguish, no inordinate number of people leaping from tall buildings (of which there are few in Provo) when Utah won three games in a row from BYU in 1993–95. A large part of Utah's euphoria was dampened by the school's ability to gain just a share of one conference title out of the three-year run. More galling was the fact BYU tied for two crowns. After the first of the three Utah triumphs, Edwards and McBride got together for a series of TV commercials for a regional bank. Construed as heresy by the radicals in both camps, the lighthearted, thirty-second spots injected a much-needed measure of levity in the heated rivalry. It further weakened one other argument of the anti-BYU element: Who in the world could hate LaVell Edwards? Hate Jim McMahon, yes; Steve Young, maybe; LaVell . . . no way.

For every Utah fan who has thrown a snowball (or mini-bottle) at BYU fans (or players) at Rice Stadium, or for any BYU fan who has thrown an apple (or a plastic thirst buster refillable) at Utah fans (or players) at Cougar Stadium, there are fans who are playing their own little games away from the stadiums.

As virulent as the epithets might be—like "BYU Sucks!" from the Ute juveniles or "You Fetchin' Sops" hurled back from impudent Cougar bumpkins,—there is a lighter side to a rivalry that most often involves ward member versus member, or a Provo Mormon versus a Salt Lake Mormon, or in the case of KSL Radio's play-by-play broadcaster Paul James, an annual Game Week lawn decoration provided by the LDS fraternity at the University of Utah.

You can talk to one hundred different fans from each school and glean an anecdote or twelve from each one.

BYU fan Bob Bills, a Cougar football player in the late 1950s and now a Provo carpet company owner, and Ute follower John Robinson, a Salt Lake surgeon, have been friends since college days. Each year, they are involved in a Game Week prank. One year, Robinson, a U of U graduate and an anesthesiologist at the University of Utah Medical Center, was in the operating room when his buddy Bills was to undergo umbilical hernia surgery. Robinson says, "I'm going to give you a shot that will make you goofier than you already are. Do you have any last words?" Bills's response: "BYU 30, Utah 0." Later, in the recovery room, his wife Carol asked him to look at his feet. "John had painted my toenails red and white and had attached red and white balloons to my ankles. And there was a red-and-white patch over my incision that said 'Go Utes!' He also had put me in a red diaper. Worse, he was letting other patients and visitors snap pictures."

Now, paybacks can be painful. In 1990, Bills learned his pal John and his wife would be out of town the week before The Game picking up their son John Jr. from his church mission. Conveniently, Bob's son, Steve, was married to Robinson's daughter, Suzanne. Voila! Instant access to the Robinson home.

Bills's company had recently re-carpeted John's whole house, including his office. Bob figured some touching up was necessary. "I had saved all the old blue carpet with Cougar heads all over it when we redid the student bowling center on the BYU campus. We had it all cleaned and transported it to Murray. We took up John's new carpet and put this blue carpet down in his office. Plus, we put up blue-and-white curtains with the block Y pattern. We hung all kinds of memorabilia on the walls. We put blue water in the toilets. Then we put a football, filled with old carpet remnants, about eight feet long and four feet wide, on the bed in his master bedroom. It must have weighed 500 pounds. We stuffed a Cougar and left it on his living room couch. We turned John's home into a BYU souvenir shop. Outside, we draped the house in a BYU flag and put a sign in the window: 'Ex-Utes for BYU sign up here.' We got forty-five signatures during the week."

Robinson, upon returning home, had a sneaking suspicion who the culprit was. The phone rang in Bills's Provo office. "Congratulations, Bob, I am thoroughly enjoying walking all over the Cougars every day."

And through all the years, Steve Bills has remained a loyal Cougar fan and Suzanne Robinson Bills still flaunts her crimson-and-white pom-poms.

In the fall of 1993, Robinson took one more shot at Bills's Provo home. "I came home from work one afternoon and my picture window had been painted red and white. And on the front lawn, which slopes down the hillside and is visible for miles around, he had painted a big red U trimmed in white—about fifteen feet by twenty-five feet. Deer came down out of the hills and ate the U. Didn't touch the grass." That week, the Utes ate the Cougars 34–17 in Cougar Stadium. "John laughed and said LaVell should have fed his kids paint for more speed," said Bills.

All this from Robinson, a former LDS bishop, and Bills a member of his stake high council.

These playful shenanigans go back and forth every year, often handed down from family to family. Gordon Oborn played for the Utes in 1955–56. His brother Kent, who still holds a school record for punt returns, played for BYU in 1964–65. Gordon, who lives in Provo, is the host of the biannual Ute tailgating party in the Cougar Stadium parking lot. Red and white utensils are the order of the day. His pregame meals are so good that he even invites the Mormon brethren to break bread—if they adhere to the crimson-and-white house rules. BYU patrons are accommodated in the Ute tailgating parking lot, with a BYU Hospitality Room. It consists of a blue-and-white tent, with a card table set up for four, including four glasses of milk and some cookies. "BYU Fans Welcome," reads the sign over the door. The milk and cookies traditionally go untouched.

For years and years, members of the Utah athletic department each November would adorn the foyer of the offices in the Huntsman Center with a stuffed blue-and-white "Betty BYU," mocking the Cougars' stereotypical stay-at-home wife and mother. Dressed in a white nightgown with blue-and-white tennis shoes and with a tray of Twinkies and Jell-O, "Betty" would welcome visitors. The brainchild of Carolyn Johnson, Evelyn O'Donnell, Linda Egger, Lisa Kelly, J. D. Davis and Robert Wiscombe, "Betty" provoked lots of laughs over the years. Until other members of the Ute staff voiced their objections. Political correctness reached all the way to the front door of the Huntsman Center. Actually, the demise of "Betty" came when members of the predominant faith cried "foul."

Larry Latimer is a BYU graduate and his brother-in-law Mark Kirk is a rabid Ute backer. Larry, a computer programmer who spent a good portion of his career in Seattle, recalls the bleaker BYU bowl days of the late-seventies and most of the eighties when he watched the BYU telecasts, mainly from San Diego, but occasionally from Florida, Alabama, and Arizona. "Every time BYU's opponent would score, Mark would call from his home in Salt Lake or wherever he was at the time. 'Hey, Larry, the kittens are getting pounded again. Nyeh, nyeh, nyeh-nyeh, nyeh.' Sometimes, there would be five or six calls a night. If I didn't answer, he would leave word of the latest opponent touchdown on my answering machine. I didn't have to actually listen to the radio or TV play-by-play. Mark was a real pest." Ohio State's 47–17 victory over the Cougars in the 1982 Holiday Bowl and Texas A&M's 65–14 Holiday Bowl romp in 1990 are two nights when Mark's calls pushed up the AT&T stock, and tested the tape capacity of Larry's answering machine.

Families are often split down the middle. Take Herb Oborn of Sandy in Salt Lake County. A cousin of Gordon, Kent, and Lynn Oborn, Herb bleeds Cougar blue; he even has his toenails painted blue and white for The Game each year. Imagine . . . a fifty-year-old man getting his toenails painted with the school logo, and bragging about it. It hardly fazes his kids Stacy, Troy, Brooke, and Todd. They are all Ute fans. Each year they decorate their dad's house with red and white streamers. "There is always a big sign, 'Utah by 3' hanging off the house, a subtle reminder of the 34–31 seasons. And they paint a big U on my lawn. It stayed on there three or four weeks. I would mow it and the darned thing wouldn't go away. That's a real bad thing in the rare years that Utah beats BYU," says Herb.

In 1989, the rivalry hit the obituary page of the *Salt Lake Tribune* and *Deseret News*. The week after BYU had lost a 56–14 decision to the University of Hawaii in Honolulu, the family of the dearly departed, obviously a Ute partisan, wrote in a final public pronouncement: ". . . he died doing what he loved most, watching BYU lose."

However, no self-respecting Ute or Cougar masks his or her feelings on this side of the veil. Take Dale J. Nielson, writing in *Cougar Sports* magazine in November of 1996:

> *I will never be one of them, but yet I am. There I sat on Friday, June 3, 1994, in the Jon M. Huntsman Center, one of a few thousand graduates of the University of Utah. I was very proud to be there, to graduate from such a prestigious institution. We were each wearing the traditional black cap and gown and I was also wearing a crimson red tie—with little BYU logos scattered over it.*

> *Virtually all of my fellow graduates cheered (and probably still do) for the Utes. But not me. Never. I have an aversion to red. But I'm a U graduate and proud of it. Red and white*

only look good when combined with another color, like blue, as in the American flag. Contrastingly, royal blue and white are a good combination, as any BYU fan will tell you.

Like many of us in that class that day, the Y continues to play a significant part in our lives. To assign a stereotype is wrong, whether it be religious, racial, athletic, etc. Whatever, we traditionally sign a good luck card to the team each year: "May U rest in peace as U lose in November."

Nielson's choice of color was taken a big step further recently by University of Utah art professor Nathan Winters in his take on the crazy feelings between BYU and Utah: "Red is a hot color, blue is cold. When you mix the two, you get a psychotic purple. That's the color psychotic people tend to choose when given the choice."

Choice is a fickle thing. Goodwill between the two schools is often counterbalanced by the malice shown way beyond the athletic arena by members of the LDS church. From Salt Lake County you hear: "I am LDS and a Ute supporter and my church is supporting BYU. What gives?" And from Utah County: "I am LDS and a BYU fan and my tax dollars to the state are supporting the University of Utah. What gives?"

McCann says religious loyalty surfaces in the strangest of places. "There have been instances where we have made efforts to send telecasts of our games into cultural halls of ward houses across the nation, only to have the idea discouraged. How? There are Ute alums who are members of the ward and vent their Utah loyalties by voicing their disapproval of the telecasts. You would think they would see the games as a positive. But to our members who are Ute alums, there is a loyalty to the church, but not BYU athletics."

Yet, TV has spread BYU athletics far and wide. McCann says for years, alums would call in from Canada, Barbados, and "many other foreign countries," relating how they had picked up the radio signal of games. "They would go to a mountaintop, or the highest place in town, and turn to 50,000-watt KSL." When Rondo Fehlberg was hired as BYU athletic director, he told of the times "I would park high on a Houston highway overpass to get the BYU athletic contests on my car radio."

Now the Blue-White TV network, originating from the BYU campus, carries their games into all corners of the country, Canada, Mexico, and South America. "We started the TV program in 1979," said McCann. "We couldn't get support from BYU, so we got some guys to put up $10,000 to televise the BYU-Texas A&M game over KBYU. It was a tremendous success. We beat A&M in a game many say sent our program on the way to the big-time. Over the years, the telecasts built loyalty and built attendance. Now there is hardly a game anyone misses." In other words, for the some 9 million members of the LDS Church, the Blue-White network is what NBC-TV is to the some 800 million members of the Catholic Church worldwide, many of whom have the opportunity to view Notre

Dame football telecasts each weekend. "Everyone has to start somewhere," says McCann.

It is that perception—that BYU is the worldwide school in the Beehive State and Utah is the regional school—that grates on Ute fans, many of whom, of course, are Mormons. And when national magazines, especially *Sports Illustrated*, make frequent trips into Utah County, Ute fans cringe, cry, and carp. The scenery has changed in the 1990s with the revival of the U program under coach Ron McBride's direction. Still, during the Bowl Alliance brouhaha in December of 1996, *SI* staffer Richard Hoffer wrote, "In truth, Brigham Young is no longer college football's equivalent of the Amish. It's a big-time program that has been bringing in junior college transfers, more minorities—more players. Half the skill positions on this year's team, in fact, are staffed by non-Mormons."

That's a scary thought for the Utes who have competed over the years, albeit it on the losing end most of the time during the Edwards tenure, with non-Mormons. That is changing also, with the Utes' burgeoning missionary program. But the only real success Utah has generated in the two and a half decades while Edwards has coached has been with non-Mormons in the skill positions. Scott Mitchell was the only LDS kid who achieved stardom. Other Ute quarterbacks finding a spot in the national statistics—quarterback Larry Egger in 1985–86, Mike McCoy in 1993–94, and Mike Fouts in 1995–96—were non-LDS. In fact, of Utah's all-WAC award winners, only defensive back Eric Jacobsen in 1987 was a Mormon. Starting Ute fullback Molonai Hola served a church mission in the early eighties.

Former Ute kicker Scott Lieber, who graduated from Highland High School in 1982, served an LDS mission to Micronesia from 1983–84 and finally started kicking in 1986, can tell you about the travails of a returned missionary playing for the Utes. It happened to him after his career was completed, a tour that included the NCAA title for field goal accuracy in 1987 (fourteen out of fifteen successes). Lieber opted to become an LDS seminary teacher. During his final interview process, he was told at the church offices that "we won't hold it against you that you played football for the University of Utah." At Granite High, the old stomping grounds of LaVell Edwards, the needling process intensified. "I would hear often from parents during parent-teacher conferences something like, 'How could they let a Ute football player teach seminary? Or, they would say, 'If you feel good about not giving your talent for God's school, I guess that's okay.'" Lieber had a photo on his seminary office wall—a collage of photos from his Ute playing days. "Parents would come in and stick Post-It notes on it every year that read Utah Sucks! All my kids liked me. It was the parents that were militant. The football connection would just send them over the edge. Football is where you see the passion in the adults."

Utah traditionally has been a running back school—Eddie Johnson, Carl Monroe, Del (Popcorn) Rodgers, Tony Lindsay, Eddie Lewis, Lewis Walker, and all-American flanker and return specialist Steve Odom. Johnson, Lindsay, and Rodgers totaled 8,810 yards in their careers—about half of what BYU quarterback Ty Detmer passed for. All the Ute backs were non-LDS, African-American, and out-of-staters. You go down the BYU roster of rushing leaders and you find Fortie, VanValkenburg, and Scott Phillips—all LDS, white, and in-staters.

Herein lies the real paradox in this unholy war. Those that were once Cougars are now Utes. Oh, Cougar assistant Norm Chow played for Utah (1965–67) and since 1978 has been an assistant BYU coach, having been anointed by *Athlon* magazine as 1993 Assistant Coach of the Year. And Edwards's current defensive coordinator and linebackers coach Ken Schmidt played at Utah (1961–63) and joined the Y staff in 1982. But the exodus to Utah, to Cougar faithful, is downright revolting.

"Don't mention the names Kaufusi and Whittingham to us," say entrenched Cougar boosters. "We don't talk to people from there," respond Ute believers of contact with folks on the BYU campus. Ute boosters just know there must be substantive reasons why families once associated with BYU now root for, even work for, the University of Utah.

Start with the Whittingham family. And start with Fred Sr., who begat sons Kyle, Cary, and Fred Jr. The elder Whittingham played for the Cougars in the 1950s (his name isn't listed among BYU's all-time lettermen although he started for coach Hal Kopp's teams) and later was the school's defensive coordinator in the early eighties. By 1992, Fred Sr. was Utah's defensive coordinator and in his three years, the Utes whipped BYU twice—the first back-to-back Ute wins over the Y in a quarter of a century.

Kyle, an all-WAC linebacker for the Cougars in 1981, is considered by many as one of the two or three all-time best BYU defenders. Many Cougars are remembered for one game—McMahon and Clay Brown, for instance, for the Hail Mary pass in the 1980 Holiday Bowl; or Steve Young for his pass reception for a touchdown to beat Missouri in the 1983 Holiday Bowl. Kyle is known for his twenty-two-tackle, four-sack game against San Diego State in 1981 for which he was accorded *Sports Illustrated* Player of the Week honors. He went on to earn both his bachelor's and master's degrees from BYU. Since 1994, he has served on McBride's staff, most recently as defensive coordinator. He doesn't have the foggiest notion of where those Y graduation certificates might be. He was 3–1 as a player against the Utes and stands 2–1 against the Y as a coach. Cary was a three-year letterman for the Cougars from 1983–85, and Fred Jr. led the Y in rushing three straight years—1987–89.

The Kaufusi story is more pronounced. Brothers Steve (1986–87) and Rich

(1989–90) both starred for BYU, with Rich gaining all-WAC defensive end honors in 1990, the year the Cougars stunned number-one Miami. But BYU didn't see a connection in the lineage and passed on offering the next Kaufusi brother, Henry, a scholarship. Henry would be a two-year starter for the Utes and a two-time winner over the Cougars. The Utes also landed Jeff Kaufusi in 1994 and he started three years. Jeff told *Sports Illustrated* in 1995 that "I hold a grudge in my heart against BYU because they hurt Henry." He intimated that Henry felt the same way. Just for good measure, Steve, the ex-Cougar, is in his third season as Utah defensive line coach. Oh, one more thing: the youngest Kaufusi football products, returned missionary Doug and freshman Jason, have cast their lot with the Utes in 1997 to follow in the footsteps of brothers Jeff and Henry.

The list of turncoats goes on and on. Glen Kozlowski was an all-WAC receiver for the Cougars on the 1984 national championship team. His brother, David, played for the Utes (1992, 1994–95). "It breaks my heart that David went to

Mark A. Philbrick

BYU's Chad Lewis became the first winner in the Lewis brothers' crusade. Mike lost all four years playing for Utah, and Chad was 0–3 before the Y won in 1996.

Utah," said Glen. "I didn't know who to cheer for—Utah or BYU—when he played there. When he was through, my allegiance was definitely for BYU." David, of course, will always cheer for the Utes.

Defections haven't been a one-way street. Orem's Mike Lewis chose Utah over the Cougars in 1986, served a mission and then started for three seasons as a defensive lineman on the Hill from 1990–92. When it came time for his little brother Chad to chose schools, he couldn't swing a Ute scholarship, so he walked on at BYU. His storied career with the Cougars culminated in 1996 with his selection to the all-WAC team as a tight end. Chad was on a team that went 14–1, was ranked number five in the country, and won the Cotton Bowl. And, for the first time in the history of the Roger and Jan Lewis family of Orem, there was a son who emerged victorious in the annual November skirmish. Mike had gone 0–4 versus BYU in his Ute career. Chad was 0–3 versus Utah until the 37–17 win in 1996. Mike was among Chad's loyal band of rooters.

Utah's recruiting surge in the Pacific has also had a major impact on BYU's program. "McBride has stolen LaVell's program," laments a gaggle of Y supporters. "McBride has installed good use of the missionary program, he doesn't hesitate to pass the ball and he has stolen the Pacific Rim from us in recruiting," they say. Utah's 1997 class of recruits included three of Hawaii's top high school prospects. And that class came on the heels of other island prizes in the nineties, including linebacker Taulia Lave. It hasn't hurt that McBride has had on his staff Sam Papalii (since returned to the islands), and currently has quarterback coach Tommy Lee, head coach at Hawaii's St. Louis High from 1966–68.

There is some reason to believe the rivalry has evened out. McBride has brought Utah back to respectability, the three wins over the Y in the nineties providing adequate testimony. But Cougar loyalists maintain the 1993–95 seasons were a mere bump in the road, that 1996's 37–17 thumping of the Utes was a more accurate barometer.

History will tell us which is true. It won't come from the Bible or the Book of Mormon either. As Utah sports information director Bruce Woodbury said so many years ago, "There's no way a person's religion could have a bearing on what happens on the football field."

No, Bruce, just what happens off the field among the Ute and BYU brethren.

We Are the Champions

Some of us saw it coming, like you might see Amtrak's Chicago-to-Los Angeles Express come roaring down the rails. Or like watching a Kansas twister sweeping across the tops of the wheat fields. There was a football storm brewing in Happy Valley. BYU had won twelve games in a row in 1983 after an opening-season loss to Baylor in Waco. UCLA and Missouri were among the victims. Utah was no more than a red ink spot after a 55–7 dismemberment in Provo.

Despite Heisman Trophy runner-up Steve Young moving on to the United States Football League as its $40-million man, and a host of other Cougars like Todd Shell, Chuck Ehin, and Gordon Hudson landing NFL or Canadian League contracts, BYU marched into the 1984 season as WAC-champions-to-be. Weren't they always WAC-champions-to-be?

There was a guy named Bosco . . . yeah, yeah, Uteski fans snickered with derision that it was really Bozo—that is until November . . . ready to take charge of the conveyor belt buttons at Quarterback U. And there were receivers Glen Kozlowski—just "Koz" to insiders—and David Mills and Adam Haysbert, heroic offensive lineman Craig Garrick, big-play running back Kelly Smith, linebackers Kurt Gouveia and Leon White, defensive back Kyle Morrell. They were report-to-work-on-time kind of guys. In fact, they were arrive-early, leave-late troopers. Opponents would discover the Cougars' work ethic was akin to that of the one-time Orem farmer Edwards, who was overseeing the nation's most successful offensive football machine.

As usual, the nation's voting geniuses were ignoring the Cougars. Figuring they had done enough in elevating Young and the 1983 Cougs into the top ten, the media (and coaches) didn't throw a single preseason vote BYU's way. Why, the conventional figuring went, BYU would come out of Pittsburgh on opening night with the number-three-ranked Panthers as just another eastern quadrant

victim. Oh, the astigmatism of the writers and broadcasters.

Doing it their way, the resolute Cougars waited until almost the final seconds to puncture Pitt's reverie and offer the opening chapter of a best seller. If there is a school that has a patent on whirlwind finishes, it is the amazing Cougars. This time, Bosco pulled the trigger with a pass down the middle on which Haysbert made a Crazylegs Hirsch–type of catch. Prancing on into the end zone, Haysbert set the tone for what would become the greatest season in college football annals. It wasn't Pitt who the

Lynn Johnson/SALT LAKE TRIBUNE

Robbie Bosco returned from injury to rally BYU past Michigan 24–17 in the 1984 Holiday Bowl win that preserved the Cougars' national championship.

nation would talk about the next week. The Cougars leaped into the top twenty. Fickle guys, these voters.

Next came a score to settle. Coach Grant Teaff's Baylor Bears had overcome a great Cougar team in 1983 to deal Young and Company its only defeat. There would be a heavy price to pay. Bosco shredded the Bears in a 47–13 victory before a sellout crowd at Cougar Stadium, and BYU edged up to number twelve in the polls. Tulsa was no more than a blip on the screen the next weekend in a 38–15 BYU victory. Are we having fun or what with the Cougars ranked number six?

Hawaii had designs on a WAC title in 1984. They had flowers to drape around the Cougars as BYU arrived at the

airport. They had nooses and the gallows readied in Aloha Stadium. And they were prepared to win a football game and spoil, once and for all, the Cougars' Cinderella season. Silly Rainbows. The Cougs had Morrell, a wild man in the defensive secondary. Just as Hawaii quarterback Raphel Cherry was ready to slip in over left guard on a fourth-down sneak to steal a victory, Morrell stole the Rainbows' hearts by timing a safety blitz perfectly and hog-tying Cherry behind the line of scrimmage: BYU 18, Hawaii 13. Cougars are ranked number four.

No one, not even the Uteskis, was denying now that a BYU team on a sixteen-game winning streak was like the proverbial downhill snowball gaining size with each succeeding weekend. When Colorado State got buried under a 52–9 avalanche, BYU fell back into non-respect land and tumbled to number eight in the rankings. Facts belied the ranking: in the national statistics, the Cougars were number one in offense, which wasn't a surprise. BYU had been number one, two, or three the five previous campaigns.

Even the two weekends that tested their souls couldn't prevent the Cougars' moving to 7–0 and a number-five national ranking. First, Wyoming tried in Cougar Stadium and saw BYU roar from behind to a 41–38 victory. Then at Air Force, BYU had to stave off the Cadets 30–25 as 1985 all-WAC quarterback Bart Weiss came close to taking the wind out of the Cougar sails. Still, the Coug record was unblemished and they were ranked number four.

The rest was, shall we say, easy. Because it was the old whipping-post teams who remained in BYU's path, and by this time they were a team on a locomotive pace. New Mexico was made to pay a horrible price for its 1981 (25–21) indiscretion as BYU rolled at Albuquerque 48–0. Then UTEP, a year removed from its 1985 upset of the century in El Paso, caved in at Provo 42–9. When San Diego State shriveled up 34–3 in Provo, the Cougars had sliced through three consecutive foes by a combined 124–12. They were ranked number three. With in-state foes Utah and Utah State the only stumbling blocks to a possible 12–0 season, this was indeed a fairy-tale wrap-up

to the regular season.

Now, Utah had shown some spunk under coach Chuck Stobart. So, too, had other Uteski teams going up against the master Edwards. But Stobart was operating under a must-win umbrella. Only ill-begotten Uteski luck—an annual lament for the Uteskis—kept The Game from being a WAC title game. However, by this time, the Cougars were playing for more than a ninth straight WAC crown. At number three in the country, a pair of wins and a bowl win—well, Happy Valley was actually preparing a national championship coronation. Always draped in an inferiority complex shawl because of the supposed Salt Lake County media bias, a season-ending BYU rush could be bigger than Brigham's entry into the Salt Lake Valley in 1847.

And so it came to pass. The Uteskis went down 24–14, again with Bozo turning into Bosco and leading a fourth-quarter charge to the winning TD. When number-one Nebraska and number-two South Carolina lost on the same weekend, the Monday polls said it all: The Cougars were number one in all of college football.

At Provo the following week, 66,000 fans paid homage to their champions-to-be as Utah State became the twelfth sacrificial lamb 38–14.

Within a month, Bosco would limp from the Jack Murphy Stadium dressing room to rally his troops to a 24–17 victory over the University of Michigan. Not even the bleatings of Wolverine coach Bo Schembechler could dilute what the Cougars had accomplished—a 13–0 season, matching the best in college history.

Wasn't it heart-warming for Bryant Gumble to utter, "They played a Bo Diddley Tech schedule?" And how about that Don James of the University of Washington and Barry Switzer of Oklahoma bemoaning BYU's "bogus" title.

The Beehive State had gone forty years without a major-sport national champion. And even the Uteskis' NCAA basketball title in 1944 was earned when many of America's heroes were off fighting in World War II.

But now, BYU, once the ugly stepchild of collegiate football, reigned over the NCAA. Seven different schools held the number-one spot during the season, but the last six weeks—through the bowl games—it was all BYU. Fifteen Cougars from the 1984 team were drafted into the NFL. Edwards was coach of the year and was last seen in January shaking hands at the White House with President Ronald Reagan.

And at Provo, in the school trophy case, is the national championship trophy. At Cougar Stadium, banners hang from the end-zone seats: 1984 National Champions. No Bowl Alliance or jealous Uteski fans who will never have one—earned or unearned—can take it away.

Fact or Fiction?

About a decade ago, while passing through the Southwest, I arrived in Albuquerque coincidentally on the same night the city's Triple-A baseball team, the Dukes, hosted their parent club, the Los Angeles Dodgers, in a one-game fund-raiser. I attended the game and saw the obviously motivated minor leaguers outhustle the Dodgers and win by four or five runs.

The Dukes went on to win the Pacific Coast League championship that season, and it made me stop and consider the circumstances:

1) The Dukes achieved everything possible at their level, albeit against opposition that wasn't the nation's best. But that was hardly their fault, was it?

2) In every game they played against top-level talent— that one night against Los Angeles—the Dukes won. Perhaps they were truly superior; there's nothing to prove that they weren't.

3) The matchup used to determine baseball's national champion, the World Series, limited itself to the two major-league champions, completely shutting out the Triple-A Dukes. Again, that can't be held against Albuquerque; nothing the Dukes could do about it.

Now, considering all those facts, and absent any shred of evidence to the contrary, what conclusion do we reach?

The Albuquerque Dukes were the true professional baseball champions!

Welcome, my friends, to the twisted logic that says Brigham Young won a national football championship in 1984. Welcome to the world where beating only four teams that had winning seasons, where playing exactly zero games against teams that ended the season in the top twenty somehow qualifies a team for a national title. Welcome to Fantasyland, Provo style.

It's a nice scam if you can work it, this whole idea of "proving" you're the best without ever playing the best. I know, Cougar fans like to shrug their shoulders, smile and say, "Not our fault that the teams we played weren't any

good. We didn't lose, so we're the champs."

It doesn't wash. The Dallas Cowboys have never lost a hockey game, but that doesn't mean they should be awarded the Stanley Cup.

C'mon, is it possible that a national title, the birthright of the Joe Montanas and O.J. Simpsons and Tony Dorsetts of the world, could somehow be stolen by a team whose most dangerous combination is Robbie Bosco to Glen Kozlowski? Didn't think so.

Yet somehow the Cougars sweet-talked the nation's sportswriters into overlooking their schedule and throwing their votes away. Forget that we played the worst and most overrated Pitt team in years, the Cougars purred. Forget that they looked inept against Utah, and lucky against Wyoming. Forget that their Holiday Bowl opponent was the Big Ten's fourth-place team, 6–5 Michigan—and that the Wolverines led by seven in the fourth quarter.

Forget the schedule full of UTEP and New Mexico and Bo Diddley Tech (thank you, Bryant Gumble).

Well, we can't forget. Making it even worse was the fact that BYU climbed into number one by winning in, of all places, Rice Stadium.

And it's not like there wasn't an obviously better choice. Washington faced three teams from the final top ten—Oklahoma, UCLA, and Southern Cal—and lost only once, to the Trojans. Think Bosco & Company could have beaten two of those three teams? Even one?

Never has a team lent so much credibility to the term "mythical" national title.

Understand, it's only fair that WAC schools should have a shot at a legitimate national championship, no question. Someday there will be a college football playoff tournament, similar to basketball, with all conference champions invited; then an unbeaten WAC school will have a chance to prove it belongs. But just because such a system doesn't exist yet doesn't mean we have to suspend all logic and good sense and hand over the trophy to a bunch of caffeine-free pretenders.

It's a surprise that the BYU "title," as preposterous as it

was, didn't spawn a tournament proposal right away, a necessary fix to a system at the mercy of the emotions of a herd of misinformed sportswriters, most of whom never saw this Triple-A "powerhouse" play.

CHAPTER 3

LAVELL EDWARDS
THE MORMON WORD FOR VICTORY

Really, LaVell Edwards has not changed much over the past, say, fifty-five years. In his teen years, he milked cows on the Orem farm of his parents, Philo and Addie, and peddled fruit from the family's orchards to such distant locales as Denver. As a collegian, he and some Utah State University friends and schoolboy buddies from Orem took a few weeks off from matching putts on the golf course to go fight forest fires in Wyoming and Montana. As a young father trying to make ends meet in the 1950s, he sold shoes at Sears.

Fast forwarding to the 1990s, we discover R. LaVell Edwards as a pitchman for the milk industry; as a meticulous green-thumber with *Better Homes and Gardens* credentials; as a gridiron battalion chief annually fanning football fires across the nation; and as a whenever-I-can golfer who, with little practice, shoots consistently in the seventies on the most challenging of courses. And yes, there is still pen money coming in from athletic-shoe endorsements.

It is safe to characterize Edwards as a college football coach who enjoys his family, church, gardening, golf, and football—probably in that order. One big addition to the list of priorities over, say, the past twenty-five years, is beating the University of Utah in football. As BYU's head coach, he has done that frequently—twenty times in twenty-five tries from 1972 to 1996.

There have been more, far more profound football accomplishments for Edwards than the near-annual pummeling of the Utes, although you would have a difficult time selling the argument to long-suffering Cougar fans who remember the lean pre-Edwards years against the Utes. Landing national coach-of-the-year honors in 1984 following his Cougars' national championship season, comes to mind. So do eighteen Western Athletic Conference championships when the school had just one in the fifty years prior to his arrival.

Through it all, including 228 career victories, coaching thirty-seven all-Americans, a Heisman Trophy winner, and two Outland Trophy winners, Edwards remains the unflappable, unpretentious, lovable granddad type—to his immediate family and to his extended football family. The laid-back, sixty-seven-year-old former Mormon bishop is as much at home in front of 65,000 fanatical fans at Cougar Stadium on any given Saturday as he is with his wife Patti, three children, and twelve grandchildren. His persona on the golf course? Says Edwards's lifelong sidekick Udell Westover, "You had better pack a lunch if you plan on beating him at golf."

In Provo, there is no more recognizable figure than Edwards, unless of course, it's Cosmo, the school mascot who is known by every grandpa and grandma, baby boomer, student, teenager, and babe-in-arms. Except perhaps for the infants, who are peripherally aware of Edwards since they are probably in the Cougar football season ticket hand-me-down line, everyone knows LaVell.

Sports Illustrated once affectionately described Edwards as a "large lumpy chap, a bit of a poet and a romantic" (which his wife translated as "a big fat daydreamer"). LaVell is the one on the sideline who twitches occasionally, shifting his weight from one leg to the other, only as often as the football crosses the fifty yard line in one direction or the other. Arms folded across his chest, his thinning hair covered by a blue-and-white Cougar cap, and a perpetual frown creasing his face—that's the unpretentious, imperturbable LaVell. No Hayden Fry–Joe Paterno designer sunglasses or BYU royal blue sportcoat and pressed slacks for this guy. Just a royal blue sweater, or windbreaker, baggy pants, and some cleatless football shoes. Oh yes, and that constant surveyor's stare at the football players racing past him to and fro on the turf of 65,000-seat Cougar Stadium. The truth be known, the towering structure that sits at the northwest corner of the BYU campus should be Edwards Stadium. Because it is the house that Rueben LaVell Edwards built.

It was a circuitous route Edwards took to football's promised land. Born—the eighth of fourteen children—and raised just a few miles north of the BYU campus, he acknowledges following BYU football regularly, often while perched in an orchard tree adjoining the practice field. While he was milking cows and picking apples, "my secret ambition was always to be a coach."

There were other trees from which he observed, developing a keen sense of what football was all about. The path from Windsor Elementary and Lincoln Jr. High in Orem took him past Lincoln High's football field. And there, "sometime around when I was eight or nine," he recalls, Edwards met Sanky Dixon, Lincoln's football coach and later Edwards's mentor and confidant. Before chores at home, came football with Sanky—and his brothers Lewis, Lamar, Don, and Max—who had passed the cow-milking duties down to little brother LaVell.

There have been reams of pages penned, writers waxing eloquently and articulately, but not necessarily accurately, on the roots of Edwards's coaching philosophy. Much of the chronicling dates no further back than the mid-sixties, when as a BYU assistant he watched quarterback Virgil Carter's prolific right arm author the first chapter of the Cougar passing revolution.

But the game plan Edwards follows today, in fact the man's concept in the fifties when he took his first head coaching job at Granite High School in Salt Lake City, can be traced to the playbook of his mind—nay, of Sanky Dixon's mind—in the early forties. "We had six basic plays for the single-wing offense. Nothing complicated. Sanky was not a complicated person," Edwards says. LaVell was the all-state center—and linebacker on defense—for Lincoln's state championship in 1947 (the only state football title ever for the school) and the state title runner-up team of 1946.

Today, fifty years later, BYU runs an offense comprised of, as offensive coordinator Norm Chow explains, "eight basic pass routes. That's the BYU passing attack—eight simple plays. A quarterback candidate comes in as a freshman, he learns the offense in two days. Then, he spends two years learning how to run it." It may be recorded in the football archives as the Edwards Plan, but look carefully at the acknowledgments. There you will find the complication copyright belongs to Sanky Dixon.

LaVell Edwards watching the game as only LaVell does.

Six basic single-wing plays for Dixon; eight basic pass plays for Edwards. Get the idea that LaVell hasn't changed much?

Oh, there has been one major change. From the 1947 championship at Lincoln, it would be eighteen years before Edwards was involved in another title. He and winning were not synonymous—not after he left Lincoln. It wouldn't have made any difference had he enrolled at BYU, a school that recruited him ever so nonchalantly since it was a given that he would walk from the family farm to the

Cougar campus to play football. The Cougars were 10–19–1 in the three seasons of his collegiate career, including 0–11 his sophomore season.

Edwards became a Utah State Aggie, the first offspring of Philo and Addie to attend college. He laughs now over one of the main reasons he left the shadow of the Cougar goalposts. "I had milked the family's two cows all my life and all I could think of was I won't have to milk those cows anymore!" More enticing was the scholarship the Logan school offered, financial assistance Edwards later credited to Mel Briggs, his basketball coach at Lincoln High. Briggs had attended the AC and, by all accounts, given Aggie brass a glowing recommendation of the accomplished three-sport Orem schoolboy.

Incredibly, considering how very mediocre the BYU program was after the war, the Aggies won only eight games, lost twenty-one, and tied one during his career, in which he captained the Aggies and earned all–Skyline Conference recognition in 1950 and 1951. He was center and linebacker on the freshman team while the Aggie varsity was 5–6 in coach Dick Romney's final year of a twenty-nine-season career. Compounding Edwards's three-year varsity frustrations were two losses to BYU and three to chief rival Utah. To further complicate matters, three coaches moved through the AC swinging doors from 1948–51: Dick Romney (1948), George Melinkovich (1949–50), and John Roning (1951). Edwards remembered that turnover rate when he signed on at BYU in 1962. When he arrived in Provo, the Cougars were on their fifth different coach in fourteen years.

Roning was a Sanky Dixon type. "Organized and a stickler for technique," says Edwards. The Aggies had surrendered thirty-one points a game in nine losses in 1950. Roning altered the landscape drastically. In addition to coaching a disciplined defense, he brought back the single-wing offense. The Aggies won just three games in 1951, but of their eight losses, four of them were by a total of twenty-one points. And nine opponents averaged only nineteen points against the defense captained by linebacker Edwards.

While Roning was providing another football building block for his student, Edwards was adding a stability dimension to his life. In the summer of 1951, he married Aggie coed Patti Louise Covey of Big Piney, Wyoming. The union would produce three children—Ann, now a freelance writer; John, now a doctor; and Jimmy, now an attorney.

Having served two years in the Officer Training Corps at USU, Edwards was dispatched directly to a two-year commitment as a second lieutenant in the United States Army in late spring of 1952. He wasn't separated from football for very long. He played in 1952 for the post team in Fort Lee, Virginia. In 1953, he coached the post team in Fort Meade, Maryland. A hint of what was to come a quarter of a century later? He posted a 3–1 record.

By August of 1954, he had returned to USU to start work on his master's degree and help Roning with the football team in a post that has since become known as a graduate assistant. By September, he had graduated to Granite High, where he became head coach for football, wrestling, golf, and tennis. He had no idea his coaching career would begin so soon. "There was a sudden vacancy at Granite and, in a spur-of-the-moment decision, I filled it," says Edwards. His first contract was for $3,500 a year—for all sports. There would be a few extra dollars from high school officiating and after-hours shoe-selling at Sears.

Later, during his early years as an assistant with BYU, he would fill out a questionnaire for the school's publicity department. In it, Edwards scribbled two notations that were indications of his three decades of witticisms to-come. Asked to list his coaching positions and overall records, he jotted down, under Granite High School accomplishments, "football . . . eight years, 31–30" and proceeded down through wrestling and golf and finally tennis. Under tennis record, he printed, "?? (poor)." On another sheet, he was asked to list his accolades. Under the high school section, he scribbled to the side of his all-region year in basketball under the heading of position: ". . . forward-guard (gunner)." But there were two things Edwards would not be for long—a tennis coach and a basketball player.

There was little humorous about his years at Granite. In fact, Edwards says, "If it is true that you learn more from defeat than victory, then my high school experience must have left me very smart." There may have been as many losses as wins at Granite, but Edwards was a voracious student of the game. His football week didn't end on Friday night. "I would go to every University of Utah home game. They had $1 seats in the end zone for coaches." There in Ute Stadium, where two decades later he would be in command of the BYU forces, he charted plays formulated by Ute tacticians Jack Curtice and Ray Nagel. "In those days . . . film and video to study weren't readily available. A guy had to take a lot of notes." Was there a rooting interest? "Oh, I guess I pulled for the Utes, except when they played the Aggies." How about rooting interest in BYU? "Really, I think I was fairly neutral. By 1959 a good friend of mine, Tally Stevens, had taken the BYU job and I started following his career." However, says Edwards, "if the University of Utah had offered me a job, I would have taken it." Oh, the course of history.

There was no such luck that the U and its new coach Nagel could be interested in a coach at a .500 high school that employed the single-wing offense, even after Edwards tutored explosive tailback Eldon Fortie at Granite. And even after Edwards earned his master's degree at the U in 1960.

But BYU took notice, especially since Hal Mitchell had become the Cougars' head coach in 1961 and Fortie became the centerpiece of Mitchell's single-wing offense. By 1962, Edwards and Fortie were reunited when LaVell was hired as a Cougar assistant, a defensive coach at that. Defense or offense, one would have thought Edwards's BYU mystique began right then and there. Fortie's 1,149 rushing yards topped the newly formed WAC, and BYU finished with a 4–6 record, the best mark in four years. Mitchell was named WAC coach of the year. The next season, Fortie was gone; Mitchell's team went 2–8 and Mitchell was gone.

Edwards stayed. And he was encouraging disillusioned freshman tailback Virgil Carter to stay with him. Carter, a Californian, had pictured himself as more of a passing quarterback, but in his rookie season, the Cougars had passed a grand total of twenty-three times. He was inclined to concentrate just on academics. "Stick with the program," Edwards counseled the young Carter. "I sense a change on the horizon." BYU football historians concede Edwards's foresight in persuading Carter to remain a Cougar altered the course of Beehive State football history, not to mention the shock waves on the national gridiron front.

Change came in the form of new Cougar head coach Tommy Hudspeth, a pass-happy Canadian. BYU's passing leader of 1963 had been Ron Stewart—ten completions, 160 yards, and one touchdown. Carter's 1964 statistics: sixty-six completions for 1,154 yards and nine TDs. He had actually become the Cougar quarterback through default. Although listed as a tailback his freshman season, Carter was the only player with passing experience, a quality imperative in Hudspeth's aerial approach.

The foundation for the passing revolution was in place. And Edwards, the Cougars' defensive coordinator, was taking offensive notes even as the Cougar defense was showing vast improvement. "We had seven games where our offense scored seven or less points in 1963. When we started scoring points with Carter, it gave the defense a big boost in morale," says Edwards.

BYU's WAC record was 0–8 over the 1963 and 1964 seasons. On opening night of 1965 at Tempe, Carter and the Cougars demonstrated to their fans there would be something special about the season. With Carter hooking up with wide receiver Phil Odle, and punishing running back John Ogden shredding the Sun Devils' defense, BYU rolled to a 24–6 victory. The win set the table for a 6–4 WAC championship season, including a pressure-steeped three-game sweep of Utah (25–20), Arizona (20–3), and New Mexico (42–8) to end the year. This title business was a novelty for all of Cougardom. Carter says there was little excitement around campus. "There were no banners or any parties on campus. We were just a bunch of guys playing football."

Oh, there was a huge difference from what had gone before. A bunch of guys had played football—sort of—at BYU for nearly half a century without winning a conference title. And they had played forty games against Utah without ever winning in Provo. They had never beaten both Arizona schools in the same season. And they had never had a quarterback come anywhere close to the bulbous numbers Carter had put up. Like twenty TD passes. Why, all six of BYU's throwers from 1953 to 1959 had only totaled twenty touchdown passes.

Football fever hit Provo. In the first three years of the WAC, BYU had only two all-conference players—Fortie and guard Roger Dupaix in the 1962 season. The 1965 season produced three—Carter, league-leading wide receiver Phil Odle, and fullback John Ogden, who was in the middle of three straight years of leading the WAC in rushing.

Fans were taking notice, too. A big football crowd, perhaps for Utah or Wyoming, was around 15,000 in the late fifties and early sixties. Often, there were fewer than 5,000 fans in the stands. In 1966, following BYU's first-ever championship, the Cougars drew a school record 38,333 for the Wyoming game and an all-time season average of 26,356 in the newly expanded (1964), 35,000-capacity Cougar Stadium. Some BYU loyalists were already crowing that the Cougars were outdrawing Utah on occasion. If only they had had a crystal ball for turnstile comparisons between the two rivals in the eighties and nineties.

Through all this, Edwards was composing offensive charts in his mind. His Cougar defenses, save for a stumble now and then, like the forty-seven points surrendered to the Cowboys in front of that overflow Provo audience in 1966, had developed a consistency that complemented Carter's offensive pyrotechnics. With Carter throwing for a career- and school-high 2,182 yards and twenty-one TDs in 1966, BYU lost just two games. While the setbacks to the Cowboys and Arizona State prevented back-to-back WAC crowns, BYU finished 8–2. The Cougars had never before amassed fourteen wins over two seasons.

BYU continued only one streak after Carter's eligibility expired. The Cougars won two more games against Utah in 1966 and 1967—three in a row in all, and that satiated BYU followers for a while. But attendance slumped to an average of 22,444 in 1968 during a next-to-last league finish. There were no eye-popping passing statistics. A 30–21 loss at home to Utah was a harbinger of a Ute revival in the series. Another seventh-place finish in 1970 left Hudspeth in a win-or-else situation. And a 5–6 record in 1971 was his Waterloo—that plus a fourth straight loss to Utah.

The public knew BYU would stay at home this time in naming a new coach. And it was a certainty the new Cougar boss would be a Mormon. As sleuths thumbed through the available data on current Coug assistants of the day, they would uncover a statistic that would lead them to the new coach. In 1971, while undefeated Arizona State was romping to the WAC title and BYU was only 5–6 overall, the Cougars allowed fewer points (199) than any of the eight WAC schools. Three BYU defenders—end Joe Liljenquist, linebacker Jeff Lyman, and safety Dan Hansen—were named all-WAC, the most postseason defensive honorees in school history. The defensive coordinator was LaVell Edwards. When spring practice opened in March of 1972, he was head coach.

In the previous twenty-three years, BYU had employed five head coaches. They had compiled an overall mark of 84 wins and 142 losses. Only two coaches—Hal Kopp in 1958 and Hudspeth from 1965 through 1967—had beaten Utah. There were rumblings—and they emanated from board rooms far removed from the coaches' football offices—that if the program was going to wallow in ineptitude, there would be no program at all. No wonder the forty-one-year-old Edwards, whose head coaching experience consisted of one year in the U.S. Army and a so-so, 31–30 eight-year run at Granite, was looking at his stay with a short-term focus.

The one thing that kept going through his mind was the excitement—and wins—generated by Carter's passing from 1964–66. Still, being the traditionalist he was, the theory that there are three things that can happen when you pass and two of them are bad kept resonating in his mind. But, he acknowledged, "When we had won consistently, we had thrown the ball. Now, being a defensive coach, I had a lot to learn about offense. The one thing I knew was we had to travel a different path." That is, he would have to seek a different path from the Woody Hayes three-yards-and-a-cloud-of-dust he had learned from Sanky and Roning. He would have to be more like Curtice, who had let quarterback Lee Grosscup unlimber his arm for the Utes.

It wasn't the name Fortie that kept tugging at Edwards's psyche, it was Carter. With the "Blue Darter" passing, BYU had won seventeen games, beaten Utah twice, and won a WAC title. Fortie had run for a WAC record in 1962, but in his three seasons, the Cougars had won only nine games. And they hadn't beaten Utah or come close to winning a conference championship.

Edwards emphasizes it was not a major decision that he opted for a wide-open style of play. "I didn't think 'wide-open' at the time. I just thought about opening up the offense." The year after Carter passed the Cougars to the WAC crown, a school-record crowd of 38,333 showed up for the Wyoming game. The school averaged a record 26,336 fans for six home games. Carter amassed 599 yards total offense against Texas Western (now UTEP) which still stands second on the all-time charts. He passed for 513. "I was no dummy even though I was coaching defense. The fans loved seeing the ball in the air," says Edwards three decades later.

BYU had films and reams of notes on Carter's exploits in the archives, but Edwards needed more to buttress his case. "I had known Stanford coach John Ralston when he was at Utah State, and even though he was a run-oriented coach, he had managed to make the transition to the passing game at Stanford with quarterbacks like Don Bunce and Jim Plunkett." It was enough of a transition to win the Cardinal two Rose Bowls. Edwards wasn't thinking such grandiose thoughts as bowl games. The Cougars had lost the last three games of 1971 to Arizona State, Arizona, and Utah, the three biggest hurdles standing between BYU and a conference title—maybe even a bowl game. By 1974, largely because of the forward pass, the Cougars had circled the track: wins over the Sun Devils, Wildcats, and Utes; a

WAC title; and the school's first-ever bowl game.

The record shows Edwards was a genius right out of the gate in the fall of 1972. But the Cougars were still more like plow horses than jets. They continued to run the ball. In his rookie season, the passing-professor's quarterback, Bill August, was hardly in the whopping statistics category. He threw 144 times for two touchdowns. Says Edwards, "It was like the Fortie days all over again . . . our running back Pete VanValkenburg led the nation in rushing (1,386 yards and fifteen TDs)." So, the heralded coaching staff of Edwards, Dave Kragthorpe (offensive coordinator), Dick Felt (defensive coordinator), Jim Criner (defensive line), J. D. Helm (running backs), Dewey "The Swamp Rat" Warren (quarterbacks), and Mel Olson (freshman coach) hadn't changed much on the BYU landscape. Except for the record.

Starting with a 32–9 win over Kansas State and ending with consecutive wins over Utah—a stunning triumph in a snowstorm in Salt Lake City—and New Mexico, the Cougars posted a 7–4 record, the most wins ever by a rookie BYU coach. Only a punishing lesson from Arizona State and their one-two all-American running back punch of Brent McClanahan and Woody Green kept the Cougars from the WAC title. Surely, once the passing game kicked into high gear, BYU would supplant the Sun Devils as league kingpin. The plans as drawn up by passing guru Warren—a pro-style attack with receivers flooding every conceivable area on the field—were in the bank. "All I could keep thinking was what a guy like Carter would have done with a plan like this," Edwards recalls.

A guy like Carter came along in 1973. But not immediately. Gary Sheide, a transfer from Diablo Junior College in California, was nursing a leg injury when the season started. BYU was limping, too, with a 1–5 record by mid-October. And hopes for a WAC title were dashed through losses to Colorado State, ASU, and Wyoming. But there was plenty of time for experimentation.

Edwards, prodded by Warren, turned Sheide loose in a formation where there were always two wide receivers. One of them was Jay Miller, who would end the season with a nation-leading 100 catches for 1,181 yards and eight TDs. "It started to get crazy," Edwards recalls. There had been a 439-yard, three-TD day for Sheide early in the season against Iowa State. In his last five games, he had hurled fifteen TD passes and had posted yardage days like 408 versus New Mexico and 354 against Utah (46–22, the most lopsided win ever for the Cougars in the series). It was indeed "crazy." But it was also a 5–6 record. And Edwards was fidgeting. Attendance had dropped by over 7,500 a game, from 28,820 in 1972 to 21,176 in 1973. "Really, I was thinking I might have just one year left in my BYU head-coaching career," says Edwards

And after an 0–3–1 start in 1974, it was more than just thinking. "I knew something miraculous had to happen to save me," says Edwards. The miracle came via seven straight wins, two of them in a three-week period over Arizona and ASU, two schools that had won the previous five WAC titles.

"Beating ASU and Frank Kush was bigger, really, than beating Utah at that time," says Edwards. The Utes hadn't been a problem the year before. Nor were they in 1974: BYU won 48–20 at Provo. A month later, the Cougars were in their first postseason game, the Fiesta Bowl in Tempe. "It was a wild ride," says Edwards. The Cougars had been picked last in the league, but had won seven games and earned a bowl bid. Not even a bump in the road—a 16–6 loss to Oklahoma State in which Sheide suffered an early injury—could mask the fact that a revolution had been spawned in Provo. Its ramifications would, to the WAC, make a monster out of BYU, make the rest of the nation think BYU when it came to any discussion of the forward pass, and make Edwards into a legend.

That Edwards would be a coach was never in question. That he would be a coach at a major university, one that had experienced at least regional success, however brief, in its Carter fling of the mid-1960s, was something of a surprise. Granted, he was well-versed in the Mormon philosophy, having been raised in a household that required, in addition to the daily ritual of milking cows, his regular attendance at church. By the time he had matriculated through high school, college, and the military, and had taken a wife, his future course was crystal clear. He would get a job, he and Patti would raise a family, and they would live happily ever after. LaVell would slip in a round of golf now and then, plant some flowers, sell some shoes, officiate a few basketball games, take in an occasional Ute football game, and dote on his three kids.

LaVell's oldest child, daughter Ann Edwards Cannon, a freelance writer based in Salt Lake City, recalled with fondness those early days with her dad in a published letter a few years ago:

> *Dear Dad,*
> *You weren't well-known when I was little. You were a high school coach holding down a couple of part-time jobs to make ends meet. On school nights I crawled into your lap and watched you scribble unintelligible patterns of x's and o's onto a yellow legal pad. During the winter when you coached wrestling, I sometimes went with you to the gym where I feared I might melt away in the hot, heavy air just like the witch from* The Wizard of Oz. *Sometimes on Saturdays, Mom took John and me to see you at Sears where you sold shoes. When things were slow we slipped over to the snack bar, long since gone, and you bought us all bags of warm popcorn, yellow with butter.*
> *When summer came you worked for Pete Carlston, teaching other people's children to swim by day, your own children to swim by night. You took us to the pool at twilight when everyone was gone and let us leap into the water. You soared off the diving board after us, caught us up and tossed us straight into the air, making us squeal with delight. Sometimes you and Mom took us to the drive-in, our faces scrubbed and our pajamas clean, where you*

pushed us in swings until the movie started. I told you I liked to go high, so you pushed me harder and harder until my stomach was in my throat—just where I wanted it to be.

On Sunday nights, you and Mom bought us strawberry ice cream cones at the ice cream parlor up the road. You loved to show us how to lick the top scoop into a swirling peak. When the two of you went out for the evening, you occasionally arranged for some of your players to tend us—big teenage guys, sweet and goofy, with crew cuts and black canvas shoes. We liked those boy baby-sitters the best because they let us tear through the house like puppies until our faces were red and sweaty, and our voices were gone from screaming. You were probably the same kind of baby-sitter when you were a kid, too.

No, Dad, you weren't famous until I was grown up and gone.

That's when people started asking me questions about you. They wanted to know who you really are. At first, I tried to answer with good humor and grace, but now I'm inclined to let you speak for yourself, so that if you wish to choose privacy, you can. I will say this, however, whenever I think of you, which is often, I always hear the remembered music of children laughing.

O X O X . . . Ann

Edwards smiles when reminded of those days. Oh yes. The smile. He has taken a lot of ribbing over the years about the non-smile. Longtime BYU golf coach Karl Tucker is credited with the much-used line, "LaVell smiles; he just hasn't told his face." Patti, who has written a column for the *Provo Daily Herald* among other free-lance assignments, says her husband has a "wonderful smile, a wonderful sense of humor and is great with one-liners."

Ann likes the one-line retort her dad used the day a big, talented, barrel-chested athlete told LaVell he was thinking about going on a church mission: "Dad looked at the player, crinkled his hazel eyes and said, 'We need a big, strong, 240-pound lineman a lot more than the Lord needs a big fat missionary.' The two men burst into laughter. The big lineman went on the mission with Dad's blessing."

A number of Edwardisms have made their way into *Sports Illustrated:*

• On the inordinate number of returned missionaries on his squad: "If we don't win our first few games, we might start looking for some hell-raisers."

• On whether speed or quickness is more important in a wide receiver: "We'd like our receivers to have both, but if they had both, they'd be at USC."

• On the spirited rivalry with the University of Wyoming, "I'd rather lose and live in Provo than win and live in Laramie." Later, to quiet a firestorm of protest from Cowboy land, Edwards did a promo for a Wyoming radio station in which he said "Hi, I'm LaVell Edwards, please come to Laramie, Wyoming, my favorite place to see Wyoming play BYU." And the Cowboy fans did, every year and in record numbers.

The one, however, that captures Edwards in a nutshell is again related by Ann, who says she first heard it from her dad: Turns out an elderly gentleman approached Edwards in downtown Provo. Understand, says Ann, that her dad, "with his craggy Mount Rushmore profile," has been fairly well known around Provo. The Utah County denizen eyed Edwards and said, "You look sort of familiar. You're an Edwards. From Orem." LaVell nodded in agreement. "One of Philo's boys," said the elderly gent. Again, Edwards nodded. "Where are you working

Mark A. Philbrick

The LaVell and Patti Edwards clan as of 1997—3 children, 12 grandchildren.

these days," the guy asked. "Oh," responded Edwards, "BYU." At this point, the man immediately knew his subject. "I know who you are. Now tell me, are you still with the maintenance department there?"

Tough thing, this advancement up the ladder to a rung that places him among the top-ten all-time winningest coaches. Just a few years before, Edwards had been selling shoes at Sears.

As hard as it may have been to make ends meet during the happy days of the fifties, there was never a dull moment around the Edwards household. Raising two kids—Jim wasn't born until LaVell and Patti were settled in Provo—holding down all those jobs and landscaping the property in Holladay filled up the days . . . and nights. "I remember we had lots of flowers and an orchard," says Ann. "And it seemed like Dad was always out there digging and pruning."

Gardening remains LaVell's favorite hobby. "Not that I have a lot of time, but I guess it's fair to say you can take the boy out of the country, but you can't take the country out of the boy. I grew up with gardening and orchards—when we had to do it to make ends meet. I love to work in the soil. I come home at night and I go out and start digging around. I guess its an escapism of sorts. I do get engrossed in it. I'm not as sharp at gardening as Ann. She's the smart one. If I have a problem, I call Ann."

That's not how his daughter tells it. "I learned from Dad over the years. I just know the varieties of flowers better. He has coached. I have read flower magazines. Dad likes to landscape and he likes to dig. He likes the architectural look. He has a lot of self-discipline. He plants flowers and shrubs carefully and at a certain distance from one another. I'm more impulsive, grouping them for instant, full color," says Ann. "We have an agreement. He's the shrub guy; I'm the flower person. Dad has really grown to love primrose. He has a whole patch of them he's quite proud of. They come back year after year and he has them spaced perfectly. He also loves daylilies."

Patti says most visitors to their home in east Provo are convinced the yard is professionally landscaped. She says "LaVell's talent for gardening has made him the friendly neighborhood consultant." Longtime neighbor Stan Collins agrees. "He could easily be a professional landscaper. People would hire him in a heartbeat. When LaVell plants something, it grows. And he gets more done in three hours than most of us accomplish in a week. There's no way to duplicate what he does. It's okay to ask questions when he's working, but that doesn't necessarily mean he'll stop while he provides the answers. We rarely talk about sports. I would want to talk football and how good his teams are. He would want to talk basketball and my days playing for Stan Watts at BYU in the 1950s. Both stories have gotten blown way out of proportion over the years."

It is no secret that Edwards is a man of deep religious conviction. As he has often said, "I don't wear it on my sleeve." But he lives his LDS faith every day. "Win or lose on the football field on Saturday, LaVell is in church the next morning teaching the gospel," says Collins. "I was his bishop—he always addressed me as 'beloved'—for seven years in the Oak Hills Sixth Ward. There is no way to adequately describe the inspiration he has been to hundreds of young men in search of a direction. He is most often referred to as a legend . . . to me I can unabashedly say he's the kind of man you hope your kids could be like one day. Of course, LaVell makes light of the legend tag. One day, on the golf course, he unleashed a drive that ended way past my sons' drives, and they are pretty good golfers. As LaVell walked away from the tee down the fairway, he turned and said to the boys, 'Don't worry, you were just out-driven by a legend.'"

Other than cranking out drives consistently in the 240-yard range, he is as unassuming on the golf course as he is about his football accomplishments. His office in the George Albert Smith Fieldhouse is adorned with various trophies, team pictures, and other paraphernalia, including a putter leaning against the wall in one corner. There is no sign of his nineteen WAC championship rings, or the national championship ring, either in a case, or on his fingers. "In the first place, I don't like rings. I've lost two wedding bands Patti gave me . . . I lost them playing golf. That's something I don't bring up very often. I wore the first WAC championship ring for a while." He is extraordinarily proud of a look-alike wedding band he has worn for several years. "Our athletic director, Glen Tuckett, gave me this ring after we won the national championship. It has diamonds running down each side in the shape of a '1.' Patti did a real nice thing a few years ago to take care of my championships rings. She had a little cabinet built with a blue velvet background with all the rings displayed in a block-Y pattern. Then she proceeded to cover it up with flowers. We finally put the ring case in a conspicuous place on an end table. And there are frequently flowers in front of it," he said with a big grin.

There are far greater callings for Edwards than rings and trophies. Long before he was BYU's head football coach, he was counseling the young people in the BYU Thirty-Sixth Ward, a student ward on campus. He had been called to be a church bishop only days after he had accepted the assistant's post for BYU football. To this day, Edwards points to his church calling in the campus ward as a turning point in his life. In fact, he acknowledges that working with athletes and learning from them, is the same feeling he experienced in those two years in the campus ward. "Sharing inspiration," is how he phrases it.

Explaining the missionary program to outsiders has consumed a lot of LaVell's time. Once upon a time, a nineteen-year-old Mormon leaving on a two-year mission was not a big deal. That is, before BYU began its winning ways. The NCAA exempts players serving church missions from the five-year window in which student-athletes must complete their eligibility. There are critics who point to the exemption as being a definite maturity advantage for BYU. "I never heard any criticism of the policy when we had all those losing seasons prior to the 1970s," says Edwards.

It hasn't always served BYU's football purposes when players leave on missions. Long-time BYU strength coach Chuck Stiggins, writing in *BYU Today* in 1991, said, "Some returned missionaries bear a resemblance to the Pillsbury Doughboy. Some of these guys, after two years away from football, look like a bowl full of jelly." Often players return only to report to Edwards that they've lost interest in football and would like to pursue other interests. In any event, it is the norm that a player serve his redshirt year after returning from a mission, if for no other reason than to get back into a football frame of mind. That's why, in a lot of cases, a BYU sophomore might be twenty-one or twenty-two years old. He would have played as a nineteen-year-old freshman, left on a two-year mission and redshirted before launching a three-year varsity career. A classic example of the seven-year BYU man was Marv Allen, who was on the roster in 1978 for the first Holiday Bowl. He served a mission to Thailand in 1979–80, redshirted in 1981, and then lettered in 1982–84, making all-WAC as a linebacker and playing on the 1984 national championship team. He also was a second-team Academic all-American and was awarded a post-graduate NCAA scholarship.

Edwards makes no excuses for the tack he took when he became head coach in 1972. Previously, a plan had been in place whereby a player who had earned a scholarship had to earn back that grant when he returned from the mission. Edwards had a better, more positive idea. "It wasn't a genius at work. I just wanted to make sure the student-athlete that left at nineteen on scholarship was still a student-athlete on scholarship at twenty-one—if he wanted to continue to play football."

Edwards finds it ironic that "few people made an issue of our missionary program when we were losing seven or eight games a year. Win seven or eight and it's because of these big, burly, old guys. I can tell you some of the same people who sympathized with our missionary plight in the sixties were critical of the system in the seventies and some of them are to this day." Many of the naysayers were Ute followers. Ironically, the University of Utah analyzed its attitude toward missionaries in the mid-eighties when Jim Fassel became head coach.

Today, coach Ron McBride's roster is nearly 30 percent returned missionaries. No one has pointed fingers at the Utes for having an unfair age advantage. Not yet.

Edwards talks often of the day Patti and he will serve a mission for the church. There are those in high places who would probably reward his thirty-five-year allegiance to the program by bidding him bon voyage for the two years and then holding the job open for when he got back. At least he would qualify on one count in the "big, burly, old guys" missionary formula of days gone by.

Consistency has been the hallmark of the Edwards Era. Granted, there were growing pains in the formative years. Yet, a four-game regular-season losing streak in 1973, three-game skids in 1975 and 1991, and a four-game drought in 1993 are, amazingly, the only blips on a record that through New Year's Day of 1997 included 228 wins, eighteen WAC titles and twenty bowl games. There have been six seasons of two or fewer losses, and thirteen campaigns with three or fewer losses. The early quest was to whip Arizona State, Arizona, and Utah. There are much broader horizons now, although Utah is in the mix of must-win games each season. During the Edwards reign, the Cougars can count among their conquests such notable football schools as Notre Dame, Miami, Penn State, Michigan, Oklahoma, UCLA, Texas A&M, Texas, Oregon, Wisconsin, Colorado, Washington, and Pitt. The only teams of national championship caliber the Cougars have played and haven't beaten are Ohio State and Florida State.

Edwards acknowledges he is constantly in awe of what has transpired in the football program, especially since he need only reflect on his first three years to recall how fragile the infrastructure was. A losing record (5–6) in 1973 and the 0–3–1 mark to start 1974 are stark reminders. It takes only an instant, however, for him to recite the reason for success. "We've been fortunate to keep the bulk of our coaching staff together."

As the 1997 season dawned, Edwards had been in place thirty-five years, twenty-six of them as head coach. But he could count at his side loyal assistants Tom Ramage (twenty-three), Norm Chow (twenty), Roger French (seventeen), Ken Schmidt (sixteen), Lance Reynolds (fifteen), and Chris Pella (twelve). Quarterback coach Robbie Bosco has been on board eight years, and if tradition holds, he will soon have a head job of his own. Kragthorpe went on to lead Idaho State to a Division 1-AA national championship, and later became Oregon State University's head coach; Mike Holmgren graduated to the San Francisco 49ers and in 1997, coached the Green Bay Packers to a Super Bowl title; Ted Tollner used BYU as a springboard to USC, where he coached a Rose Bowl champion; and Doug Scovil moved from Cougar play-calling to the head job at San Diego State.

Kragthorpe, who was in on the ground floor of BYU's success in the seventies, said, "I'd be surprised if I couldn't go back there today and recognize the playbook. Coaches stay there and don't have to reinvent the wheel every year. LaVell gives his coaches tremendous leeway. He has never interfered. When I was there, he never came in to any position coach's meeting with their players and said anything that made it look like he knew more than we did."

To this day, be they veteran assistants or newcomers, Cougar coaches are allowed their say and often see their ideas implemented into the system. Felt served twenty-six years with Edwards before retiring after the 1993 season. Says the former BYU and pro standout, "LaVell gives you a job and lets you do it. I feel strongly about him for his loyalty." Edwards says as a bishop he learned that a successful leader surrounds himself with outstanding people and then allows them space to work. He guides, but does not dominate. Chow, who played at Utah, says every assistant is encouraged to contribute. "We're all aware of who the boss is, however, and that's crucial to our success."

Patti has been around for all thirty-five years of her husband's tenure—including the twenty-five he's served as boss. "He lets the assistants do what they were hired for. I feel the way he has delegated authority is one of his biggest strengths."

Along with keeping assistants in the fold, Edwards's forte has been keeping players content in an atmosphere that includes not only adherence to the school's strict code of honor, but a divvying up of playing time among marquee players. "My strength is in one-on-one associations with my players. You always have to relate to them. You have to keep your thought processes open. The majority of my work is not done on the field. It's in my office, suggesting a direction for the players. You have to have a good feeling, or a confidence in what you are doing. To do that, you have to keep thinking a little bit like they do."

This philosophy quite possibly kept all-American-to-be Jim McMahon in the program in 1978. When it became obvious that Marc Wilson would be the Cougars' starter, a restless McMahon began sending out transfer feelers. "Coach asked me where I'd go. He reminded me I'd have to sit out a year regardless. Then he outlined a program he thought would help my career and the BYU program as well. I guess he was right." Two all-American years and a sixteen-year, Super Bowl-studded NFL run for McMahon was the evidence.

Then the buck does stop on the desk of Edwards. "Whether you feel like it or don't feel like it, it does stop here. When I first became head coach, I thought, man, I know what pressures Tommy was going through. When I was an assistant and some player came to me with a problem, I could say 'you better go see Coach Hudspeth on that one.' Now, when they come to see me, or someone calls up with a problem, I'm the guy who has to help resolve it."

Other than quarterbacks, few players have left LaVell's program once they have signed on. Honor code violators are the exception. In 1982, star California receiver Glen Kozlowski was removed from the team for one year because of an honor-code violation. He was reinstated on the squad in 1984 and was named to the first-team all-WAC, functioning as a key cog in BYU's national title run.

Part of the BYU code of honor forbids sex outside of marriage, the use of drugs, alcohol, or tobacco, and the consumption of coffee or tea. Football players and regular students alike have felt severe repercussions from violations. "Probably the most frustrating aspect of the whole job is seeing kids who just won't recognize the opportunities that they have and what they ought to be doing with them, both on and off the field," says Edwards. Yes, there is intense pressure, the kind that has caused him to have a headache nearly every day of his life—"a penetrating, throbbing ache just behind my left ear." Is it any wonder? "Today's coach must monitor his players' conduct and academic performance, be responsible for winning and losing, appeasing alumni groups, making special appearances, helping with fund-raising, and the whole ball of wax. These are the kind of outside pressures that detract from the job of coaching. But there's nowhere I would rather be than on the sideline at Cougar Stadium on Saturday afternoon."

Thousands of BYU faithful share his sentiments—that he be on the their side-line on Saturday afternoon. By 1975, his fourth season in the head football chair, crowds of 30,000 were commonplace. By 1979, the season average turnstile count reached 35,357. By 1981, school officials were setting up temporary seating in the end zones and the average attendance shot up to 40,640 fans. Expansion plans were drawn up, and following the final home game of 1981—naturally another victory over Utah—Edwards donned a hard hat and pulled the handle on a bulldozer that took the first bite of sod from the old stadium to make room for expansion to 65,000 seats. Not bad for a city whose population, outside the student enrollment, was around 74,000 at the time. No wonder that an awestruck Edwards walked into the jam-packed stadium the next September and wept tears of joys. It was, after all, the stadium he, his staff, and a pocketful of passing wizards had made possible.

To think that just ten years earlier the Cougar football program was wallowing in virtual obscurity, a distant third behind the University of Utah and Utah State.

Steve Griffin/THE SALT LAKE TRIBUNE

Cougar players douse their coach with Gatorade to celebrate their 1994 victory over New Mexico, making LaVell Edwards the fourteenth coach in NCAA history to collect 200 wins.

Even the Aggies, under Chuck Mills and Phil Krueger, were churning out four straight seasons of seven or more wins, including four straight wins over BYU. Yet, a simple device known as the forward pass had catapulted the Cougars to the front of not only the Beehive State football pack, but into the national spotlight. As early as 1974, the phrase "national rankings" crept into the Utah County football lexicon.

Edwards, to this day, cites luck as a key ingredient to the renaissance. "I was lucky to get a couple of very good football coaches early in my career as head coach, and that had a big impact on our success." Dewey Warren and Doug Scovil were among them. Warren drew up the original pro-style passing attack in 1972. Scovil, who had extensive pro experience and who was the QB coach at Navy when Roger Staubach won the Heisman Trophy in 1963, entered the scene in 1977.

"Doug's system, which incorporated a lot of passes to the running backs, is essentially what we are still using in the 1990s," says Edwards. He freely attributes the Cougars' yardage and scoring "craziness" to Scovil. In his first year on the job,

Scovil created a furor in the game against Utah when he called for Wilson to re-enter the game to throw "just one more pass" for an NCAA record. It launched Utah's "I hate BYU" crusade, with Utah coach Wayne Howard the head cheerleader. The crusade has been effectively sustained by Ute fans through fourteen Cougar wins over the last eighteen years.

If there was any luck involved, it was with BYU's first two passing quarterbacks. Sheide matriculated from Diablo Junior College, where he was injury-prone, a jinx that hounded him, even with eye-popping statistics thrown in, throughout his two years with the Cougars. Then came Gifford Nielsen, who prepped just across the street from BYU at Provo High School. Nielsen's first love was basketball and it was pure happenstance—the hiring of Frank Arnold to replace Glen Potter as hoops coach in 1975—that prompted the two-year BYU basketball letterman to switch sports. Without Sheide leading the Cougs to a 7–4 record in 1974 and without Nielsen's heroics in rallying BYU to a 6–5 mark in 1975 and then a 9–3 record and a WAC title in 1976, there's no telling what might have happened to Edwards.

What did happen was that a Washington schoolboy named Marc Wilson applied for passing membership; and so, too, did a phenomenal Roy High School phenom named Jim McMahon; and a California whiz kid named Eric Krzmarzick; and a Skyline High School free-spirit named Gym Kimball; and a Connecticut youngster named Steve Young, who was a state rushing champ and whose dad, LeGrande, had played at BYU in the late 1950s and whose great-great-great-granddad was Brigham himself. "As we started throwing the ball and started getting proficient at it, we got better athletes and we just stayed with it. I guess the timing was just right," says LaVell.

It would be convenient to claim Edwards and BYU sprung a surprise on the nation with a passing attack that often found the Cougars throwing forty-five or fifty times a game (McMahon threw sixty times against Hawaii in 1980). But by 1981, just nine years after Edwards turned Sheide loose through the airlanes, Cougar quarterbacks had finished in the top four nationally in passing, including two number-one seasons by McMahon in 1980–81. What Warren and Scovil had concocted, the likes of Tollner, Holmgren, and Chow perpetuated. Consistency? Most every starting Cougar QB since Carter—and all the all-Americans—has thrown for over 400 yards in a game, some of them several times. And against top-flight teams.

Edwards watched his teams switch from everyone's must-play list—"In the old days we were everyone's homecoming opponent," he says—to a team schools avoided like the plague. The Arizona schools hightailed it to the Pac-10 in 1978. By 1979, the Cougar athletic director had to branch out and sign up intersectional foes like Texas A&M, Wisconsin, and Colorado; BYU whipped them all and approached the nation's top-ten rankings. "We were doing the same things on offense—with minor variations," says Edwards.

Like in 1979, in a nationally televised game with San Diego State from Jack Murphy Stadium, Scovil made an ever-so-slight alteration in a down-and-out pattern. Two Cougars went to the same zone, with one breaking to the sideline and the other faking to the outside and going deep. Wilson's first four passes went for touchdowns in a 63–14 win. It was that single game that left Bosco near speechless in his family's home near Sacramento. "All I could think was, wow! What an offense for a quarterback. That was when I started thinking seriously about BYU as my collegiate home."

Chow, like Holmgren and Scovil before him, speaks what is on LaVell's mind. "The key to our system is repetition. You can beat us 50–0 and the next week, we'll be back running the same offense." Case in point: In 1982, Steve Young made his second start of the season and only the fourth of his career (he was a starter in two games when McMahon was injured in 1981) against Herschel Walker's Georgia Bulldogs in Athens. In the first half alone, Young threw five interceptions. But he was still executing the same passing schemes in the second half of a 17–14 loss. While Scovil, Holmgren, and Chow have basically called the plays, Chow says it's all Edwards-inspired. "He might tell people he doesn't understand the offense, but he's the one who put it in here twenty-five years ago when nobody thought it would work. He's the one who had the courage to stick with it, no matter what."

Opposing coaches wish there hadn't been so much glue. Since the parade of all-American quarterbacks began marching down Cougar Boulevard, starting with Nielsen in 1976 and continuing through Steve Sarkisian and the Cotton Bowl victory of 1997, BYU won two hundred games, lost just sixty and tied two. In twenty-one seasons, BYU quarterbacks have led the nation in passing eight times and finished second four times. Again, Edwards invokes the "aw shucks" defense. "We got very lucky; it seemed like everyone we brought in to the program connected. And once we started getting better athletes, we stayed with the passing game."

There have been few how-to books written about BYU's defense in the Edwards regime. Most of the time, the Cougars have merely outscored the opposition. Only once, in 1993, has a BYU team averaged fewer points per game than its opponent since LaVell took over. And then the disparity was only an average of 37.0–35.5. But amazingly, twelve times, the ex-defensive coordinator has had teams give up fewer than 20 points a game in a season, including the championship season of 1984 (13.8). "We have rarely signed the outstanding defensive players in the nation, but they've done pretty darned good once they get here," he says. Four ex-Cougars defenders were playing in the NFL in 1996, including former Pro Bowl linebacker Kurt Gouveia. Defensive tackle Jason Buck won the 1986 Outland Award as the nation's top lineman.

Once the custom wheels were on BYU's streamlined passing machine by 1976 when Nielsen was in full blossom, the nation began to take note of the Cougars. For the first time in history, a BYU quarterback was named all-American, with the Football Writers Association of America bestowing the honor. It began a string of five all-American QBs for BYU in ten years, an unparalleled collegiate achievement. The Cougars began a streak of ten straight WAC championships in 1976.

Still, as the decade of the seventies ended, Edwards and his Cougars were still empty-handed when it came to post-season victories. They had come close in the Fiesta Bowl in 1974 and in the Holiday Bowl in 1978 against Navy, 23–16, when they frittered away a 16–3 lead. However, the 1979 Holiday Bowl against Indiana remains the single worst experience in Edwards's collegiate career.

In a weak moment, when he has come the closest to comparing his great teams, he'll refer to the 1979 crew, his alibi being it was the first of the really great teams. "We went undefeated [11–0] for the first time ever in the regular season. We had an exciting 18–17 win over Texas A&M to start the year and then we won our next ten games, often in blowouts." There were thirteen Cougars who made first-team all-WAC, including Wilson, whose ten NCAA records earned him consensus all-American honors. The Cougars were ranked number nine in the nation, their highest perch ever to that time. But unranked Indiana overcame a brilliant 380-yard passing performance from Wilson to secure a 38–37 win in the Holiday Bowl when BYU kicker Brent Johnson, who led the nation in scoring in 1979, missed a twenty-seven-yard field goal as time expired. "We beat ourselves," said Edwards. "We lost to an inferior team."

The eighties would treat Edwards and BYU to more thrills than most of the nation's schools have experienced in all their history. It started quickly. As devastating as the Holiday Bowl had been in 1979, the 1980 event in Jack Murphy Stadium will rank as one of the top three BYU football accomplishments of all time. And when Hail Mary conversations unfold, minds of football-savvy Mormons will always flash to the haze of that December 18 night when McMahon heaved a forty-yard pass that his tight end Clay Brown snatched away from an end-zone collection of five Indiana defenders. Kicker Kurt Gunther's extra point, with no time left on the clock, capped a twenty-one-point, four-minute BYU rally that produced a 46–45 victory. Edwards wasn't watching. He was preparing his concession speech for Mustangs' coach Ron Meyer. Edwards got a good view of the midfield meeting. He was atop the shoulders of his victorious Cougars.

Milestones came as fast as mileposts, starting with that first-ever twelve-win campaign of 1980. McMahon's first-round NFL draft selection in 1982, following his engineering of a second straight bowl win—38–36 over Washington State in the 1981 Holiday Bowl—was followed by Steve Young's second-place finish in the Heisman balloting in 1983. Then came the 1984 national championship of 13–0 under field general Bosco and a national coach-of-the-year honor for Edwards.

After a three-year hiatus from the WAC throne room (1986–88), Ty Detmer led the Cougars back to conference superiority with a 10–3 campaign. The decade closed out with BYU offensive lineman Mohammed Elewonibi winning the school's second Outland Award of the eighties.

There was serious speculation that Edwards would bow out of coaching in 1990, after another WAC title and the Heisman Trophy and Davey O'Brien Award for Detmer. He was sixty. And what other honor could he and his players possibly achieve? The response from LaVell: "I can't imagine coaching when I'm seventy."

And so on he went, continuing into the last decade of the millennium like a spring chicken, with 1991 bringing another WAC title and one of the most spectacular seasons ever for any quarterback. Detmer rallied an 0–3 Cougar team with a ten-game unbeaten streak and finished his career with sixty-two NCAA records.

As 1992 dawned, Edwards was welcoming a flock of record-breaking prep quarterbacks into the program. Guys like John Walsh, Steve Clements, Tom Young, and Ryan Hancock arrived to pass. And for only the third time in history, Edwards brought on a junior-college transfer, Steve Sarkisian, to steer the ship in 1995. So what were the spoils for the guy quickly becoming of Social Security age? Four more WAC titles—"marred" only by a second-place finish in 1994 and a string of three straight losses to Utah (1993–95)—plus a five-year contract to coach until 2000, at least. The long-term pact was a novelty. Since time began, BYU coaches had always worked with one-year contracts.

Outside the 1984 national title season, the 14–1, number-five-ranked BYU team of 1996 that distinguished itself with a come-from-behind 19–15 victory over Kansas State in the Cotton Bowl on New Year's Day of 1997 ranked among the three highlights of his star-spangled career; the other two being surpassing Arizona State as WAC kingpin in 1974 and the undefeated regular season run of 1979.

So what of this legend? Is the sun setting on this cinch National Football Foundation Hall of Famer's college career? Negative. "I want to coach. I love to coach. I have good health—always been lucky in that respect, except for the darned headaches, and a couple of Advil take care of those. Recruiting is not a problem. I'm always ready for spring practice. I truly love to go out there and see what progress we can make in spring ball. And I don't ever remember a spring when we didn't have a lot of work in front of us. This 1997 season is no different. We've got to find us a quarterback." Which was the cue for him to rise from his high-backed leather chair in his office and head to the coaches' locker room for a quick change of clothes. As sure as cherry blossoms were popping out all over, so too was the adrenaline flowing for the legend.

The last image of the Mt. Timpanogos football giant was of him putting the pedal to the metal of the golf cart and heading in the direction of the 120 spring-practice candidates who would be writing the twenty-sixth chapter of the Edwards

Epic. He had his eight basic passing patterns in his pocket.

EDWARDS ON UTAH

No BYU football coach has ever been hired with the sole directive to beat Utah. Hudspeth's Cougar teams had beaten the Utes three straight years (1965–67) and in four of his eight seasons, BYU had finished ahead of Utah in the WAC standings. It was a 6–16 record against perennial WAC powers Arizona State, Arizona, and Wyoming, as much as anything, that did in the second-winningest coach in school history (39–42–1).

When Edwards was named coach, BYU was in the midst of a six-game losing streak to Arizona State. At least the four losses to Utah from 1968–71 had been close—a total difference of twenty-five points. In that same time span against ASU, the average losing margin was twenty-five points. "Early on, we had a two-pronged goal—to catch Arizona State and then, with any luck, be in a position to beat Utah for the WAC title." The ASU assignment came first in 1972 and, as Edwards says, "We found out we had a long way to go." Even though BYU had the nation's leading rusher in Pete VanValkenburg, Frank Kush's Sun Devils had a pair much like him in Brent McClanahan and Woody Green. ASU demolished the Cougs 49–17 in Provo, a loss that ultimately prevented BYU from winning the WAC title under its rookie coach.

Edwards and his Cougs did take care of business in late November in Rice Stadium. The Cougars stifled the Ute offense in a 16–6 victory, the closest Utah would come for six years of the rivalry. "Looking back, I can tell you that was one of the biggest victories of my career. Utah had dominated us for so many years and we had come so close to them for three years. It was a major, major victory."

No other first-year BYU coach had ever emerged victorious over the Utes (interim coach Floyd Millet, filling in for Eddie Kimball who was serving in World War II, brought BYU its first-ever win over the Utes in 1942). The only downer for the Cougars, who finished 7–4 overall and second in the WAC, was the Utes' Don Van Galder winning first team all-WAC quarterback honors. It was the last time a Utah signal caller would win the award. The Cougars were applying for a patent on the position. And the copyright papers were in order on the outcome of their annual in-state grudge match.

The BYU-Utah rivalry has never been a feudin', fussin', and fightin' affair—not judging by LaVell's perspective. He has had a cordial relationship with all the Ute coaches, even though his school's dominance of the series has probably meant the downfall of three of them. Utah's Bill Meek had a 7–5 record in 1973, finished 4–2 in the WAC, and had a career mark of 33–31. But the Cougars' 46–22 shellacking of the Utes in Salt Lake in 1973 sent him packing. Edwards, like so many Utah fans did at the time, shakes his head. "Bill was a good coach . . . won some big games." The problem was, the last game anyone remembered—especially the big boosters who still figured the good ol' days of kicking BYU's rear end would return soon—was the Cougars' twenty-four-point win in Ute stadium.

And when Utah-born Tom Lovat, the Ute lineman from Bingham High, took the Utes' reins in 1974, Edwards would come face to face with another lifelong friend. "I watched Tom play at Utah in 1959 and 1960. And he was on Ray Nagel's staff before he took a high school job. He was a good man, too." As far as the rivalry with BYU was concerned, Lovat came in at precisely the wrong time. "It was the year we really started throwing the ball," says Edwards. "And by the time we played the Utes at our place, we were on a roll with Sheide and they were coming to the end of a bad year." It got worse as BYU lowered the boom in a 48–20 win. Two years and a 94–42 combined margin of victory left no doubt that the pendulum had swung in the series. BYU's three straight wins in the 1960s were far more competitive.

Edwards remembers clearly the euphoria he was feeling at the sudden domination of the Utes. Longtime Cougar coach Eddie Kimball, who had never beaten Utah in eight tries, brought him down to earth. "I was talking to Eddie one day after our third or fourth win against the Utes, telling him how they weren't really very good at the time. I guess Eddie figured I was taking the wins in our biggest rivalry for granted, or something like that. He glared at me and said, 'LaVell, don't ever, ever take a win over Utah for granted. View it as a very special thing to beat Utah.' I suppose his feelings were mainly a result of all those years of losing to the Utes. Anyway, I never forgot the conversation. Any win over Utah became special."

And the wins over Utah kept coming and by larger margins. In 1975, Cougar running back Jeff Blanc ran for 163 yards and two TDs as BYU routed the Utes 51–20. In 1976, the two teams played their closest game since 1972 with the Cougars winning 34–12 in Salt Lake. Again, it was too much for big bankrolling Ute boosters to stomach. Lovat was jettisoned. And Edwards remembers commiserating with his foe. "It was a tougher game than the score indicated. I honestly believe Tom had things heading in the right direction."

It was Lovat's successor, Howard, who really started to shake up the rivalry again. "Wayne was a good recruiter. He had some great contacts in California. They came close to getting Jim McMahon, you know." But in his rookie Utah season, Howard, often referred to as a "wild man" on the sidelines, got caught up in the emotion of the rivalry. A 38–8 loss at Provo was exacerbated when Cougar quarterback Wilson was reinserted into the lineup late in the fourth quarter to go for a passing record. Wilson not only got the record, but BYU scored another touchdown in the process, sending Howard into a postgame "I hate BYU" tirade.

Edwards says he understands now a lot of what Howard was venting over. "I don't blame Wayne. I've been on the other side a few times. You know the Terry Donahue episode [a 31–10 UCLA win in 1986 when the Bruins were passing for TDs in the fourth quarter] and then Texas A&M throwing that halfback pass when they were ahead by forty-five points [in the 1990 Holiday Bowl]. We invited some of the criticism on ourselves in those crazy early years. But when I've been aware that our quarterback was going back into a game just to set a record, we haven't done it."

A case in point was 1990 when Ty Detmer was within eleven yards of breaking McMahon's NCAA season passing mark. The Cougars had a 48–27 lead over San Diego State in Jack Murphy Stadium when Edwards figured enough was enough. Detmer ended with 4,560 yards for the year, just shy of McMahon's 4,571. Witnesses say Detmer's dad, Sonny, was so livid his son didn't get the record that he drove non-stop from San Diego to his home in San Antonio, Texas.

Edwards says a lot of what happened in 1977 was a result of he and Howard "not being very well acquainted." Not that he would have allowed quarterback coach Doug Scovil to send Wilson back in had he known Howard any better. Scovil, who marched to his own drummer, sent Wilson back in on his own. "Wayne wasn't around much. He didn't mix in coaching circles and we met only briefly at Salt Lake media events. After that year, Wayne and I got to be pretty good friends . . . not that we were buddies, but there was no animosity."

It would have been LaVell's turn to vent in 1978 had he been the emotional type. Caught up in an alternating quarterback morass between Wilson and McMahon, the Cougars blew a 22–6 lead and lost at Utah 23–22. Says Edwards, "I tried to tell anyone who would listen that Utah was playing better and developing a solid defense under Wayne. I never had any trouble after that of convincing my coaches or fans that Utah would always be ready for us." The Cougars had already locked up the WAC crown by the time they met the Utes, but the loss prevented the school's first-ever undefeated, untied conference mark. They would have to wait a year.

BYU really gave Howard something to moan about from 1979–81. Even though the Utes went 13–6–2 in the span and contended for the WAC title in 1981, BYU outscored its arch rival a whopping 139–34, including a 27–0 whitewashing in 1979, the Cougars' first shutout over Utah. Recalls Edwards, "I still find it amazing where some of those games got away from them. In 1981, we had to beat them to win the WAC, but win 56–28?" That runaway Cougar win drove Howard over the edge. He had made the Utes a contender, but never a champion. And the combined score of his five games against BYU was 199–65.

Although he never beat BYU, Howard's successor Chuck Stobart (1982–84) gets Edwards's nod as the toughest to coach against in the first seventeen years of his tenure in the rivalry. "He was a good coach of the fundamentals, a no-nonsense guy right out of the Bo Schembechler school. We got together a lot . . . compared notes on what was going on around the country." Stobart didn't have any offensive secrets, leaning on the running of Carl Monroe in 1982. But he did know defense. "He made it hard, very hard, on people with his defenses," says Edwards. Utah led the WAC in defense in 1982 and took BYU to the wire before losing 17–12 in Salt Lake. "That was one of those games we had to win to take the WAC title," says Edwards. "And believe it or not, that wasn't the most important game, or the toughest, we won against Chuck."

That one would come in 1984 in Salt Lake City. The Cougars had swept unbeaten through ten foes, but a loss to Utah would surely end any hopes of a national title. "Utah took us to the wire. We were leading only 17–14 in the fourth quarter before we got a late score," says Edwards. "Utah gave ground very grudgingly." BYU's eventual 24–14 win elevated the Cougars to number one in the nation, a perch they preserved with a win over Utah State and a Holiday Bowl win over Michigan. Stobart was not so lucky. After posting a 16–17–1 mark and playing BYU to two games decided by ten points or less, the Utes ended their handshake agreement with Stobart. His last in-state visit was a good-bye chat with Edwards in Provo.

The Utes, now faced with having lost to BYU twelve times in Edwards's thirteen seasons, figured they would fight fire with fire. They hired Jim Fassel, a passing tactician who had never been a head coach, but who had tutored John Elway at Stanford in the late seventies and early eighties. "We could see where Utah wanted to go. Basically, they were where I was with BYU in 1972. Their crowds were down. They wanted some excitement. They wanted some passing offense. I liked Jim . . . I liked him a lot. If he had done with the defense what he did with offense, there's no telling how good Utah could have been." Edwards was implying that while passing totals at BYU had been calculator-crazy, the Cougars almost always had good, if not excellent, defenses.

Ironically, during the first four years against Fassel, BYU was made to look almost human. Of course, after Robbie Bosco's senior season in 1985, the Cougars fell on some lean QB times of their own. "We had some very tough games with Utah while Jim was there," Edwards concedes. One was in 1985, a game BYU won in Provo 38–28 to secure a tie for the WAC championship. While Fassel didn't go into an "I hate BYU" harangue, he did question the impartiality of the officiating. The Cougars added to Utah's 1986 misery (a 2–9 season) with a 35–21 victory in Salt Lake, and in 1987 the Utes unveiled Utah County–raised freshman quarterback Scott Mitchell in a game won by BYU 21–18. "You could see the Fassel stamp all over Scott," says Edwards.

BYU saw all they needed of Mitchell in Rice Stadium in 1988. With the Cougars again enmeshed in a quarterback quandary between Sean Covey and Ty Detmer,

Utah unleashed a decade of frustration in rolling up a 57–28 victory with Mitchell throwing for three touchdowns. It was BYU's first three-loss WAC season since 1975. The Edwards reaction at the time: "If this is a cycle [losing to Utah for the second time in sixteen years], I like the cyclical nature of it."

Edwards, to this day, is not surprised about what happened the following November in Provo. "First of all, we needed to beat Utah to keep our hopes alive for the WAC title. Second, I know the players were thinking a lot about what had happened the year before." Edwards says he has never been a coach to hold grudges, nor has he based a whole season on beating Utah. "And I've never employed the battle cry of 'remember what they did to us last year.'"

But he acknowledges his team went into that 1989 game with tunnel vision. "I never would have thought, even without them having Scott [Mitchell was on the sidelines on crutches following a practice injury], that we would win like we did." It was a 70–31 decision, but it was also 49–0 in the first half. And there was no basis for a pouring-it-on fit from Ute coaches. Detmer played only one series in the second half. Again, Ute officials had seen enough. Following a 42–38 loss to Air Force the following week and after a season in which the Utes had surrendered a last-in-the-nation 43.5 points-per-game average, Fassel was gone. He had gone 1–4 versus BYU and could finish no better than third in the WAC.

With attendance hovering around an average 64,000 at Provo and around an average 25,000 at Utah, the Ute hierarchy needed quickly to find a competitive coaching match for Edwards. Surprisingly, for the second straight time, they turned to another veteran assistant with no previous head coaching experience— University of Arizona assistant Ron McBride. "I had known a lot about Ron. He had been an assistant twice at Utah, and most of those years the Utes had been pretty darned good, both on offense and defense. It wasn't a surprise to me that Ron dug in really quick on defense. We had talked about it. When we were good, we were usually one, two, or three in the WAC in defense. Hey, we were 14–1 in 1996 largely due to a good defense."

It took McBride three years to make inroads against the Cougars. "We knew he was coming on strong," says Edwards. "We knew he was getting some tough defensive kids and he was getting great kids out of Hawaii, some that we would normally get." It didn't happen as fast as Ute fans would have liked. BYU, with Detmer at the controls, laid the heavies on the Utes 45–22 at Provo in 1990, and again in 1991 at Utah 48–17. Each time, the Cougars needed the win to clinch an outright WAC title. It was 1992 in Salt Lake when Edwards saw the real fruits of McBride's labors. "Again, we had to beat them for a share of the conference title. We led 31–0, but we had to hold them off at the end for a 31–22 win. Utah got a bowl bid because of that late scoring surge."

Finally, in 1993, Edwards watched what he knew deep inside was bound to happen eventually. The Utes got a late fifty-five-yard field goal from Chris Yergensen to secure a 34–31 victory, their first win in Provo since 1971. "We had escaped so many times to beat them and win the WAC title. But this time, Ron's team kept us from the throne room." Incredibly, the Utes had not only won, but piled up a 629–501 total-yardage advantage. What in the name of the Heisman Trophy was going on here?

In retrospect, the Utah victory did more to cement relations between the two schools than anyone could have remotely expected. Prior to the 1994 season, Edwards and McBride signed to do a series of commercials for Arizona-based Bank

Mark A. Philbrick

LaVell is a voracious reader, and his wife Patti loves to have him home.

One, which was attempting to gain a foothold in the Salt Lake market. In the thirty-second spots promoting the bank's mortgage loan services, they made famous the "buddy-pal" exchanges, playing mainly on the Utes' 34–31 victory in Provo. The commercials won a regional advertising award. One spot showed Edwards tossing and turning in bed, agonizing over a nightmare in which McBride is at once a tailor measuring Edwards for a 34–31 pair of slacks, and in another, as a waiter presenting a tab totaling . . . you guessed it, $34.31.

In the irony of the century, Edwards's nightmare was played out for real in Rice Stadium in 1994 with the Utes winning again, and just as the commercials had said in a three-month saturation of the Wasatch Front market, it was . . . 34–31. "I didn't see any real humor in it at all," says Edwards, a slight trace of a smile tugging at the corners of his mouth. There was a reason. The Ute win again denied BYU a piece of the conference title. What's more, even after beating

Oklahoma in the Copper Bowl 31–6, BYU (number twelve) ended up ranked lower than the Utes (number ten) in the national polls. The loss to Utah and the Utes' subsequent 16–13 victory over Arizona in the Freedom Bowl was a parlay the Cougars couldn't overcome. "Look at the defensive totals," Edwards says. "Utah led the league in defense." The Utes had also led the WAC in offense. "That got our attention, too," said the Cougar coach.

The Edwards-McBride television commercials attracted even more viewers in the months leading to the 1995 campaign. Some Ute fans viewed them as some sort of magic since Utah hadn't beaten the Cougars twice in a row since the late 1960s. The coaches looked at them as a lot of extra money in exchange for very little time. "We had to memorize maybe six lines for each one," says Edwards. And it is common knowledge around the WAC that LaVell is only in the middle of the league's pack of sixteen coaches salary-wise. But the goodwill fostered by the spots far outweighed any other benefits. For BYU fans, it was merely a formality that with Utah coming to Provo, the Ute two-game streak would be over.

Again, the Cougars' eleventh game was for at least a share of the WAC title and a return to the Holiday Bowl for the eleventh time. After a slow 2–3 start, the 5–1 Cougars had a get-even party planned. But this time, the Utes had something to play for. A win would assure the Utes at least a share of their first WAC championship in thirty-one years. Utah had lost four of its first seven games—all by a touchdown or less, but had spun off three wins in a row, including an improbable one-minute, fifteen-point rally that stunned Air Force 22–21. "It was our worst game of the year; it was impossible to explain," says Edwards of Utah's easy 34–17 victory. Three Utah wins in a row—over the once-invincible Cougars. "I guess that's why you play 'em," said Edwards.

The TV spots ended for McBride in 1996, ostensibly because a big Ute booster and coincidentally the owner of a competing bank, threw water on the deal. Edwards spent a good part of the early summer in commercials searching for a new "buddy." He found one in a youngster named Sparky. But there was no comparison with the viewer appeal of his old pal McBride. "I found out about on-screen chemistry and how sometimes it works and sometimes it doesn't," joked Edwards. There was no clowning around in BYU's season. For the first time in history, the Cougars were picked second in the new, expanded sixteen-team WAC. Behind Utah of all teams. "That's pretty interesting," dead-panned Edwards at the summer WAC meetings. "Remember, you [media] picked Hawaii to finish eighth one year and they won the Holiday Bowl."

Perhaps it was the magic of those TV ads that had inspired Utah. Perhaps it was a guy named Sarkisian who inspired BYU. By November, it was obvious the WAC Mountain Division title was going to come down to a November 18 meeting in Salt Lake City. The rampaging and seventh-ranked Cougars versus the twice-beaten Utes who could win the Mountain title and advance to the WAC title game in Vegas. "Hey, Mac had won three and I had won three in the 1990s. But he had won the last three. It was my turn," says LaVell, looking back on a magical season that was finished off with three momentous wins.

The Cougars unleashed a powerful running game to subdue Utah in Rice Stadium 37–17; scored a near-miraculous come-from-behind 28–25 win over Wyoming in the WAC title game in Las Vegas, and carrying a number-five national ranking, downed favored Kansas State in the Cotton Bowl on New Year's Day 19–15, again in a come-from-behind effort. "I honestly can't think of a bigger three-game finish in my career," says Edwards.

On and on it goes for the ageless Man of Mt. Timpanogos. They thought they had him cornered in 1974. But like Houdini, he slithered out of a 12–13–1 career start and ended up winning a WAC title in his third year. Utah thought they had him figured out in 1978, but it turned out to be their only win of the rivalry in seventeen years.

No one dreamed a school from the tiny unknown community of Provo, Utah, would win a national title (1984), produce a national coach of the year (1984), churn out two Outland Trophy winners (1986 and 1988), and then be left for the bone pile after failing to win the WAC title (1986–88). But Edwards rallied his troops to produce a Heisman Trophy winner (1990) and five more WAC titles in succession. And a 7–4 record in 1995? Surely this would be the end of the trail for the sixty-five-year-old Edwards. Then came 1996 and, arguably, the best college football season in history. BYU became the first school ever to win fourteen games in a single season. The Cougars' 14–1 record left them ranked number five in the country and a New Year's Day winner for the first time.

"We've had a lot of luck on our side," says Edwards. "The key thing is we've had good coaches and good athletes who have always been able to adhere to the standards of excellence we require on the field and in the classroom and in everyday life. I wouldn't have it any other way, win or lose."

Then, the million-dollar question. How long will he keep on coaching? "I feel good. As long as I can feel good in March [spring practice], in August [the beginning of fall drills], and in December [the end of the season], who knows? They may want to get rid of me you know." Yeah, LaVell, like in 1974, some 217 victories ago.

Has there ever been a seventy-five-year-old coach in the history of Division I football?

The Best Quarterback of Them All

There has always been an argument in Provo on just which quarterback of the six BYU all-Americans was the best ever in the Beehive State. It is unanimous that all six were better than anything Utah could offer up, mainly because no one at Utah could bring the Uteskis a conference title. All six Cougs did. Still, who was the best Cougar field general?

Was it hometown hero Gifford Nielsen, the Provo High School star who became the Cougars' first national QB legend and sixth-place finisher in the Heisman balloting?

Was it Marc Wilson, who led the Cougars to their first-ever undefeated regular season (11–0) and finished third in the Heisman chase?

Was it Jim McMahon, the free-spirit Catholic kid from Roy High School who was spurned by Notre Dame and the University of Utah and became the first Cougar signal caller to throw for over 4,500 yards and forty-five touchdowns and bring BYU its first bowl victory?

Was it Steve Young, who completed an amazing 65 percent of his passes over two seasons and finished second in the Heisman voting?

Was it Robbie Bosco, who led the Cougars to their only undefeated, untied season (13–0) and the national championship, finishing third in the Heisman race two consecutive years?

Or was it Ty Detmer, the Texas wizard who played more games (46), threw more passes (1,530), completed more passes (958), rolled up more yards (15,031), threw for more TDs (121), compiled the best pass efficiency mark in NCAA history (162.7), and set fifty-nine NCAA records, tying three others. And who won the Heisman Trophy?

Now, surround yourself with experts—and there will be as many clever analysts as there are people in the room—and you will hear arguments for all of them. Some might even take you as far forward as John Walsh, who led the

31–6 assault on Oklahoma in the 1994 Copper Bowl. There may even be a couple of votes for Steve Sarkisian, who amassed the most wins ever by a college QB (14) and spearheaded what many contend is the most monumental victory in BYU history—the 19–15 conquest of Kansas State in the 1997 Cotton Bowl.

Giff enthusiasts separate themselves from the pack by leaning on the hometown-boy-makes-good hypothesis. And you have to concede that Nielsen, who was a Cougar basketball standout before he became a hero of the grid-iron, was the local kid who launched BYU to its first back-to-back WAC titles. And he was the first Cougar alum to hit it really big in the pros as the Houston Oilers' starting QB.

Wilson gets his votes, too. Three reasons really. One, he was the on-field architect for the unbeaten season that pro-pelled BYU into the top ten for the first time. Second, he won a pair of the biggest games in school history—18–17 over Texas A&M and 63–14 in a nationally televised rout of San Diego State. Third, he was, to that time, the highest-finishing Heisman candidate (third).

McMahon is the most intriguing of the whole lot. He wasn't Mormon; in fact, he proclaimed himself Catholic. His real religion was throwing the ball. He was the first Cougar QB to lead the nation in passing and he did it two years in a row. As a starter those two seasons, he was 21–2, including two bowl wins. He remains the only Cougar QB to ever leave school undefeated as a bowl game starter, win-ning the classic "Hail Mary" Holiday Bowl game against SMU and piloting the Holiday Bowl win over Washington State. By the time he left, Cougar followers had even for-given him for the 23–22 loss to Utah in 1978. Because in his last two seasons, he beat the Uteskis by a combined score of 112–34. He was third in the Heisman balloting in 1981 but was a first-round draft choice by the Chicago Bears (fifth pick overall) in the 1982 draft.

Young was probably the most undisciplined onfield QB of the bunch, what with his play improvisation and unbridled desire to run. Still, his 3,902 yards offense and

71-percent pass completion mark in 1983 led the nation, capped by a rousing 21–17 win over Missouri in the Holiday Bowl. And who could argue with the $40-million pro contract he landed from the Los Angeles Express of the United States Football League?

All Bosco did was lead the Cougars to their only national football title. He wins the gumption title hands down for

Mark A. Philbrick

Ty Detmer threw for over 15,000 yards and won a Heisman Trophy. Any arguments as to who is number one?

jumping off a gurney, limping back into Jack Murphy Stadium, and leading BYU to a come-from-behind win over Michigan that ultimately clinched the national championship. Still, he could finish no better than third in the Heisman race.

I'll settle the argument. The king of them all was Detmer. At six-foot-nothin' and 175 pounds (including equipment and the football), the San Antonio whiz kid left BYU and all of Division I football with records by which all others will be measured.

It was his durability that was admirable if not heroic. From the time he came off the bench to rally BYU to a 20–17 win in the 1988 Freedom Bowl, Detmer made thirty-nine starts, and they weren't against Little Sisters of the Poor.

By the time Detmer took the controls at Quarterback U, pundits figured it had all been done. McMahon had done 4,571 yards and Bosco almost 4,300. Detmer did 4,560 his sophomore season. By the time he was through, he tacked on an NCAA-leading 5,188 yards in 1990 and another 4,031 his senior campaign.

Detmer, gets the slim nod over McMahon for the "best ever" at BYU and in the state of Utah because he played in an era when the Cougars were upgrading their schedule. He came face to face with number-one Miami in 1990 and sent the Hurricanes packing with a 28–21 loss. During his tenure, he was also tested by the defenses from Penn State, Washington State, and Oregon. In three full years as starter, he guided BYU to a 28–9–2 record and three WAC titles.

As coach LaVell Edwards has written about Detmer's Heisman season, "When Ty came along and had a big junior season, he was able to stand on the shoulders of all those BYU quarterbacks who came before him."

Detractors will note that he lost most of the games against high-level opposition. Three of the losses came on consecutive weekends in 1991—in the Pigskin Classic against Florida State and at UCLA and Penn State. He was leading a very inexperienced offense that after the opening three losses, jelled into an 8–0–2 team. His performance, though lacking in numbers, could well have been better than in his Heisman campaign. To begin with, Detmer had to undergo rehabilitation for off-season shoulder surgery that was required when he was crushed under the Texas

A&M avalanche in the 1990 Holiday Bowl.

Detmer, who relieved Sean Covey in the 1988 University of Utah game, never lost to the Uteskis as a starter. In fact, teams under his direction rolled up a 163–70 margin against the Uteskis. Detmer remains the only BYU quarterback in the history of the rivalry to own three wins over the Uteskis.

He remembers the one as a sophomore in Cougar Stadium. "They had beaten us the year before and some of them were jerks about it. We had a score to settle." It was settled in the first half, when BYU led 49–0.

The idea, at least for the Utes who lost games of 70–31, 45–22, and 48–17 to the Texas Tornado, is to keep the lips zipped up. Before a Cougar quarterback throws a football in their collective mouth.

It's hard to believe there could be someone better than Detmer. But that's what we heard after Nielsen, Wilson, McMahon, Young, and Bosco.

Stay tuned.

Great Scott!

When they're finished balancing the budget, feeding the world's hungry and rebuilding I-15, somehow those gallant souls in blue find time to play football, no doubt donating their salaries to some noble charity (the ninety percent that doesn't go to the church, of course). Yes, those BYU quarterbacks can do anything, can't they?

Welcome to Smugville, where the myth of the BYU Quarterback lives on stronger than ever.

Don't believe it? Just think back to March 1996, when a newspaper poll of Cougar screwballs in Provo revealed Gifford Nielsen, midlevel BYU quarterback of the mid–1970s, to be the most popular candidate for the school to hire.

As the basketball coach.

Granted, he had no coaching experience anywhere, at any level, in any sport. No, he had never recruited before, never run a program, never tried to motivate athletes. Okay, he hadn't even played college basketball. But if anyone could turn around the 1–25 Cougars (my, how I enjoy reading those words), surely a BYU quarterback could do it.

Couldn't he?

He certainly won the endorsement in about five seconds of every Utah basketball fan, every brave soul who ever bought those sorry three-rows-from-the-top Marriott Center tickets, watched Majerus or Archibald or Pimm whip the Cougs, then tried unsuccessfully to find a beer to celebrate. With Nielsen on the sidelines, the seats would probably improve as the Cougars failed to, and the game's outcome obviously would be in no doubt. Maybe Giff could even help with the beer problem.

Anyway, that's the level of blind faith and irrational esteem that people put in the quarterback down there. It's so prevalent that even the players eventually buy into it, producing circus-sized egos in shoulder pads. Nielsen, for example, started believing he could coach basketball, even if he couldn't fool Rondo. John Walsh declared early for the NFL draft, somehow convinced his WLAF talent would go

undetected by the pros. And Jim McMahon, well, let's just say that "ego" doesn't do justice to the self-absorbed worship he descended into after Mike Singletary and Richard Dent earned the punk bystander a Super Bowl ring.

But that's the way things are at the school that gave us Bob Jensen and Steve Lindsley, where the system makes the players look good rather than vice versa. Devise an offense that passes on every down and steamrolls lesser opponents into stat-enhancing pulp, and let the quarterback collect the glory. It's like letting Manute Bol shoot 1,200 three-pointers a season and when he leads the league in three-point baskets proclaim him the new Downtown Freddie Brown.

Normally it's harmless, or at least easy to ignore. But occasionally, inattentive, gullible, or short-sighted sportswriters somehow buy into the idea, and in the process embarrass themselves and college football. The worst example, of course, is the season when the six-foot pip-squeak from Texas had one good game on national TV, then started running up the score on Colorado State and Air Force. His reward was the Heisman Trophy's lowest moment, lower even than the year voters chose something called a Gino Torretta as the winner.

Of course, comeuppance was sweet. The moment Ty Detmer, wearing an idiotic lei and an even more idiotic grin, accepted the Trophy, the Hawaii Rainbows suddenly found the resolve to administer a thirty-one-point whipping that night. Same thing three weeks later in the Holiday Bowl, when Texas A&M made Trophy Boy's shoulders their own trophies in a 65–14 party.

And the "Ty for Two" campaign got off to a delightful start the next fall when BYU lost its first three games. Funny how hard it is to look immortal when you're not picking on UTEP's secondary, isn't it?

Yes, it's a proud history, all right, going all the way back to Gary "Next Stop Canton" Sheide and Marc Wilson, the man who ruined Al Davis' reputation and personally kept the Raiders out of two or three Super Bowls. Sean Covey was a favorite of Ute fans, for the pleasing way he could be

plastered into the Rice Stadium turf in 1988. And John Walsh, well, we can't thank him enough for delivering not one, but two 34–31 losses.

To be fair, even Salt Lakers have to concede that Steve Young has turned out to be a decent quarterback, though Frank Layden could probably pass a team into the Super Bowl with Jerry Rice hauling in everything thrown into his time zone. We don't have to like it, though, and we don't; just notice sometime how few 49ers jackets and hats you see in Rice Stadium.

Amid all the numbers and records and hype, however, one quarterback stands out in the memory banks. One individual stands alone as the greatest passer ever to come out of Utah County, to emerge from the shadow of Cougar Stadium: Scott Mitchell.

How that must sting. The man who passed for an NCAA record 631 yards in a game, who propelled a high-powered offense on the strength of his passing arm alone, who earned victories without an ounce of help from the defense, and who almost single-handedly won a Utah-BYU game—was a Ute.

He attended Springville High, within walking distance of Cougar Stadium, and was expected—practically ordained—to attend BYU. But he considered the alternative (and, one can assume, experienced some sort of epiphany, though he's never mentioned it) and told Jim Fassel and LaVell Edwards that he would prefer to attend Utah.

Mitchell turned out to be probably the biggest talent ever to wear a U on his helmet. The tragedy is that Fassel never provided a defense that could compete; just imagine such a talent in command of a Ron McBride–coached team. But there were still plenty of memorable moments, like that incredible 631-yard performance (and before Cougar fans holler about running up the stats, consider this—Utah lost that game 56–49 to Air Force). Or the six touchdown passes against UTEP in a game Utah barely won 50–45.

Or 57–28, the greatest football game ever played. The quarterback was brilliant that day, throwing for 384 yards and three touchdowns. Think he regretted his decision that day? "It doesn't get any better than this," he said.

He left a year early after an injury and a sub-par offensive line made him concerned about blowing a pro career. His

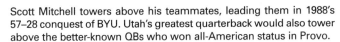

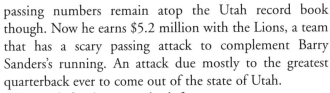

Scott Mitchell towers above his teammates, leading them in 1988's 57–28 conquest of BYU. Utah's greatest quarterback would also tower above the better-known QBs who won all-American status in Provo.

passing numbers remain atop the Utah record book though. Now he earns $5.2 million with the Lions, a team that has a scary passing attack to complement Barry Sanders's running. An attack due mostly to the greatest quarterback ever to come out of the state of Utah.

So much for the quarterback factory.

CHAPTER

RON McBRIDE
THE WALKING SUPERSTITION

There's dark, and then there's dark.

There's the kind that surrounds you and penetrates you and miniatures you, so dark that even sound seems suffocated by the monstrous absence of light and motion. That's the darkness of a new moon's summer night in Price, a small southeastern Utah town where twilight's end seems to freeze the surroundings in place, where the wee hours are as black and starless as the coal dug in the mines that honeycomb the nearby soft-rock mesas. That's the darkness that clings to the landscape this night, long after the few thousand townsfolk and the several dozen football players making their annual sortie into town have turned in.

But this night's calm is suddenly disturbed. In one window at the front of a dormitory, a light goes on. Moments later, there is stirring in the building. Quickly, it spreads to the floor above, and to a neighboring building, and to its neighbor. Within minutes, the calm is shattered, a general alarm sounded. Every door is pounded on, and the slumbering collegians slowly awaken. In one corner of Price, the nighttime is suddenly alive with activity. It's 3 A.M.—and it's time for football practice.

There's dark, and then there's dark.

And then there's Ron McBride's mood.

The University of Utah football coach brings his team to Price every August, in hopes of separating his players from the distractions of home and molding them into a self-contained, self-reliant unit. At McBride's Camp Carbon, the Utes transform themselves, through equal parts isolation and hard labor, from a disparate group of selfish individuals into a dedicated and cohesive cooperative. At least that's the theory.

But this fall, the autumn of 1993, McBride is unhappy with how his team has come together. The drills and scrimmages seem normal, and the conditioning undertaken with the standard workmanlike if unenthusiastic attitude. The weights are being lifted, the playbooks memorized. Yet McBride senses things are not right in his team's huddles. Two weeks of two-a-day practices have yet to meld his squad into the football machine he had hoped. Worse, word has reached the coach that some of his players have violated training camp rules, that curfew is not being strictly observed, and that some of Salt Lake City's distractions have been imported to Price. But most troublesome of all to McBride is the nagging feeling that his players don't yet feel like teammates, that the ideal of cooperation hasn't quite taken hold.

"In order to get something done, you all have to be on the same page," McBride lectures his yawning charges as they stand limply together at the edge of the practice field. "We can't accomplish anything unless we're together." That means no cliques, no resentments, no artificial divisions, he tells them. Black or white, Hispanic or Pacific Islander, McBride says, it doesn't matter. In his eyes, they are all Utes, working toward a common goal of winning football games. If they are to succeed, they all must have that mind-set, he says.

Everyone must dedicate himself. And if one strays, McBride says, they all must serve the penance. Which is why their night's sleep is being interrupted.

The football players look at each other numbly. They're tired. But they understand.

"He got his point across," says center Lance Scott. "We all make up the power of one. So everyone pays when someone screws up, not just one guy. . . . We're a team."

And as a team, the players jerk through a brief set of calisthenics, then slowly run laps around the field. There are no lights, so the predawn practice is limited to a Marine bivouac-style jog, a half-hour or so of effort to emphasize the coach's lesson.

"It doesn't hurt to make the players a little uncomfortable sometimes," McBride says. "It helps keep them mentally tough, mentally alert." Even if it's hard to tell at 3 A.M.

Okay, even McBride will concede that's a little early to hold football practice, but only by a couple of hours. Once the season begins, after all, the coach's day normally begins at 5 A.M., for a few hours of solitary film study. It's his way of trying to guarantee that nothing has been overlooked, an impossible urge to know everything and foresee every possibility. It's a consuming life, especially during those three fall months when McBride has no life outside football.

"I'm not the smartest guy out there, I know that," he concedes. "You are what you are. Some guys have brains, some have a knack for the job."

Utah's coach has effort.

That's why, during the season, McBride's days are a blur of calculated activity, from studying film at dawn to hours of meetings with assistants to addressing his players to overseeing practices. The only breaks in the schedule are annoying but necessary appearances before boosters and the media—he's almost always gracious and genuinely friendly, if anxious to resume his labors—and a daily ritual of swimming seventy-five or so laps to help clear his head.

He also personally grades every film of every game and every practice, sometimes three or four times. His assistants will study the video and zero in on their own players, but McBride wants to see it all for himself.

Click. Offensive lineman slow to move his feet. Make a note. Rewind. Click. Tight end not keeping his hands up, not holding his block. And why is the full-back standing so far from the quarterback? Watch that defensive end, he's trying to circle behind the tackle. Write it down. Watch it again. Click. Click. Click.

"There are no secrets in football. It's all on the tape," McBride believes. "You have to teach the kids how to do things, how to block, how to tackle, and make sure they do it right, every time. It's all technique, first. And then it's all work."

Which isn't a bad description of Ron McBride and his tenure as head coach at Utah. When he took over the program in 1990, his first head-coaching job after twenty-five years as an assistant coach, McBride mapped his way to success the only way he knew how. Technique first. Then work.

The technique for shoring up a crumbling football foundation was a traditional one, and an obvious one for the Salt Lake City situation McBride inherited: Start with defense.

There wasn't much mystery about that in 1990, not after Jim Fassel presented Ute fans with the most porous eleven-man unit in the nation, 105th among the 105 Division I schools in 1989. Only twice in Fassel's final season did Utah hold its opponent to fewer than five touchdowns; even the slick Scott Mitchell-led offense couldn't overcome that sort of support very often.

McBride instructed his recruiters to focus on quick, strong athletes who could stand up to the WAC's offensive machines. And he vowed not to pluck the best players out of the defense and remake them into offensive weapons, as Fassel often had. You can just keep trying to outscore opponents, and maybe you'll win as often as you don't, McBride figured. But prevent a team from scoring, and there's no way to lose.

Sounds like a simple concept, and it is. Like he said, there are no secrets in football. It just seemed like a revolution after the pinball games that characterized Ute football in the late 1980s.

But McBride added another element to the program, one he feared had been missing for years. He didn't just want talent; that wasn't enough. Fassel's yo-yo Utes had been plenty talented, after all. The missing ingredient, McBride knew from his years on the sidelines, was attitude—a dedication to winning no matter what. Tough guys who would respond when challenged, who would rely on guts as much as talent.

"We started to pay attention to personality a little bit more," says McBride. "We were looking for work ethic and commitment. I love a guy who might not be the most talented guy ever but who will bust his butt to make a play. He'll work to improve, and maybe by the end he'll be just as valuable as the guy with all the natural ability."

A commitment to work. Just like his coach. In fact, McBride sought out players who had overcome hardship, who had persevered through difficult circumstances to make themselves better.

Players from broken homes, or rough neighborhoods, or backgrounds of poverty—those recruits had added incentive to succeed, the coach decided. "If a guy is really hungry, he'll respond when you show him what he needs to do," McBride says. "A guy who has always had everything handed to him, maybe he doesn't want to run those extra laps or lift weights a little longer, or watch film every day."

So the coach watched for his chance to scoop up those self-motivated talents.

He recruited a defensive lineman who was a ferocious pass-rusher but got little recognition because he played on a bad team in a dusty corner of Colorado. He signed an offensive lineman who wasn't big enough for his position but excelled anyway on an overmatched team through sheer force of will. He added a linebacker who excelled in junior college but was passed up by California schools near his hometown because he was judged too small for big-college football. He took on a quarterback stranded by the elimination of another school's program, a smallish specimen recruited by nobody, who had walked on and turned himself into a football player through study and effort.

He put together a cast of players as unlikely to win Division I football games as he was to coach them, then watched them feed off his energy and become all-conference performers.

In his fifth year at Utah, Luther Elliss, Lance Scott, Mark Rexford, and Mike McCoy presented McBride with a 10–2 record, the school's first bowl victory in three decades, and its first top-ten ranking.

"This team is a reflection of its coach, and they would all tell you that," said athletic director Chris Hill at the time. "They are his kind of players, and he is their kind of coach."

It's difficult to tell who would be more flattered by the comparison.

By all accounts, McBride was that type of player as well. He grew up in Los Angeles and played both baseball and football at South Gate High School.

Displaying a natural athletic ability, he was named all-city in both sports in 1957.

He left Southern California for San Jose State soon thereafter and impressed his fellow Spartans with his dedication to winning.

His wife Vicky remembers having to kill time outside the Spartans' locker room after losses; so bitterly did he take losses, McBride would mope around for hours, long after everyone else had gone, before finally heading home.

"It was so pitiful to see him that way," she says. "I'd try to tell him not too take it too hard, but you could see that the hurt was genuine." His teammates noticed

After defeating BYU 34–31 in Provo in 1993, Ron McBride celebrates "my biggest win ever" with his biggest fan—his wife Vicky.

it, too, and chose McBride as their team captain for his senior season in 1962.

His coaches noticed as well. After McBride gave pro football a shot as a linebacker in the semi-pro USA League, San Jose State welcomed him back as its linebacker coach and head of the freshman team in 1965.

He's been on the sidelines ever since.

"It's what I know how to do. I didn't go into this to be some famous coach or something," McBride has said. "I just got a few chances early on and stayed with what I know. I've been pretty lucky that way."

He first tried using his degree in secondary education by teaching at a San Jose high school while also serving as the school's defensive coordinator. But three years later, that luck kicked in. Gavilan Junior College in nearby Gilroy hired him as a defensive line coach, then promoted him to offensive coordinator.

Three years later, McBride began climbing the college football ladder, first at Cal-Riverside, then Long Beach State under head coach Wayne Howard. Finally, in 1977, McBride's life changed with a phone call from Howard, who had just been hired as Utah's new head coach. Come along and be my offensive coordinator, Howard told him. You'll love this place.

He had no idea.

McBride arrived, looked around for a day, and realized he was home. The city was picturesque, the mountain setting spectacular. The people were friendly and the campus a landmark. The four-season weather, the wide streets, the big-but-not-too-big metropolis and the laid-back unpretentiousness—"I knew right away this is the place I wanted to be," he says.

Vicky and the four kids were tougher to convince. "I was a Californian, and I always expected to be a Californian," she says. "I thought he was crazy. But I saw what it meant to Ronnie. And he was right."

Professionally, it seemed like a good move, too; Utah's football program had bottomed out under Tom Lovat's three-year reign, which produced just five victories. But Howard saw great possibilities for a school with so many advantages—Utah was a growing state, the WAC was beginning to gain respect thanks to Arizona State and the rise of Brigham Young, and the state school and its boosters seemed willing to spend the money necessary to reverse the Utes' direction. After all, if the Cougars could be winners, why couldn't the Utes?

Sure enough, in 1978, Howard's second season, Utah suddenly blossomed to an 8–3 title contender (admittedly aided by the departure of Arizona and Arizona State from the WAC), and the new coach seemed settled in for a long reign.

But Howard soon grew frustrated by the difficulties of trying to build a program in the increasingly long shadow of Brigham Young University, by now a national player under LaVell Edwards. A pair of annoyingly mediocre seasons convinced Howard to quit coaching, and even a bounce-back 8–2–1 season couldn't change his mind, not when it was punctuated by a disheartening 56–28 finale in Provo.

McBride applied for Howard's job, but the school instead chose a disciplinarian from the Midwest, Chuck Stobart. The new coach allowed McBride to keep his coordinator position, but the two were never really comfortable with each other's styles, and after a year, McBride faced a difficult career crossroads.

He finally concluded that Stobart deserved to hire his own staff, even if it meant McBride had to leave his adopted hometown. Reluctantly, he accepted a job as offensive line coach at Wisconsin. It was the Big Ten, and thus the big-time, but McBride spent two seasons waiting for a chance to return to Utah.

That chance arrived in 1985, when Stobart's style was deemed too dull and his record too mediocre. McBride applied again for the head coaching job, hoping the connections he made during his six years in Salt Lake would pay off.

No such luck, not when the school decided to go with a passing wizard who promised to sell tickets with an exciting team. Jim Fassel, a former quarterback with a score, score, score! philosophy, got the job.

As a consolation prize, and because Utah donors had lobbied on his behalf, Fassel offered McBride a job on his staff. Not as coordinator, mind you; that was too sophisticated a task to be left to a lineman. Fassel suggested McBride could take charge of the blockers.

Oblivious to the inherent insult and eager to return to Utah, McBride wanted to jump at the job. Vicky didn't. They're sending you a message by not hiring you for the head coach's job, she told her husband. Forget Utah; go where you're wanted.

McBride took the job anyway. He had never sold his house in Salt Lake, figuring on returning at some point, if just to retire. Wisconsin was okay, but Utah was home.

It wasn't long before he realized that Fassel's strategy of pass first, ask questions later, wasn't going to work. In 1986, one of the most promising Utah teams in years fell flat on its face with an 0–7 start, finishing 2–9.

After that season, Dick Tomey asked McBride to join him at Arizona, where he had ended up after a successful tenure at Hawaii. McBride was tempted, but refused. Tomey called back, offered more money. Still McBride said no. Tomey invited him down to take a look around. McBride was impressed but said he couldn't leave home. He couldn't leave his players.

Which was exactly the attachment Tomey wanted on his staff. Finally McBride accepted, and immediately regretted it. His good-byes to his players were tearful, but everybody wished him well. "The day he left, he felt really awful," Vicky says. "I wasn't sure he was going to go."

He went anyway, and quickly earned the respect of his new players in Tucson. "There aren't many assistants like Ronnie," Tomey says. "I've never seen a guy more loyal to his players, and vice versa. . . . Nobody works harder, and nobody makes his guys work harder. But they respected him so much, they would do anything he asked."

Once, according to a story in the *Tucson Citizen*, McBride called his linemen together at the end of a tough two-and-a-half-hour practice in the brutal Arizona sun. Everyone figured he was sending them home. But the coach had one more drill.

"Coach McBride has an idea," said fellow assistant Rich Scherer. "We're going to set up a line of blocking dummies ten yards apart for eighty yards. You're going to run full speed, hit each dummy, jump up as fast as you can and do it again. Then you're going to sprint back one hundred yards as fast as you can and do it again. Then you're going to sprint back and do it again."

Before anybody could start complaining, one of McBride's linemen, John Fina, began shouting "Yesss! Yesss!"

"Whoooooohooo! Let's do it!" chimed in Rick Varna.

"It looked like an invasion force and the Dummy Corridor became the day's most enthusiastic exercise," the *Citizen* reported. "Never had fifty or sixty football players had so much fun doing something so dreaded."

"He makes you love practice," says Glen Parker, another former Arizona offensive tackle. "We would go to war for Coach McBride. Every day he dreams up something like this and every day it has a purpose. He gets the most out of everybody he coaches."

Those Arizona players hung a bad-taste nickname on McBride, calling him "Kool-Aid," a reference to Jim Jones's poison drink that killed hundreds of his cult followers. The reason? Said Parker, "This offensive line would follow him just about anywhere, even to hell."

That sort of devotion finally convinced Utah's hierarchy to give McBride a chance, once Fassel flamed out in a sea of missed tackles. In December of 1989, the University of Utah invited the prodigal son home.

Utah's football fortunes turned around in December 1989, when Chris Hill gave Ute fans an early Christmas present by hiring Ron McBride as head coach.

Steve Griffin/THE SALT LAKE TRIBUNE

The welcome was tearful, with McBride trying to explain how much the school and the opportunity meant to him. He promised to reward the faith the Utes had put in him by leading his team to bowl games and conference championships.

"I'll get you to the top, I guarantee that," he said at his introductory press conference, beneath a banner reading Welcome Home, Ron. "But it depends on how we all hang together. You give me your support and I'll get it done for you."

That was welcome news to fans of a program that was gradually accepting mediocrity as its lot. As Edwards kept raising the level of his Cougars' aspirations in Provo, Utahns were becoming restless at the series of raised hopes and wasted talent.

It was also pretty big talk for a guy who had never run a program before, especially at a school that, his predecessors had concluded, was jinxed. Beat BYU? Win a WAC title? The man doesn't realize what he's up against.

Or, maybe he just didn't care. McBride was as convinced as ever that if he could find good, dedicated players who were willing to work as hard as he, that winning football games would happen naturally.

He believes in aggressive defenses and a dependable running game, but that's about as deep as his coaching philosophy goes. Don't expect McBride to try to revolutionize the game, because he has neither the expertise nor the inclination for it. As he says, there are no secrets in football.

"You have to have kids who want to play, first of all. They have to be totally committed to the program, and that includes the academic part of it," the coach explains. "If a kid isn't going to put the effort into class, he's not going to be willing to do the other things it takes to excel. They have to give their best."

Rather than a playbook full of secret weapons, McBride's fundamental key to winning football exists in an acronym that succinctly summarizes what he asks of his players, and himself. It's called MAFU, a foreign-sounding word that is emblazoned on hats and T-shirts and wall posters all over the Utah football offices.

It stands for the four tenets of McBride-ball: mental toughness, aggressiveness, fanatical effort, and unity. He came up with the concept while an assistant coach, and preaches it to his team every chance he gets. "That's all you need—those are the things that separate the successful teams from the rest," he says.

He has managed to instill those tenets by demonstrating to his players that he is as dedicated to them as he demands they be. Successful coaches are as much evangelists as field generals, spreading their gospel and inspiring zealotry. In a state known for its religious fervor, McBride certainly has the knack.

"Ron doesn't have former players; he has disciples," said one of those brethren.

Added Luther Elliss, before graduating to NFL football, "There was never a day where Coach couldn't make you excited about practicing. It could be raining, snowing, windy, whatever, and he could convince you it was football weather. Actually, I think he believed it."

And because he is as hard on himself as on others, it makes the hectoring and vilifying and nit-picking worth it. Make no mistake, he is his players' best friend. But he is also their harshest critic.

At practice—quite possibly his favorite activity in life—McBride has a comment on everything, from the pass coverage to the linemen's footwork. He'll carry on a conversation with visitors, sometimes two or three at once, but punctuate every other sentence with a shout toward his players.

Mostly it's positive reinforcement—"Way to go, baby, way to work!"—to let them know he's still got an eye on the proceedings. But when he detects someone coasting, or not concentrating, or using sloppy technique, McBride spares no decibel in making his point.

"He's got that raspy voice, but he can get it about as loud as a jet airplane," smiles Harold Lusk, who spent five years listening to the rants. "He can get pretty mad. But I believe he honestly does it out of caring and compassion for you as a player."

Compassion is a frequent word to describe McBride's demeanor—though it can be hard to accept when he turns into a raving lunatic and assumes a three-point stance to badger a half-hearted lineman into improvement.

Certainly his Arizona Wildcats noticed. The school's 1989 football media guide describes the coach this way:

> McBride is sort of an anti-leader figure. He's not too tall, not to lean, not too mean and not too much in between. He's got this great laugh, great smile, great knowing eyes and great compassion—unbelievable passion.
>
> His players say he can look right through them and know their guts. He seems to reach players at different levels than most coaches. Mac does it on the strange brotherhood of the frog.
>
> It's like, "Hey, you remember me. I was the guy who taught you how to catch frogs and make bread into fish bait balls when you were a little kid. I was your childhood. I was your fun buddy, but I need some help now, see. I need you to go out and repay the debt. I need you to kick some butt for me now."
>
> Or as guard John Brandon said, "We all love him; we adore him. He's like an older brother more than a coach. He yells at you but you know he cares."

Nothing changed once he got the head coach's job, his Utah players attest.

"I have never known anyone who yelled as much as Coach Mac," laughs Henry Lusk, the all-WAC receiver. "He's absolutely crazy sometimes. But we all love him."

It's reciprocated, if the time he takes to talk to every player individually is any indication. McBride remembers details of people's lives, and is genuinely interested in them. He asks about parents, greets children by name, keeps track of all sorts of problems, from grades to girlfriends.

"You know those files people use to keep phone numbers, a Rolodex? Coach Mac has one of those in his head," marvels longtime assistant coach Sean McNabb. "He remembers names and faces and details of every single player without hesitation. It's not phony at all, he's really interested. It's amazing to watch."

He gets a chance at every practice, when McBride wanders among his troops while they stretch and asks after the family, inquires about injuries, just jokes around and lets them joke back.

"They know he cares," says Manny Hendrix, who works in the athletic department. "It works because he's authentic. You don't fake caring about people."

So when they excel on the football field, he's one of the guys, as happy for them as they are for him. In 1990, McBride's first year as head coach, the Utes traveled to Minnesota the second weekend of the season for a difficult road game. The Utes played inspired football, and surprised the Gophers and their Metrodome crowd by keeping the game even down to the final minute. But with the scored tied 29–29 and time running out, Minnesota positioned itself for a chip-shot field goal that would win the game.

On the game's final play, LaVon Edwards blocked the kick and returned it ninety yards for a touchdown, giving the Utes an unbelievable 35–29 victory and turning the end zone into a pile of delirious Utahns.

In jubilation, McBride sprinted down the sideline himself and launched himself atop the scrum. "He hobbles around like an old man, and suddenly he's running for his life," recalled Charlie Brown, then a freshman. "There was more shouting and hugging than you can imagine, and here in the middle of it is our coach. It made him one of us."

Recruits know it too, which is one of the reasons Utah has attracted some of the best athletes ever to its campus since his arrival. McBride offers what every college coach is selling—a good education, a chance to play in an emerging program, perhaps a championship or bowl appearance or two, and the opportunity to better oneself and create a future.

But he also can offer four years of Ron McBride, which is a unique enticement to many players. Indeed, most recruits who commit to Utah, especially the ones sought by other, bigger programs, say they make their decision because of the coach. First, McBride's earnest nature comes through during home visits, when the coach outlines Utah's program and, more importantly, tries to connect with the parents.

"Parents have to trust you, that's the bottom line. They're sending you their kid, they want to know they can believe what you're saying," McBride explains. "I want to convince the kid, but it doesn't do any good if the family doesn't trust you. I'm just honest. I say what I believe and either they like it or they don't."

Those who do are invited to dinner at McBride's home during the recruiting season, by all accounts an eclectic experience. The recruits and their parents get to meet fellow future Utes and get to know their new best friend.

"Those nights, when we have six or eight recruits all together, are my favorite part of all this," says Vicky McBride. "There's a lot of laughing. You can really feel friendships forming."

Think of a football coach and the icons come to mind: Vince Lombardi, Tom

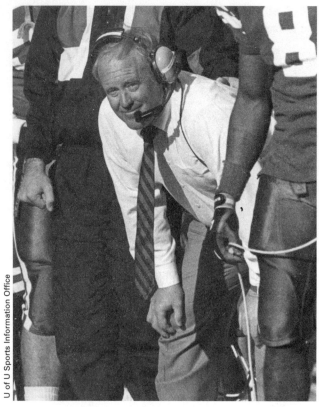

U of U Sports Information Office

No coach is more intense (or superstitious) on the sidelines than the hard-working Ron McBride.

Landry, Bear Bryant, George Halas. Men who ruled with an autocratic style, who motivated through fear, who were respected but rarely loved.

In more recent times, the stereotype more resembles a CEO, a man atop a corporate structure who regards his players almost as products to be marketed. Bill Walsh, Tom Osborne, and Jimmy Johnson come to mind.

Now consider this slightly pudgy specimen limping around the Ute practice field wearing shiny plastic jogging pants, a gray-and-red T-shirt under a wrinkled baseball jacket, and a bent-up cap that fails to keep locks of mussed, gray hair from escaping in every direction. His right hand is curled in an uncomfortable-looking mangle, the result of arthritis that he will rarely acknowledge. He hobbles gingerly from drill to drill on a foot afflicted by gout three summers ago. He yells in a coarse voice made raspy by years of trying to make his screams heard above the roar of a crowd.

In an age where coaches become celebrities with endorsement contracts, nobody will ever mistake Ron McBride for Pat Riley. Which suits him just fine. "I'm not going to pretend to be something I'm not," he says. "I'm just me."

Hey, it's worked so far.

But maybe not without some help, as he would be the first to admit. After all the work, all the preparation, NCAA coaching is still a career built around the whims and decisions and vagaries of teenage athletes, kids just a few years out of high school.

And it's a game decided to a certain extent by the bounce of a strange-shaped ball. In other words, luck plays a bigger role than the fans realize, certainly a role that makes football coaches uncomfortable. Even the biggest control freaks can't control everything. Not that McBride hasn't tried.

See, maybe Chris Fuamatu-Ma'afala, Luther Elliss, and Chris Yergensen were responsible for part of McBride's 49–34 career record. But keep an open mind. Isn't it also possible that the coach's lucky coin helped break the Utes' bowl jinx? Or that a certain black-and-white shirt kept a three-game winning streak intact? And those miraculous last-minute comebacks against Fresno State and Air Force in 1995—those might be the best ones of all. Those victories can be traced directly to magic mud.

Or maybe not—there are plenty more lucky totems and mojo makers around McBride's neck or in his pockets or on his schedule, and who can say where the luck lies? Hats, sweatsuits, necklaces, bears—Utah's coach has a talisman for every occasion, from the simplicity of a lucky lapel pin to the more elaborate mud concoction.

"He's been superstitious all his life," says Vicky McBride, who has given up trying to keep track of all her husband's various eccentricities. "He was that way when he coached high school ball. He wore a pair of pants that had a big hole in the back all season. He wore them forever, and the team won a championship."

To some, all the reliance on luck and omens may sound silly, but there is a sound principle at work here, too. Given the capriciousness of football bounces, there is a comfort zone in knowing everything is in order. "It makes him feel safe, makes it easier to think clearly on the field. You can concentrate better," explains Vicky. "If everything is right, then you'll have a better chance to win."

And so Utah's coach keeps track of who drives him to media luncheons and what food his team eats before games. Others join him in superstitions—for instance, he always stays in the same hotel room at the University Park Hotel the night before home games, with management's cooperation. Once during the Utes' win streak in 1994, the hotel staff, taking no chances, had to talk a guest who had extended his stay into moving to another room.

His players and fellow coaches are in on it, too. At Long Beach State, the 49ers once refused to take the field until McBride's lucky hat, inadvertently tossed in the trash, was located.

And at Cal-Riverside, a cocktail waitress at a tavern where the coaching staff gathered for beers convinced McBride she could guarantee the outcome of games by stabbing voodoo pins into a doll dressed like the opponent's mascot. The waitress seemed vaguely unbalanced and unnerved the coaches a little. But the team kept winning about 90 percent of the time over two years, so the tradition couldn't be halted.

McBride is normally reluctant to discuss his superstitions, especially during the football season; see, talking about them might keep them from working. It's just plain bad luck. All he'll say on the subject is that "some things do work. They make you feel good, like everything is going right, like you can't lose."

But it's no coincidence when Utah switches to white uniform pants after two home losses in red, or that his administrative assistant had to quit accompanying him to Crimson Club meetings after she missed one and the Utes won the next week. Or that fans are not allowed to photograph players as they board team buses; something about removing their energy.

Or, most notably, that the Utes have a habit of walking barefoot through a tub of mud the afternoon before night games, presumably while avoiding stepping on any cracks.

Keeping it all straight? Don't worry, even the reverent coach has trouble following every bit of McBride Mojo. He also would dispute the idea that it's all silly superstition, too.

Take the magic mud, for instance; it's supposed to provide additional energy to each player's legs. There's a certain amount of truth to that, insists Jerry Mika, the University Park Hotel director of marketing who gets his hands dirty for the team before each home game.

"This is not voodoo or hocus-pocus stuff," Mika says. "It's strictly medicinal. Soft mud on the foot's pressure points can do wonders for a guy."

Mika won't reveal the recipe, introduced to McBride by a Hawaiian he knows only as "the seaweed man," but some players, willing to go along with their coach's wishes, have recognized parsley and mushrooms in the odd mix.

The mud sometimes presents a challenge on the road. In El Paso in 1995, for instance, Mika couldn't find the appropriate type of dirt around the team's hotel. He finally found the necessary soil about twenty miles out of town, by digging under a eucalyptus tree. The Utes ran their toes through it before the game and won 34–21.

McBride doesn't just believe in walking through strange concoctions from the Orient, though. He drinks them, too. The coach is a regular consumer of Kombucha, a smelly mix of mushrooms, tea, brown sugar, and assorted vitamins and minerals. By sipping it slowly every day, the tonic promises "youth, beauty, vitality, longevity."

Sometimes that longevity must apply to his wardrobe, too. Wearing the same clothing as at the previous victory is a fairly common idiosyncrasy in the coaching profession, and its a longtime favorite of McBride.

"I used to get mad at him. I told him, 'For Pete's sake, it takes you three hours to get ready for a game,' " says Vicky McBride. "There's not enough room in the damn suitcase." Not when there's certain pants, and shirts, and sweatsuits, and shoes to wear at kickoff. "I packed a sweatsuit for him to wear after swimming in the hotel one time, and he crammed another one in his suitcase," says the coach's wife. "I asked him why and he just said 'never mind.' But I knew. The man takes two sweatsuits to a city where it's going to be 95 degrees."

Weather is much less important than karma, though. In 1993, when his suit coat was arguably responsible for igniting a three-game winning streak, McBride insisted on wearing the heavy jacket on the sidelines in Honolulu.

Not the first time, recalls Vicky McBride. While an assistant at Arizona, McBride wore a jacket to a night road game—a victory. "He wore that warm tweed coat for weeks—even in the UCLA game," which had been switched to an afternoon kick-off in the Tucson sun for television. "It was 120 degrees, and he's in a jacket."

Superstition even became a medical issue in 1995. During the first week of training camp, McBride was standing on the sidelines, his back to the practice field, while chatting with visitors. A swing pass to Fuamatu-Ma'afala came his direction, and the freshman tailback, all 270 pounds of him, crashed into the coach at top speed, breaking McBride's ankle.

Doctors placed McBride's ankle in a walking cast, which they said he would have to wear for a month. Just days before the soft cast was to be removed, the Utes defeated New Mexico for their first victory. Suddenly, McBride couldn't find the time to have his ankle reexamined. "He keeps putting it off. He's always got some reason he can't take the cast off," laughed trainer Bill Bean. "I suspect it'll stay on as long as we keep winning."

Sure enough, after three extra weeks of wearing the protective gear, Utah lost a disappointing home game to San Diego State. By that Monday, McBride's ankle was out of the cast for good.

Sometimes, however, the charms, clothes, and mud aren't enough. For crucial moments during games, McBride saves the hex. By flicking his finger in a half-circle motion and calling out a player's number, bad karma is transmitted to an opposing player.

Think it doesn't work? Neither did Chris Service, until Oregon kicker Josh Bidwell shanked a field goal in Utah's 1995 season-opener, with McBride yelling his number all the while.

"I thought he was calling the player over. He was calling him loud," said Service, Utah's outdoor-equipment manager at the time, who was responsible for carrying McBride's headphone cord during games. Utah's coach uses the hex on third-and-short situations, or fourth-down plays, Service said. "At first, you might giggle to yourself . . . but sometimes it works."

McBride picked up the practice from Bryan Rowley during the all-conference receiver's playing days. And Rowley, now KALL radio's sideline reporter, still has the touch, some Utes say. McBride sought out Rowley during BYU's final drive in the teams' 1994 game in Rice Stadium, so the story goes, and the two focused on Cougar quarterback John Walsh. Moments later, Walsh was sacked and fumbled, and Utah's 34–31 victory was preserved.

"I'm not saying we caused the sack or anything," Rowley demurred. "But focusing that kind of energy can't hurt."

And it's hardly the most outlandish sideline stunt McBride has ever tried, anyway. At Cal-Riverside, an equally superstitious booster gave the Irish coach a shillelagh to carry on the sideline. He swore that if McBride pointed it at the other team's fullback, the lucky stick would cause a fumble.

It looked and sounded pretty silly, but what choice did McBride have? Turning down a lucky totem could doom his team to bad luck. So he gave it a try. It didn't work, though, and McBride went back to his "normal" collection of superstitions. Like the coins he keeps in his pockets, the ones he has owned for years. Or the red-and-white beaded necklace, given to him by a booster's son, that he wears under his game-day shirt.

On his lapel is a pin that says 110 Percent and is always worn upside down. Mind

U of U Sports Information Office

Utah players carry their coach off the field after pulling off a 16–13 upset over Arizona in the 1994 Freedom Bowl.

you, it's the original pin—not the replacement one that cost the Utes a home game against Stanford in 1995 because a desperate search failed to turn up the real pin by game time.

His own personal talismans aren't the only important ones. Certain people must sit in certain spots on the team's plane or at booster luncheons, and when Allison

Stone, daughter of KALL radio personality Brad Stone, showed her red-and-white teddy bear (named Mac, of course) to the coach, a smiling McBride made her promise to bring the bear to every Ute game, for luck. Just in case.

"His philosophy isn't that every single one is going to be good luck. He wants to repeat what worked," says the nonsuperstitious Vicky McBride. "He says, 'If I'm comfortable carrying forty-two lucky charms, what do you care?' And he's right. If he feels more positive, that's what is important."

Call it luck or superstition if you like, but it didn't take long for McBride to become a historic figure in Utah football. His teams won eleven games in his first two seasons as coach, a debut bettered only by Ike Armstrong, the winningest coach in Utah history, in 1925–26.

Two seasons after Utah fielded the nation's worst defense, McBride coached the WAC's most stingy squad in 1991.

The 4–7 record he turned in his first year, using mostly inherited players, is the only losing season McBride has ever suffered. The six straight non-losing seasons, with six or more victories each year, is the greatest stretch of winning the University of Utah has seen since Armstrong retired in 1949.

Until McBride, the Utes' bowl history was brief: just a pair of games, the 1938 Sun Bowl and the 1964 Liberty Bowl. The new coach inaugurated a new post-season tradition, taking Utah to four bowl games in the past five years. Oddly, the year the team stayed home was another milestone occasion for Utah—in 1995, it claimed a share of the WAC championship for the first time since 1964.

It will be difficult, however, for the Utes to top their 1994 team, McBride's Masterpiece. Those Utes combined the WAC's most reliable offense with one of the nation's best defenses. The team won its first eight games, beat the eventual conference champ (Colorado State), produced a Freedom Bowl victory over Arizona, and finished the season ranked tenth nationally.

That stands as the greatest season in Utah history—but McBride says it required little coaching. The senior-dominated squad, which produced seven all-WAC players and four NFL draft picks, was self-motivating, self-disciplining, practically self-coaching.

"That team knew what it had to do every week, what it took to win, and it went out and did it," the coach said the following spring. "I never had to tell them anything. I didn't make any great speeches or that stuff. They were probably harder on themselves than I ever was."

McBride's remarkable accomplishments at the Utah helm has reenergized a large following of football fans left mostly discontented by decades of mediocrity. Season-ticket sales surpassed Rice Stadium records, and donors became more willing to pony up for the athletic department.

That's because in 1993, McBride's mainstays began to receive a donation in return—one of the most precious bestowals a Utah coach could ever proffer.

The Utes beat BYU. In Provo.

"This is the biggest win of my life," McBride said with what was left of his voice moments after Utah's 34–31 win at Cougar Stadium on November 20, 1993. "I can't describe this feeling. This is everything to us."

It had been twenty-two years since the Utes had left Provo winners, before most of the players who broke the jinx had been born. So the coach had ample reason to hug his players, his coaches, his wife, the band, the media, seemingly every one of the 1,500 Utah fans in the stadium that day.

"There's no better feeling you get in your lifetime as a coach, because this has been a burden on our backs for a lot of years," he explained, choking on his words. "And to win down here is even more important. I can't tell you how big a thing this is for me, for our team, and for our fans."

Funny thing. Just days earlier, McBride had assured broadcasters and writers that the BYU game was no bigger than any WAC game, that the biggest thing was to win and stay in bowl contention. Sure we'd like to beat BYU, he and his staff kept telling the world. Just as much as we'd like to beat Air Force or Hawaii.

He even said it with a straight face.

Newspaper reporters tried to pry a little honesty out of McBride, but he stuck by his Milquetoast story. Well, mostly. Finally, McBride winked, looked both ways as though expecting LaVell Edwards to jump out from behind a tree, and said softly, "If we win this game, I'll give you the best quotes you ever had." Then he resumed his say-no-evil stance. And when the Utes won, McBride obliged by telling everyone who would listen that it was the greatest day of his football life.

It's a habit straight out of the coaches' handbook: Speak ill of no opponent. McBride is one of the commandment's chief adherents and expects his players to be as well.

The schedule may say Texas-El Paso and San Jose State, but the wary coach sees nothing but Notre Dames and Florida States. Ask about Fresno State and he'll compare them favorably to an NFL team. East Dakota Tech? Sure, they haven't won a game, but they look terrifying on tape.

"I can't tell you we should kick somebody's butt, because the minute you start to think that, you're in big trouble," McBride says. "Everybody is good enough to beat you, and if you go out and give them a reason to, it helps them do it."

Not that BYU and Utah need any extra reason to try to beat each other, of course. But McBride especially has reason to respect the Cougars' football system.

In many ways, he copied it.

McBride established the basic four-three defensive alignment as his standard, as they did in Provo. He made the pass his principle weapon but resurrected Utah's stagnant running game for balance—a blueprint that BYU spread to the entire conference decades ago.

He determined to compete for the best Mormon athletes and encouraged them to fulfill two-year LDS Church missions, a market that the Cougars had once cornered. And to run his program and compete with the league's long-dominant power, McBride recruited a handful of coaches familiar with BYU's system—because they had been part of it.

Fred Whittingham was hired in 1992 as Utah's defensive coordinator, a position he held for four years under Edwards at BYU. Two years later, McBride added Fred's son Kyle, who played four seasons and coached one in Provo, as his defensive line coach. When Kyle succeeded his father, who moved on to the NFL after one year, McBride hired another Cougar alum, Steve Kaufusi, to take over the linemen.

"They do things the right way at BYU. They know how to attract good kids and they know how to teach them. That's why they've been successful for so long," says McBride.

That respect carries over to the coach's relationship with LaVell Edwards; he can relate to his rival, even joke around with his "buddy," as a series of popular bank commercials portrayed them, while still trying to beat him at his own game.

It's difficult to quantify how important winning is to Ron McBride, but Tomey, his boss at Arizona, is impressed. McBride is willing to sacrifice anything—time, effort, even his own blood—to earn a victory, Tomey guarantees.

He means that literally. Tomey recalls with amazement a summer vacation his family took to Hawaii with the McBrides and other friends, to a house he owns on the Islands. One night Tomey organized a game of Capture the Flag for the group, which involved creeping around in the dark on land surrounding the house. When the game ended a few hours later, McBride emerged streaked in blood. He had accidentally run through a patch of thorns and slashed his skin open in several places.

"We had to take him to the hospital for stitches. He still has a scar on his face from that night," marveled Tomey. "But Ron never said a word until the game was over. He didn't want to hurt his team's chances. He wanted to win."

And if winning at Utah means expending a little blood, some sweat, a few tears, Ron McBride is ready and willing.

A Coach for All Seasons

When a group of sports aficionados gathered in Salt Lake City in 1996 during the state's centennial celebration to select—among a plethora of legends—Utah's outstanding college coach of the twentieth century, the name in the hermetically sealed envelope read LaVell Edwards.

Nine million Mormons worldwide stood to rise and shout. Many of them were Uteski football fans.

Because, you see, Edwards not only revived a flagging BYU program starting in 1972 but stirred the emotions of Uteski brass to the extent that five coaches and eighteen years later, the U administration finally made a long-term commitment to improve the floundering Uteski program.

As the sun rose on the 1997 football season, Edwards's influence had spilled over into Ute coach Ron McBride's program to the extent that some Cougar faithful were heard to exclaim, "Mac has stolen Edwards's program!" That the hustling McBride was using the missionary program to enhance his foundation, that he was pursuing pass-happy quarterbacks, and that he was establishing a recruiting monopoly in the Pacific Rim seemed like a carbon copy of what made Edwards and the Y system so solvent.

What a compliment! That Utah could emulate—well, sort of, considering one WAC co-championship and one bowl win out of four tries is the extent of the McBride Revolution—what BYU has achieved in the last quarter-century.

Mac was no dummy. Edwards is the IBM of college coaching. Buy into his system—even as a coaching challenger—and your stock goes bonkers. In McBride's seven seasons, the Utes' record is 49–34. The record of his two predecessors, Jim Fassel and Chuck Stobart, in eight seasons is 41–50–1.

Now that's pretty fair country teaching. And country is what Edwards is made of. Born on a farm, raised on a farm, attending an agricultural college, and retaining country roots through a love of the earth is what LaVell Edwards is all about.

Since 1954, he has never been anything but a coach. Oh, there were odd jobs to make ends meets for his wife, Patti, and children Ann and John during the formative years at Granite High School. But selling shoes at Sears and officiating high school basketball games were means to an end. Most of his waking hours out of the workplace were devoted

Mark A. Philbrick

LaVell Edwards: The General in charge of the troops can bark orders when necessary.

to a coaching journal. One day, these X's and O's will add up to wins and losses, he must have told himself.

By the time he graduated from the prep ranks to become a BYU assistant, there was a third child, Jimmy, and more responsibilities. But there was still that coaching journal. And there were daily entries. Some people thought Edwards was plotting running plays. He hit a golf ball 280 yards

through the air. He always did relish the way the ball flew through the air with the greatest of ease. Shame on those line-drive strikers. Get the ball into the air, watch the graceful arc and ultimately the roll of the ball toward the green.

Man, oh man, imagine getting a football to do the same thing. Fling it into the air, get it in the hands of a fleet receiver, and watch him roll toward the end zone. Hole-in-one, eagle, birdie, touchdown. Now, that's sports jargon I could live with said the former Utah State center/linebacker who is fond of saying his only passing experience in college was centering the ball backwards out of the single-wing formation.

The most exasperating quality about "Nosey," as he is known in more intimate circles, is his nonchalance. To see him on a sideline is to see the school president observing a graduation processional, or the chemistry professor measuring a beaker of water. Tight-lipped, arms folded, the body moving imperceptibly as the ball changes ends of the field. He might seem detached, but the mind is whizzing at computer speed and precision.

The unflappable Edwards is calling on all those years, all those entries from the coaching journal as the play unfolds. It would be one thing to claim this is a flash-in-the-pan experience. But on and on it has gone for twenty-five seasons. Tight-lipped, arms folded, the body moving almost imperceptibly as the ball changes ends of the field, Edwards has observed 228 victories—an incredible average of nine per season.

Something is right here. Very right. And very irritating to Edwards's detractors. How could someone so placid, someone in a pressure cooker like a football stadium filled with 65,000 what-have-you-done-for-me-lately, lathered-up fans, seem so unruffled while, on the other side of the field, his coaching counterpart is going through all sorts of frustrating pyrotechnics?

Well, for one thing, Edwards doesn't wear a headset. He coaches during the week in practice, devising new variations off the eight basic passing formations the Cougars have been employing now for nearly twenty-five years. And

on Saturday, when the information highway has been solidly implanted in the minds of the offensive executioners, Edwards slips into his relaxation mode.

No big show from this guy. Same character you might find on the golf course, ripping a 275-yard drive, followed by a 150-yard approach shot and a 10-foot birdie putt. Just as his quarterbacks so effortlessly throw for 300 yards against the Uteskis, Edwards can pull the clubs out of mothballs and saunter onto any golf course and shoot in the seventies. Think Mac has a tough chore on the sidelines in football? LaVell dishes out lessons on the links, too.

Take the BYU-Uteski game of 1996, for instance. It didn't take a rocket scientist to figure out the Utah defense was vulnerable to the run. So LaVell issues the directive that the Cougars' game plan will feature the run. It featured the run for four quarters—376 yards worth. It didn't take a headset. During the Cougars' defensive stands, LaVell looked at offensive coordinator Norm Chow and said keep the pass under wraps. No one in the college game today knows the ebbs and flows of a game better than Edwards. And on November 23, 1996, the Cougars had the Uteskis at low ebb.

One thing about LaVell. He is stubborn. After the Cougars soundly whipped the Uteskis—again, and for the twentieth time in twenty-five tries for Edwards—he rewarded his troops with a week off, just two weeks before the WAC championship game against Wyoming. Assistants begged for a continuation of the Cougars' hard work that had earned a 12–1 record. Boosters were aghast. The biggest game of the year and we're resting? On days besides Sunday? Well, the sage of the Wasatch struck again. With a week off, the Cougars were emotionally sharper for the Cowboys. Edwards the clairvoyant couldn't have known there would be an overtime. Could he? In any event, BYU won a 28–25 overtime decision. The guy just has a feel for the game.

So, the Cougars have themselves an unflappable, unpretentious football genius. There is no emotional roller-coaster at Provo like you find with the Uteskis. Get bombed on Saturday and the Uteskis are hustled into

practice on Sunday. BYU gets bombed on Saturday and the Cougars rest on Sunday and have the same practice ritual on Mondays. Heaven knows, the kids that got bombed on Saturday are well aware of their shortcomings. A five-hour practice on Sunday will not cure Saturday's ills.

LaVell just ambles along like old man river. He wins nine or ten games a year, wins a championship nine out of ten years and every year except 1995, has taken his team to a bowl game for nineteen straight Decembers. At sixty-seven, he has seen top-flight assistants come and go—one of them, Ted Tollner, to a Rose Bowl championship coaching USC; another, Dave Kragthorpe, coaching a Division I-A national champion at Idaho State; and yet another, Mike Holmgren, coaching a Super Bowl champion at Green Bay in 1997. Yet, the coaching staff remains much the same as it has nearly three decades. It will be that way until somebody finds some way to figure out what the secret is. Perhaps it will be the day LaVell writes his book on football techniques and strategies. Coaches of the Uteskis should buy the first copy.

Edwards is an icon in the coaching profession. He'll say he surrounded himself with genius assistants. Yet, he was sly like a fox. While others ran, he passed . . . and passed . . . and passed. And be darned if anybody has figured it out to this day. National coach of the year in 1979 and 1984, WAC coach of the year seven times, head coach in the East-West Shrine game four times, the Hula Bowl three times, and the Blue-Gray Game twice, he has brought more glory to the WAC and to BYU than any coach in history.

They may say that LaVell was confused during that three-year stretch when Utah won three games in a row. The only confusion was when, as a WAC tri-champion in 1995, the Cougars weren't invited to a bowl game. Big mistake. Everyone knows that now. LaVell didn't get mad. He got even. And that's why one day soon, ol' Smiley will become the first modern-day Beehive State coach to be inducted into the National Football Hall of Fame. It's the natural spot for the state's outstanding coach of the twentieth century.

Doctor Mac

Imagine you need surgery, and the hospital gives you a choice of doctors.

You can have kindly old Doctor Ed, they tell you, or the maniacal Doctor Mac.

Ed has been around for years, about as long as anybody can remember, and has this incredible national reputation. He's famous for this fancy style of stitching he popularized, the kind that seemingly revolutionized his field and has become the norm in operating rooms all over the country today. Few have as good a record of saving patients as he does. You're lucky, friends tell you, most hospitals don't have such a well-respected surgeon on staff.

Doctor Mac, on the other hand, has been around a long time, too, but only recently became a surgeon. He's been doing the drudge work of the profession for years, letting inferior doctors lose patients he could have saved. There's nothing notable about his techniques, not much really notable about him at all, especially considering he's in a profession with so many famous specialists. He's saved quite a few lives, some miraculously so, but he's lost some for no apparent reason.

Not much of a decision, is it? Where do I sign, you ask?

But wait, your nurse tells you. Forget about the image, the TV personality these two project. Before you let them cut you open, perhaps you should look a little closer at your choices.

Sure, Ed has national renown and a big paycheck to match. He seems like the wise old country physician, able to put even the most skeptical minds at ease with just a few well-chosen words. But once you're on the operating table, you ask, just how steady are his hands?

Not to worry, you're told. Ed doesn't actually hold a scalpel much anymore. He mostly hangs around to elaborate on his philosophy of surgery, wear a gown and a concerned frown, watch what goes on, and then speak to the family afterward.

It's still his operation, you're still his patient, but Ed won't

actually scrub up. He's got a staff full of interns who handle the actual surgery for him, freeing Ed up to go home at noon and have a quiet lunch with his wife. And Ed's hospital has plenty of cash available to provide state-of-the-art instruments, monitors and facilities.

No, Ed doesn't remember many of the details of surgery, but he can usually find the hospital by himself. And as long as everything is done in his name, and the patients mostly pull through, who cares who does the actual cutting and stitching? He picked the staff, after all, even if it was about twenty years ago for most of them.

The truth is, Ed doesn't even know your name exactly. But there's no better surgeon in the business, right?

Suddenly, that appendix feels a lot worse. Something as important—as life-and-death—as your health deserves the best care money can buy.

Perhaps you should consider Doctor Mac, volunteers the nurse. He's taken on a lot more serious cases lately, and the results have often been spectacular.

Just be ready for the most intense experience of your life. Mac approaches his cases with a remarkable focus; there's literally nothing in the world more important than that next procedure. He'll spend hours and hours, often starting before sunup, poring over X-ray after X-ray to make absolutely sure there's no detail he has overlooked. He'll obsess over the tiny things, and lecture and harangue and motivate his assistants until they are totally prepared. The operation will so consume him, Mac will even search for good karma in the form of every lucky charm he can find.

Come the day of the operation, he'll insist on overseeing every facet, taking responsibility for every move. He's been training to be head surgeon all his life, after all, so Mac knows how difficult success is to achieve. It's all he can think about, and he is willing to sacrifice whatever it takes to get there.

He's had his failures, too, but look at what he had to work with. His hospital was in pitiful shape when he arrived, a real St. Elsewhere that few patients wanted to entrust with their emotional well-being. Through hard

work, he has slowly established his employer as the best in the state, even better than Doctor Ed's more prominent institution to the south.

Even through the haze of anesthetic, the pain is growing fierce. The operation can be put off no longer.

The surgeons are in the scrub room, Doctor Mac memorizing your medical history and Doctor Ed napping peacefully in a motorized wheelchair.

It's time to choose.

He's a better coach than band director, but McBride leads the Utah band in "Utah Man" after every game.

(Author's Note: In no way did the previous essay intend to imply that health and medicine are somehow equivalent in gravity to football. As anyone who has been to Rice Stadium in late November can attest, football is considerably more important.)

CHAPTER

1990–1992
LOW RUMBLINGS OF A RIVALRY

As 1990 dawned, it seemed like just another typical chapter in the life of BYU-Utah football. On the cover of the Cougars' annual press guide was a full-length color photo of quarterback Ty Detmer, his right leg planted firmly on the Cougar Stadium turf, a football gripped tightly in his Texas-sized hands, and his blue eyes intently surveying a field of receivers. Below his left elbow in quarter-inch-high lettering was the inset "Ty Detmer, Heisman Candidate." On the cover of the Utes' media publication was a photo collage of returning starters—linebacker Kava Afu, kicker Wayne Lammle, wide receiver Darrel Hicks, and running back Clifton Smith. But there was nothing, not even a snapshot, to note the arrival of new head coach Ron McBride.

Of course, it made sense. Detmer, just a junior, was coming off the second-best season of passing in school history—4,560 yards, just eleven yards shy of Jim McMahon's all-time record. The six-foot, 175-pound co-MVP of the 1989 Holiday Bowl in which he set NCAA postseason records in passing (576 yards) and total offense (594) in a 50–39 loss to Penn State, had come out of nowhere to finish ninth in the Heisman balloting after only two seasons. His 175.6 passing efficiency mark was the second highest in NCAA history—again second only to McMahon's 176.9 in 1980.

With two years left, the son of Texas prep coaching legend Sonny Detmer was poised to eclipse every offensive record of his all-American predecessors. And every Cougar quarterback from Marc Wilson in 1979 through Robbie Bosco in 1985 had finished at least third in the Heisman voting, with Steve Young second to Nebraska's Mike Rozier in 1983. The key for school publicists was to get the word out early on Detmer. The ninth-leading vote-getter, given anywhere near his statistics of 1989, could surely jump to the top three this season, what with the top five Heisman finishers of 1989 having completed their eligibility. Plus, there was a marquee game looming for the Cougars, a nationally televised game in Provo with preseason number-one Miami. Summer chatter centered on it being the make-or-break game in the Heisman chase that would include the likes of Colorado's Eric Bieniemy, Virginia's Shawn Moore, Notre Dame's Raghib Ismail, Houston's David Klingler, and Miami's Craig Erickson.

With McBride taking the Ute helm, Utah had changed coaches for the sixth time since Edwards assumed the reins at BYU in 1972. And, for the third time in that coaching merry-go-round, the Utes were handing control of a struggling program to a guy who had no major college head coaching experience. Utah had struck out with hometown product Tom Lovat (1973–76) and had minimal success with Jim Fassel (1985–89) in their previous stabs at elevating assistants.

McBride did, however, bring a sparkling portfolio of assistant coaching accomplishments, having helped Wisconsin (1977–82) and Arizona (1987–89) to bowl successes. It wasn't too difficult for many Ute heavy hitters to conjure up enthusiasm for McBride, whose previous two tours at Uteville (1977–82 and 1985–86) had produced a total of forty-five wins and five of the seven winning seasons since 1977. In the eight total years, his coaching helped seven Utes gain all-WAC honors, including Dean Miraldi, Wayne Jones, and Dave Cullity, who were drafted into the NFL. Still, many Ute alumni didn't know whether to laugh at the choice of their young athletic director Chris Hill or to cry that the school hadn't reached out for a more high-profile leader. After all, bypassed in the selection process was Keith Gilbertson, who had experienced resounding success as head coach at the University of Idaho and who had Pac-10 assistant experience with veteran Don James at the University of Washington.

McBride started in a hole of Grand Canyon proportions. When he took command of the Utes in his first spring practice in April, it had only been five months since BYU had administered one of the worst beatings in the history of the rivalry—70–31—at Provo, with Detmer throwing four touchdown passes in just over one half of play. In fact, no Cougar team had scored more points against the Utes although there had been bigger point differentials. McBride remembered one of the horror shows—a 56–6 Salt Lake City shellacking in 1980 when he assisted Wayne Howard. Not only was Detmer returning at the wheel of the high-octane Cougar offense, but at Utah, prolific signal caller Scott Mitchell had opted to forego his senior season for the NFL draft. The ex-Springville High School star, who was the subject of a bitter recruiting battle between BYU and Utah in 1985, had engineered a stunning 57–28 upset of BYU in 1988 but was sidelined with an ankle injury and missed the 70–31 shellacking.

McBride and his new staff, which included holdover assistants and close McBride friends Fred Graves and Sean McNabb, were not faced with a major offensive makeover. Mitchell's leadership had helped Utah to an average of 441 yards per game, 338 of it through the air and an all-time single-season Ute mark of thirty-one TD passes. He left with twenty-four school records, including a 631-yard passing afternoon against Air Force in 1988 and a six-TD game against UTEP in 1989. Of Hall of Fame stature, though, was the three-TD, 384-yard day against BYU in 1988.

Rick Egan/THE SALT LAKE TRIBUNE

Utah began to make defensive strides in 1990 under new coach Ron McBride with Greg Reynolds (96) and Pita Tonga (49) two of the mainstays.

Defense was Utah's Achilles heel—and had been through most of the Fassel years. In 1989, the Utes allowed 541 yards per game—last among 105 Division I schools. How scary was it? In the last four games, Utah surrendered 2,520 yards offense—a whopping 630 per game. And there were two other black eyes in the season—a 659-yard yield to San Diego State and 633 to Fresno State, the latter annihilation prompting veteran Bulldog coach Jim Sweeney to observe: "That's the worst Division I defense I've ever seen." Sweeney didn't see the Utes when BYU racked up 750 yards on November 18. "We will eventually give you solid defense, lots of emotion, and smash-mouth football," said Mac.

The means to the end McBride was seeking began at Camp Carbon in Price, on the campus of College of Eastern Utah. The new Ute coach wanted his troops as far from the Salt Lake City distractions as he could get them. Price was 120 miles to the southeast with about the only after-hours activity being a wild-wave swimming pool four short blocks from the school dormitories. It was there Mac instilled his philosophy of mental toughness, aggressiveness, fanatical effort, and unity

(MAFU). He endeared himself to his players when one night after a constructive practice, he jumped up on a table, gave a typical lathering-up speech, then leaped headfirst into a mass of chanting Utes screaming "This is how close I want to be to you!"

The camaraderie theme spilled over into Utah's first two games. In McBride's head coaching inaugural, the Utes marched north to Logan, where they promptly shut out their Beehive Boot rival 19–0. Ecstatic Ute followers fawned over McBride like a father over a newborn son. A shutout. Why, there hadn't been one of those from the Utes since . . . well, since McBride was an assistant in 1982. Imagine, from the last game of 1989 and a seventy-point yield versus BYU, to a 1990 lid-lifting shutout. The Aggies managed just 172 yards. And Utah was getting a pair of field goals from Wayne Lammle and rushing TDs from Steve Abrams and Clifton Smith. The new quarterback on the block, Jason Woods, a towering Mitchell look-alike transfer from Lamar University, was not spectacular, but he was error-free in a 16-for-29 performance. That he was as slow as molasses was of some concern, but he had delivered a victory.

The win over the Aggies would pale by comparison to the next weekend's proceedings in Minneapolis. Never mind the Golden Gophers were picked for a down season. It was the Big Ten after all, and McBride remembered all too well his last foray into Big Ten country with the 1986 Utes—a 64–6 shellacking at the hands of Ohio State in Columbus. Even a decent Ute showing in the Metrodome would leave McBride on track in his rebuilding program.

Incredibly, by the end of the first period, Utah had a 19–0 lead with Dean Witkin scoring on a twenty-two-yard run, Mike Angelsey reaching pay dirt on a seven-yard pass, and Abrams plunging in for a two-yard TD. That lead—and a 317-yard passing exhibition by Ute senior Mike Richmond, the QB-apparent to Mitchell who had lost the spring battle to Woods—would evaporate, and the two teams were tied 29–29 as the Gophers lined up for a potential game-winning chip-shot field goal of twenty-eight yards. With the clock reading 0:03, Minnesota kicker Brent Berglund's attempt was blocked, with the loose ball scooped up by Ute cornerback LaVon Edwards and returned ninety-one yards to deliver the Utes a 35–29 win. McBride raced fifty yards down the sideline to launch himself onto the pile of Utah humanity in the end zone in a scene that was replayed over and over on national TV that night. But there was another TV highlight being beamed nationwide by then. Naturally, the undefeated Utes' titanic victory would be upstaged by . . . BYU.

The Cougars could hardly be expected to pick up where they left off in 1989. In consecutive games against Utah, San Diego State, and Penn State in the Holiday Bowl, BYU had rolled up total offense marks of 750, 559, and 641 yards respectively. Detmer's 576 yards passing against Joe Paterno's Nittany Lions in a 50–39 losing effort at Jack Murphy Stadium were the most ever in a bowl game by anybody from any league in any bowl.

But with fourteen starters back, including most of the fearsome offense, BYU had plenty of bullets in its six-shooter, and they had the Texas gunslinger Detmer with a full season and a couple of bowl games under his belt. UTEP discovered early on that the Cougars had indeed lost very little, if anything, surrendering 553 yards as BYU romped to a 30–10 win in a Sun Bowl skirmish on opening night. Peter Tuipulotu moved up to take the running back spot of the graduated Fred Whittingham and gained eighty-nine yards against the Miners. Detmer was deadly, hitting thirty-three of forty-six passes for 387 yards, with tight end Chris Smith and wideouts Nati Valdez and Matt Bellini showing they would be favorite targets for the season.

The win over downtrodden UTEP was expected, since BYU had thrashed the Miners four straight years since the 23–16 El Paso "upset of the century" in 1985.

The victory over defending national champion University of Miami in Provo seven days later was about as expected as a snowstorm on Maui. Coach Dennis Erickson herded his haughty Hurricanes into Cougar Stadium for their opener with thirteen returning starters, including QB Craig Erickson, who, as a starter, hadn't lost a game in eight tries. There were a few other Hurricanes who would receive all-American recognition, including defensive lineman Russell Maryland and linebacker Maurice Crum. BYU had met Miami one other time, a 41–17 skewering in 1988's regular-season-ending game at the Orange Bowl.

This was a litmus test for the Cougars. The Hurricanes' last two victories of 1989 had been over Notre Dame 27–10, and Alabama 33–25 for the national title. Many of the faithful were praying for the ESPN encounter just to be close, and as a bonus, that Detmer would experience a get-out-the-Heisman-vote type of night.

The Cougars ordered some mesmerizing late-summer weather—93 degrees and bone-dry air—and proceeded to show Miami's air-oriented attack a thing or two about the nuances of the passing game. Detmer would throw fifty-four passes—two more than the Hurricanes' Erickson—for 406 yards. Mainly, it was Detmer's ability to rally his troops each time Miami threatened to pull away. Trailing 7–0, Detmer led the Cougars on a seventy-yard scoring drive, capped by a fourteen-yard TD strike to Bellini. Behind 14–10, with just under two minutes to play in the half, Detmer completed eight straight passes with the payoff to Andy Boyce, and, following kicker Earl Kauffman's PAT—to go with his other extra point and thirty-two-yard field goal—the Cougars led at intermission 17–14. Down 21–17 in the third period, Kauffman delivered a twenty-nine-yard field goal, and then Detmer engineered a forty-three-yard drive capped by a seven-yard scoring strike to Mike Salido. A two-point conversion pass to Boyce left BYU on top 28–21, and that's where it stayed through a scoreless fourth period.

Despite five turnovers, four of them lost fumbles, BYU had prevailed in their biggest game since a 28–14 Kickoff Classic conquest of Boston College in 1986. As BYU fans uncharacteristically stormed the field, the verdict was in on Detmer: 406 yards and three touchdowns. With a distinct advantage over Erickson and establishing a tough-nut persona in the face of a savage Miami pass rush, the wiry, leather-tough Texan had leap-frogged over several Heisman hopefuls and established himself as the early front-runner as college player of the year. There was more—much more for the 2–0 Cougars. A number-sixteen preseason pick, they jumped all the way to number four in the polls. Of course, with the stunning win over Miami and the lofty ranking, BYU had effectively neutralized the luster of its upstate rival's 2–0 start.

Essentially, after September 8, Utah's season fell into a familiar rut—obligatory victories over UTEP and New Mexico by a total of sixteen points, but a with a diet of the same ol', same ol' black eyes. Like, for instance, a 52–21 whipping at the hands of Air Force and a 66–14 embarrassment dished out by San Diego State in Navytown.

But overall, there was a discernible difference in McBride's inaugural season and the preceding four years. The Utes, playing the more aggressive defense that Mac had promised, were competitive against teams their own caliber, losing to WAC foes Hawaii, Wyoming, and Colorado State by a total of thirty-nine points. And they rarely surrendered one of those unseemly offensive totals as in years past with Fresno State's 514 and SDSU's 523 yields the exceptions. Plus, at year's end, linebacker Anthony Davis and senior defensive back Sean Knox would earn first-team all-WAC defensive honors, the first for Utah since 1987.

As McBride and his Ute staff sifted through the rubble with one hand keeping the ship on course and the other charting an off-season recruiting regimen that would bring more defensive reinforcements on board, the Detmer-led Cougars were making national waves for Edwards—again.

Buoyed by the Miami victory, the Cougars overcame a 29–7 halftime deficit to blow Washington State away with a thirty-six-point fourth quarter and win 50–36 in Provo on September 15. Detmer's five passing touchdowns to five different receivers led to a 448-yard afternoon, giving him over 1,300 yards in his first three games. The September revelry continued the next week with a third straight home game and a 62–34 bombardment of San Diego State on CBS-TV. For those viewers who stayed around, plus the 66,044 fans in Cougar Stadium, it was offensive pyrotechnics par excellence. Detmer hurled three TD passes to Boyce and amassed 514 aerial yards while Aztec QB Dan McGwire set a stadium record with fifty-nine pass attempts. With a second straight national telecast of his considerable aerial skills, Detmer moved farther up the Heisman ladder and the Cougars retained their number-four poll standing.

Not for long. Neither Detmer nor BYU would be able to take the pressure from a crush of media-types wondering if indeed this was going to be a replay of 1984 when Robbie Bosco led the Cougars through a rugged opening and into a marshmallow-soft schedule.

Leaving their cozy Provo bailiwick and landing in University of Oregon's Autzen Stadium in Eugene, a hobbled Detmer, suffering from a ligament strain in his throwing hand, and the Cougars ran into a Ducks buzz saw. Namely, quarterback Bill Musgrave and a swarming Oregon defense that sacked Detmer for a safety and left BYU with a minus forty-seven yards rushing. Detmer threw for 442 yards and two touchdowns, but he had a career-high five interceptions. It was Musgrave who monopolized the ABC-TV highlights with three touchdowns and a rushing TD of his own. The resounding defeat, in which BYU managed just one highlight—Detmer's sixty-nine-yard-TD bomb to Micah Matsuzaki—saw the 4–1 Cougars tumble to number eleven in the polls. No one had an accurate handle on how much damage Detmer had suffered in the Heisman hunt.

Whatever psychological wounds he incurred, the gritty Cougar leader healed them over the next four games—just in time for The Game. In consecutive wins over Colorado State, New Mexico, Air Force, and Wyoming, he continued his torrid pace, hurling fourteen TD strikes and throwing for 1,576 yards.

The Cougars, seemingly incensed at being held to sixteen points by Oregon, steamrolled past CSU 52–9, then toyed with the Lobos 55–31, annihilated Air Force at Colorado Springs 54–7, and buried Wyoming in Laramie 45–14. The nationally telecast triumph over the Cowboys, in which Detmer threw for 484 yards and two TDs, was sweet retribution for his worst collegiate performance. During his freshman season in 1988, Detmer was intercepted four times by the Cowboys. This day, he would leave the field as the all-time leading passer in BYU history, surpassing McMahon's old mark of 9,536 yards. McMahon took thirty-six games for his record. Detmer had broken it in thirty-two games. He would get much, much more in Rice Stadium one week later.

The Utah reconstruction program had been slow and torturous for McBride, who sent his troops into battle against the Cougars with a 4–6 record. True, the Utes had matched the previous year's win total, but the memory of the blowout loss to San Diego State two weeks previous hung over the program like an early winter storm cloud envelopes the Wasatch Mountains. San Diego State's McGwire had thrown four touchdown passes, and the sixty-six points reminded McBride all too much of the 2–9 Utah campaign of 1986 when the Utes gave up forty-five or more points five times. And now came BYU, with Detmer chasing the Heisman Trophy, the Cougars ranked number four in the nation, averaging nearly forty-three points a game and needing one win to clinch the WAC title and a thirteenth straight bowl appearance.

Utah's 29–27 win over New Mexico the week before in Albuquerque had pumped some life back into the team, but it took a twenty-nine-point, second-half rally to achieve the victory and keep McBride's charges from falling into a tie for the conference cellar. Even then, the Utes managed only 129 yards passing from Richmond and 267 yards total offense. Still, that fifty-two-point loss to San Diego State, a team BYU had waxed 62–34 earlier, kept Utah fans from entertaining any 1988-type upset hopes. That year, in finishing with a 9–4 record, BYU was alternating quarterbacks between Sean Covey and Detmer. The Utes knew it would be Detmer from start to finish this time, and 1989 was fresh in their minds—Ty's four-TD, 358-yard exhibition in just over one half of action. Could it get worse?

The sixty-fifth renewal of The Game, which had been won by BYU seventeen of the previous nineteen times in Edwards's reign, began under a heavy overcast. In the first two minutes there was heavy-handed play by both teams: a personal foul for a face mask violation on Utah, and an unsportsmanlike conduct on the Cougars. All was well with these two bitter combatants who had a combined 121 yards in penalties in their 1989 meeting.

Detmer wasted little time. On second down from his own seventeen, he flipped a swing pass into the right flat to his tight end Chris Smith, who galloped down the sideline all the way to the Utah thirty-seven where the facemask penalty was tacked on. Detmer's pass to Tuipulotu for seventeen yards set up Stacey Corley's five-yard TD sweep off the right end only ninety-nine seconds into the game. Kauffman's PAT made it 7–0. It had taken the Cougars a minute longer to score the year before when they got twenty-eight points in the first quarter.

But by the time Utah got a thirty-one-yard field goal from Lammle on the first Ute series at the 10:09 mark, the Utes were closer than they ever got in 1989. And after Utah's defense held the potent Cougs on the next series, Richmond unloaded a fifty-six-yard post-pattern TD pass to wideout Bryan Rowley. With Lammle's PAT, it was Utah 10, BYU 7. A crowd of 33,515, which showed an awfully lot of blue at the kickoff, was suddenly an awfully raucous red.

And it got really wild on the third play of BYU's next possession when Knox picked off Detmer's pass at the Utah twenty-three. But the Utes' flubbed their biggest opportunity of the day when Richmond gave it right back six plays later with Tony Crutchfield stepping in front of his pass and returning it to midfield. Again aided by a late-hit flag on the Utes, BYU struck quickly, when on the fourth play of the drive, Detmer hooked up with Matsuzaki for a twenty-five-yard TD pass. Kauffman's PAT spread the margin to 14–10 with 2:02 to play in the quarter.

Utah was still close in the penalty-marred game midway through the second quarter, but a BYU bounce on a Kauffman punt left the Utes in a hole at their own two yard line with 8:45 to play in the half. Working out of the shadow of their goal-line to the twenty-three, Richmond went up the sideline where Cougar cornerback Josh Arnold intercepted the pass. On second down, Boyce cut to the corner of the end zone, where he collected Detmer's perfect missile for a twenty-one-yard TD. Kauffman's PAT spread the margin to 21–10 with 7:03 left in the half.

Again the Cougars held. And again, they pounced quickly. On first down from his own forty-five, Detmer lofted a completion to Brent Nyberg who stepped out of an attempted tackle by cornerback Mark Swanson and scampered fifty-five yards for the TD. Kauffman's PAT left it 28–10 with 5:20 to go in the half.

As befits a matchup between an opportunistic, number-four-ranked, 9–1 team and an identity-seeking 4–6 team that is playing it close to the vest, this one was put to bed on a weird sequence just before half. The Utes were given a big break when Smith fumbled the ball after a thirteen-yard pass from Detmer with 1:05 on the clock. On second down from the BYU 43, Richmond bobbled the snap from center and the Cougars' Rocky Biegel recovered at midfield with forty-six seconds left. Detmer's twenty-two-yard pass to Salido advanced the ball to the U twenty-two and a sixteen-yard Detmer-to-Nyberg aerial left the ball at the Utah six with twenty seconds left in the half. Then Detmer whipped a pass over the center to Smith for a TD. Kauffman's PAT gave the Cougars a 35–10 halftime lead. The Cougs had reeled off twenty-eight straight points. Utah had controlled the clock 17:20 to 12:40, but the quick-strike Cougars had charge of the score. The Cougars had been intercepted twice and lost a fumble and still led by twenty-five.

From there, the powerful Cougars, who would see Arnold recover a fumble and Brian Mitchell intercept another Richmond pass—giving Utah five turnovers for the day—toyed with the Utes. Utah would get a pair of Lammle field goals and a late, four-yard TD pass from Richmond to Mike Angelsey, but Kauffman's thirty-three-yard field goal and a Detmer-to-Eric Drage four-yard TD pass kept the Utes in their place.

Knox offered the best assessment of the Cougars' domination. "Detmer is so tough. That's his best asset. We got after him and put him on his back a couple of times, but he kept coming back. He's a great quarterback in a great offensive scheme. And remember, he has a lot of good people playing around him." Eleven different Cougars caught passes, led by Smith's 125 yards and Nyberg's 116. Five different BYU players caught TD passes. Said Detmer, "This is a better team than the one that played here two years ago." Said Edwards of his thirteenth WAC gold trophy, "I can't think of a better place to clinch the conference title than in Salt Lake City."

Despite the loss, the Utes had 436 yards total offense and outgained the Cougars on the ground 114–86. That rushing advantage didn't mean much in a 45–22 rout, but it would be significant considering what happened later in December.

Any minor shortcomings the 10–1 Cougars had were pushed into the background the following week when BYU demolished Utah State in Provo 45–10 to earn the Beehive Boot, emblematic of in-state supremacy. Saturday, November

24, was another record-shattering day for Detmer, who broke the NCAA record for most passing yards in a season (4,869) set the previous season by Houston's Andre Ware (4,669). Detmer's five TD passes and 560 yards passing would be his final contributions to a Heisman bid that found him as the front-runner for the December 1 announcement.

Detmer had eclipsed a bushel of records held by previous Cougar icons— among them nineteen straight 300-yard passing games to surpass McMahon's twelve. And Detmer's twenty-four 300-yard passing games overall eclipsed Young's mark.

Mark A. Philbrick

BYU continued to dominate the Utes in 1990. Here Alema Fitisemanu manhandles Ute quarterback Mike Richmond in the Cougars' 45–22 win.

When the nationally-televised Downtown New York Athletic Club Heisman announcement came, Detmer was surrounded by teammates and coaches— Edwards sat proudly at his side—at a hotel in Honolulu where the Cougars would meet University of Hawaii that night in Aloha Stadium.

Intoned New York Athletic Club president C. Peter Lambos, as Notre Dame's Ismail, Virginia's Moore, and Colorado's Bieniemy sat at rapt, hopeful attention in New York City, "For the fifty-sixth time since Jay Berwanger won the award in 1935, it is the special privilege of the Downtown Athletic Club and its membership, composed of thousands of men and women residents throughout these United States, to join me in letting the country know the name of this year's greatest football player—the winner of the 1990 Heisman Award . . . whose name is Ty

Detmer . . . Ty Detmer of BYU, Ty Detmer!"

In a span of nine hours, BYU's first-ever Heisman winner would experience the gamut of sports ecstasy and agony. When he appeared in Aloha Stadium, a crowd of 45,729 applauded politely. Whether it was for winning the Heisman or that the fans remembered the year before when their Rainbow Warriors drove the Texan nuts with five sacks is a matter for conjecture.

In three hours, it was left for Hawaii fans to chant appreciation for a Heisman-like performance from their team. The UH defense, captained by linebacker Mark Odom and cornerback Kenny Harper, replayed the 56–14 Rainbow romp of 1989 by stuffing the Cougars, 59–28, mainly through a twenty-eight-point first quarter blitz. Harper collected three of the Rainbows' four interceptions off Detmer. In a final blow to the Cougs' egos, Hawaii showed a 667–439 yardage advantage with UH quarterback Garrett Gabriel out-passing his more decorated counterpart 359–319. However consolation-like, there were more record numbers for Detmer and his mates. He ended the season with an NCAA record 5,188 yards. His NCAA record onslaught reached forty-two with five others tied. Detmer helped Boyce to a single-season school receiving mark of 1,241 yards and Smith finished with an NCAA record 1,156 yards for a tight end.

As it turns out, Honolulu was paradise for the Cougars, and Detmer compared to December 29 and the thirteenth annual Holiday Bowl in San Diego's Jack Murphy Stadium, where Texas A&M was waiting. The Aggies continued what Hawaii had done, shredding the Cougar defense for 680 yards including a 200-yard rushing night for all-American running back Darren Lewis. By halftime, A&M led 37-7, and not even the most optimistic Cougar follower was thinking of a repeat of 1980's Holiday Bowl III in which McMahon rescued the Cougars from a 45–25 hole in the last five minutes for a 46–45 win over SMU.

The lopsided score was bad enough. More insulting was A&M quarterback Bucky Richardson throwing for 324 yards—far out-distancing Detmer. There was a reason. Entering the game with a slight left shoulder separation, Detmer was finished off by a crunching sack by Aggie defensive end William Thomas early in the third quarter. This time, it was Detmer's right shoulder. Led from the field, Detmer would later undergo surgery to repair both shoulders. Having sunk from number four in the nation to a final ranking of number twenty-two in the span of two games would necessitate major surgery of another kind. Why, even Utah fans were figuring there was hope on the horizon. They had, after all, lost by only twenty-three points to the Cougars.

In a span of seven years, the BYU football program had produced a national champion (1984), a national coach-of-the-year (1984), two Outland Trophy winners (Jason Buck in 1986 and Mohammed Elewonibi in 1989), and a Heisman

Trophy winner (Detmer in 1990). Detmer's accomplishment was judged so profound that the only significant alteration to the front of the Cougars' 1991 press guide from the 1990 edition was a color change putting him in visiting raiments—white jersey and blue pants. Otherwise, practically the same stance, the same intense, surveyor's-type stare downfield, and, although covered by pads, two healthy shoulders. Oh yes, the small type in the bottom right-hand-corner had one major substitution—the "Heisman Candidate" of 1990 now read "Heisman Trophy Winner."

And McBride had made progress on the Ute brochure. At least he was shown, familiar headphones and all, in a two-by-two-inch black-and-white snapshot on the back cover. His one small step—transforming a decrepit defense from 105 and last in the country to eighty-first—in 1990 had led to a bumper recruiting campaign, especially from Hawaii, where island native and assistant coach Sam Papalii enticed the likes of Louie De Castro, Toele Fa'amoe, and Roy Ma'afala to cast their lot with the Utes. And McBride literally got tongue-tied extolling the attributes of a strapping all-around athlete from the tiny southwestern hamlet of Mancos, Colorado. "Luther Elliss will be the best lineman who ever played at this school," said Mac of the tight end/defensive lineman for whose services Utah out-recruited mighty Colorado of the Big Eight.

McBride admitted to a shade of tunnel vision in making defense a number-one priority in his rookie season. But after his predecessor made a habit of transferring many of Utah's best defenders to offense, there had to be a quick-fix to yielding forty-three points a game. Utah shaved that generosity to thirty-one points in 1990. Nine of the top twelve tacklers would return for McBride, including Davis, an all-WAC first-team linebacker. The Utes would get far more stingy defensively.

But it was time to strike a middle-ground stance. "Our offense must become aggressive, hard-nosed, and fundamentally sound," McBride emphasized, an offensive variation of his "smash-mouth" defensive stance of the previous season. He would turn to junior college quarterback Frank Dolce to lead the forces. Utah mined from the same El Camino JC where they had earlier struck QB gold. Larry Egger's two-year (1985–86) passing totals still stood as number two in school history. Dolce had displayed his mettle in spring ball by winning the starting job from Richmond who had averaged nearly 200 yards passing in back of a makeshift offensive line in 1990.

There were few question marks in Provo. "Having Ty back is a great place to start," said Edwards, seeking his thirteenth WAC title. Also returning were Peter Tuipulotu, the team's leading 1990 rusher, and the leading scorer in all-WAC first team kicker Earl Kauffman. Micah Matsuzaki, with six TD catches, was the leading pass receiver back, but Nati Valdez, Eric Drage, and a pair of returned missionaries, Bryce Doman and Tyler Anderson, would provide attractive targets.

Defensively, second-team all-WAC selections Rocky Biegel (linebacker) and Tony Crutchfield (cornerback) and the WAC's leader in interceptions with six, corner-back Derwin Gray were back. Still, it was Detmer, needing only 426 yards offense to become BYU's all-time leader, who would spearhead this team, if he was healthy. The toughest three-game start in Cougar history—Florida State in the Pigskin Classic in Anaheim, plus UCLA and Penn State on the road—would test his durability.

Detmer's physical stature endured. Mentally . . . that was another question. FSU running backs Edgar Bennett (98 yards), Amp Lee (75), and Sean Jackson (75) punished the young Cougar defensive line. And quarterback Casey Weldon out-dueled Detmer through the airlanes 268–229, in a matchup of Heisman Trophy candidates as the top-ranked Seminoles routed the Cougars 44–28 just across the San Diego Freeway from Disneyland. The offensive totals were BYU-like, except they were reversed: FSU had 543 yards, BYU had 262. Detmer would have to wait ten days for his career-yardage record.

Moving across town to Pasadena, the Cougars redeemed themselves—sort of—by pushing UCLA to the limit before losing 27–23 at the Rose Bowl. Detmer became the greatest yardage man in BYU history with 377 yards passing. But it was his counterpart, Tommy Maddox, who threw two TD passes to Sean LaChapelle, and running back Kevin Williams who rushed for 135 yards and scored the win-ning TD in the fourth quarter and helped drop the Cougars to 0–2. It got worse before it got better.

A week off to heal their wounds and shore up the beleaguered defense went for naught with a record crowd of 96,034 and an ABC-TV audience looking on at Beaver Stadium in University Park, Pennsylvania. Penn State thrashed the Cougars 33–7, with unheralded QB Tony Sacca out-passing Detmer 187–158. The Nittany Lions also rolled up 292 yards rushing, while the Penn State defense gave up zero yards rushing to BYU. What's more, the Cougars lost Doman for the season. Doman caught a seventeen-yard TD pass from Detmer in the second quarter but suffered a broken collarbone on the play. For the first time since 1975, and for only the third time in the Edwards era, BYU was 0–3.

The early season in-state bragging rights belonged to the Utes. By the time September 22 dawned, Utah was three wins ahead of the Cougars. The only loss in their first four games was 24–21 to Air Force when the Falcons overcame a 21–14 Ute lead in Rice Stadium. Utah's resurgence went much deeper than a 3–1 record, including victories over the Pac-10's Oregon State and Oregon. In down-ing Utah State 12–7, Oregon State 22–10 in Corvallis, and Oregon 24–17 in Salt Lake, the Utes were rock-solid on defense, allowing only 184 yards per game and racking up twenty-five sacks. Even Air Force's vaunted wishbone was limited to 300 yards offense. Rabid Ute fans knew this was unheard of from Utah football.

At least since 1981 when Utah had posted three shutouts in their first four games—when McBride was a member of Wayne Howard's staff.

It started innocently, if not dramatically, enough with a 12–7 come-from-behind win over Utah State. In a play that ended the first half and one that will live in infamy in the minds of Aggie fans, Dolce connected on a sideline streak pattern to Bryan Rowley, who at the Aggie nine yard line was wrapped up by USU tacklers. Rowley managed to shove (TV replays showed it as an illegal forward lateral) the ball to fellow wide receiver Greg Hoffman, who strutted the final nine yards to pay dirt. Added to Chris Yergensen's two field goals, the Utes overcame a four-yard TD pass from Ron Lopez to Tracey Jenkins, and, after a scoreless second half, salvaged a 12–7 win.

Utah faithful, so hungry for success, had seen this opening-win stuff over the Ags before—just one year earlier. And they had seen it followed up by an emotional inter-sectional win the week after in Minnesota. This time, the Utes gave McBride a 2–0 start with a victory at Oregon State. With the Beavers losing five fumbles and the Utes piling up eight sacks—four by Sharrieff Shah—the Utes escaped with a 22–10 win fueled by three Yergensen field goals, a one-yard TD pass from Dolce to Scott Murray, and a two-yard run by Keith Williams. Even though Dolce was twenty-one of thirty-two in passing for 238 yards, the Utes were zero for eleven in third-down conversions. But they were 2–0 and the defense had been superb—again.

Even in the loss to Air Force, the U offense/defense balance was encouraging—373 yards gained, 300 given up. There had been past AFA games when Utah coughed up over twice that amount. The Utes built a 21–14 lead behind Yergensen's two field goals, Dolce's one-yard TD sneak, and Williams's four-yard TD run, but the Falcons won on Antoine Banks's third-quarter TD run and a field goal by Joe Woods in the fourth quarter. A week later Ute fans cheered wildly at Rice Stadium when the Penn State thrashing of BYU was announced. And then they watched their gridders pile up a 24–0 lead over Oregon behind a pair of Dolce-to-Rowley TD passes, Yergensen's twenty-three-yard field goal, and Dolce's one-yard run. The Ducks made it close only through a fourteen-point fourth quarter. Again, it was a nine-sack Ute defensive performance, fueled by Blaine Berger, Jimmy Bellamy, and Dave Chaytors with a pair each that held Oregon to 247 yards offense. Utah hadn't set the world on fire on offense either with 279 yards, but they were 3–1. That was bonfire enough for Ute fans.

As expected—as was traditional—BYU returned to its WAC sanctuary and in four straight Cougar Stadium games chalked up four wins. Three of them came easily—over Air Force 21–7, Utah State 38–10, and Hawaii 35–18. Detmer was steady but not spectacular as he had been in his Heisman-year run. It was against woebegone UTEP on October 12, the day after Edwards turned sixty-one years old, that BYU struggled. Trailing 17–7, Detmer led the Cougars to three straight TDs and a 28–17 lead. But trailing 31–29, the Miners had a shot at victory when Jason Gillespie lined up for a forty-five-yard field goal with fourteen seconds remaining. Cougar linebacker Scott Giles managed to deflect the kick and BYU pulled even for the season at 3–3. The next week against Hawaii, Detmer threw a season-low twenty passes for 225 yards. However, BYU unveiled freshman running back Jamal Willis who gained eight-five yards and scored two TDs. After a miserable start, the Cougars were back in familiar territory—4–3 overall and atop the WAC at 3–0, and ahead of Utah . . . again.

The Cougars had been picked to sit at the head of the WAC class. Utah had been picked seventh. But after taking their 3–1 mark to Arizona State, where three turnovers and a rash of penalties cost them dearly in a 21–15 loss to the Sun Devils, the Utes began to make serious rumblings of their own. Five games deep into the season, four of them non-conference games, it was apparent Utah had taken on a new persona. No team had surpassed 400 yards total offense against Utah, and the Utes' point yield of sixteen points per game was the lowest in ten years.

When they did get into a shootout in game six at Wyoming, they were able to flash the potency of old, rallying for thirty-five points in the second half to secure a 57–42 victory. It was Utah's first win at Laramie since 1972. Dolce threw three interceptions, but he also had four TD passes in bringing the Utes back from a 36–22 deficit. One Ute highlight among many was Shah's sixty-nine-yard TD return of an interception off Tom Corontzos. For future reference, the rookie Elliss had his first sack. Utah was 4–2 overall and 1–1 in the WAC.

Over the next three weeks, the Utes would show how far they had come and how much further they had to travel. Utah turned in some payback time as Dolce was interception-free with a touchdown pass to Sean Williams in a 21–16 win over CSU. The Rams had humbled the Utes 50–10 in 1989. A 115-yard rushing day gave Williams two straight 100-yard games and three for the year. Perched at the threshold of a 3–1 WAC mark with a 21–10 fourth-quarter lead over the Aztecs, the Utes surrendered two late touchdowns to let SDSU off the hook 24–21. Dolce's 316-yard, two-TD day and Rowley's 157 receiving yards were not enough to overcome a 153-yard rushing exhibition by SDSU's Wayne Pittman. It got much, much worse in Hawaii's Aloha Stadium on November 2 when the Rainbows erupted for twenty-one points in the final ten minutes to overwhelm the Utes, 52–26. Dolce passed for 373 yards and three TDs, but he was also picked off three times and the Utes lost two fumbles. It was the first defenseless outing of the season for the Utes who gave up 622 yards offense. The Utes fell to 5–4 overall, 2–3 in the WAC.

Meanwhile in a buildup to The Game, BYU was up to its old offensive tricks with Detmer in the Heisman groove of 1990. Few Cougar faithful will ever forget what he did on the night of November 16 in San Diego. Following the season low-point against Hawaii, Detmer lit up University Stadium in Albuquerque for 375 yards and four touchdowns in a 41–23 win; undressed CSU with a 343-yard, three-TD performance on ESPN with the Cougars winning 40–17; and led the Cougars to a 49–10 fourth-quarter lead over Wyoming with a pair of TD runs himself, with BYU ultimately prevailing 56–31. The Cougars had scored 137 points in three games, built their record to 7–3 overall and 6–0 in the WAC, and then came an ESPN game for the ages in Navytown's Jack Murphy Stadium.

Cougar fans thought they had seen the granddaddy of all comebacks in the 1980 Holiday Bowl when McMahon rallied BYU from a 45–25 deficit to a 46–45 win over SMU with three touchdowns in the last four minutes. This night, Detmer brought BYU from twenty-eight points down with a quarter to play. With a shot at clinching at least a WAC title tie, San Diego State built a 35–17 halftime lead behind David Lowery's passing and ballooned that to 45–17 with a minute to play in the third period.

But Detmer, who had had a split cheek stitched up in the first half, unlimbered in the final sixteen minutes to pull BYU even. The senior QB, in surpassing previous NCAA marks for career plays, attempts, and completions held by the Aztecs' Todd Santos, finished thirty-one for fifty-four and 599 passing yards—the bulk of BYU's 767 yards for the night. SDSU got 695 yards of their own with Lowery throwing for 568. The Y's Willis had 163 receiving yards and 66 on the ground and totaled three touchdowns. It was the highest-scoring tie game in NCAA history and earned BYU (7–3–1 overall and 6–0–1 in the WAC) at least a share of the conference title heading into The Game.

Utah would be playing for something itself. By thumping New Mexico in Rice Stadium 30–7, and slipping past UTEP 10–9 in El Paso on a fourth-quarter field goal, the Utes stood at 7–4 overall and 4–3 in the WAC. It was their best record in six seasons. Utah had lowered the rushing boom on the Lobos in Salt Lake with a school record 478 yards, fueled by 191 yards and two TDs by Keith Williams, with Charlie Brown chipping in 107 and a TD. Dolce, slowed by an ankle injury, would throw only nine times for fifty yards. The Utes harassed the Lobo QB all day with eight sacks, including two each by Elliss and Shah. Williams continued his running onslaught in El Paso with 142 yards, and Rowley caught a twenty-two-yard pass from Dolce, who again threw just seven passes, as the Utes might have been guilty of looking ahead by one week. Three interceptions, two of them by junior cornerback Ed Miller, saved the day. Assured of a first-division finish and shoot, with even a shot at an 8–4 season and perhaps a bowl game, Utah went into closed practices for the Cougar showdown.

Much as in 1989 when an injured Mitchell was on the sidelines, Dolce was side-lined with a broken ankle as the Utes moved into Cougar Stadium, where they hadn't won since 1971. A crowd of 66,003 ignored 38-degree weather to see Detmer, still a long-shot for his second Heisman Trophy, play his final home game. Opposing him would be Richmond, who had thrown for 326 yards against the Cougars the year before but who had ridden the bench behind Dolce all season. The Utes were buoyed by two straight WAC wins, and who could ignore, except for the one stumble in Hawaii, the defensive transformation in just two years under McBride. BYU, on the other hand, had yielded eighty-three points and 1,225 yards of offense in its two previous games. Of course, the Cougars had amassed 108 points and 1,332 yards offense of their own. Still, in the days leading to The Game, Detmer was asked one more time about that 1988 game in Salt Lake when both he and Covey were roughed up in a 57–28 Ute romp. "It still kind of haunts me," he said of being upstaged by Mitchell. Having thrown nine TD passes in the two games since hadn't exorcised the demons; three and a half hours on November 23, 1991, would.

Game sixty-seven in the series will be remembered for one of the wildest opening quarters in the rivalry's storied history, with thirty-one points scored and the Utes, remarkably, holding a 17–14 lead. It will also be remembered for one of the meekest finishing three quarters ever for the Utes and a typical finishing blitz by the Cougs.

Richmond hadn't thrown a pass all year. He had been involved in five mop-up running plays for a minus five yards. And yet, for the third time in three years, the senior from Reedley, California, would be thrust into the Ute-Cougar cauldron—the second time as a substitute. And on this occasion, he was facing the Heisman Trophy winner bent on compiling enough statistics to perhaps influence some last-second voters for Heisman II.

You would have thought Utah would want to keep the ball away from Detmer as long as possible. But no, the Utes won the toss and deferred to the second half. So Utah's Dan Pulsipher booted the opening kickoff to Eric Mortensen, who promptly fumbled with Ute Jeff Kirkman recovering at the BYU nineteen. On first down, Richmond dropped back, set, and rifled a pass to Rowley. Boom! Eleven seconds gone, one offensive play, one Ute nineteen-yard TD pass. Yergensen's PAT made it 7–0 with 14:49 on the clock. Cougar Stadium was as quiet as a Mormon sacrament meeting. Not even the hootin' and hollerin' from 500 or so Ute fans could cut through the deadening anguish.

Give our Ty the ball. Just get him the dad-blasted ball. They did. And on his first pass, he threw a completion—to Utah's Todd Lawson. Taking over at the Y nineteen again, Utah was less successful as Richmond threw four incomplete passes. A succession of penalties (there would be twenty-one on the teams for a combined 200 yards) had made it a nine-play drive that was capped by Yergensen's twenty-eight-yard field goal. With just under three minutes gone, the seventeen-point underdog Utes led 10–0.

Get Ty the ball again, Cougar faithful prayed fervently. They did. And he was promptly sacked for an eight-yard loss at his own three yard line by Preston Christensen. This couldn't be. BYU is down 10–0, the Cougars are at their own three yard line and are reeling in the face of a wild-eyed Ute defense. Detmer had done a lot of things—he would end the day and his career with fifty-nine NCAA records—but he had never hooked up with a receiver for a ninety-seven-yard TD pass. Drifting deep into his own end zone, he spotted Drage with a step on his Ute defender down the left sideline. It was a no-contest foot race. The Cougars had recorded the longest TD pass of 1991 in the NCAA and the longest in school history. Keith Lever's PAT left it Utah 10, BYU 7. The teams had played four-and-a-half minutes.

Mark A. Philbrick

The Cougars flexed their muscles again in 1991 with this reception by Byron Rex helping BYU to a 48–17 win over the Utes in Provo.

Somehow, Ute return specialist Vernon Shaver got caught up in the hysteria. He shouldn't have. Fielding the kickoff in his own end zone, Shaver made it all the way out to his two yard line. And Utah could do zilch against a BYU defense that now smelled blood. Steve Young's (that's Utah punter Steve Young . . . no relation) punt was a forty-nine-yard beauty, so was the Cougars' next drive. With just one Detmer completion—nine yards to Matsuzaki—BYU used nine plays to take the lead with Detmer skirting left end for fourteen yards and the TD. With Lever's kick, the Cougar fans were breathing again and sipping on their hot chocolate. The boys in blue were ahead 14–10. All was well again in Cougarville . . . for two minutes.

Faced with a third-and-six from his own sixteen, Richmond found Rowley streaking behind the Y defense and eighty-four yards later, Rowley—who had been recruited out of Orem High, right in BYU's backyard—was in the end zone. Following Yergensen's PAT, Utah led 17–14. The teams had played just over twelve minutes and had combined for thirty-one points. A shootout no one really expected—in view of Dolce's absence—was well underway. Unfortunately, for Utah, there would be just one marksman—that rifle-toting Texan.

Young's punt left BYU at its own ten with 13:30 left in the second quarter. Detmer then orchestrated a masterful ninety-yard drive, aided by a pass interference call on Utah. Detmer hit four different receivers along the way and got the go-ahead score by finding Matsuzaki for an eleven-yard scoring toss. Lever's PAT was blocked, but BYU had once again wrested the lead from the pesky Utes. Suddenly, the Cougars were having fun again. Utah wasn't laughing.

Especially when, on the third play after the kickoff, Richmond's pass was intercepted by Cougar noseguard Lenny Gomes at the BYU forty-three. Four plays later, it was Detmer to Drage again, this time for thirty-three yards and a touchdown. Drage would end the half with three catches for 137 yards and two touchdowns. And BYU would end the half with a 27–17 lead. The Cougars had been intercepted twice, lost a fumble, and had thirty-eight yards rushing—and had a comfortable lead. It was because the BYU defense had two interceptions of its own, plus the Ute running game showed a minus five yards against a BYU front led by Gomes, Giles, and Biegel.

If Utah's dobber was down, Gomes buried it on the fifth play of the second half with his second interception of the game, prompting Edwards to say postgame, "Lenny may have set an NCAA record for most interceptions by a noseguard in one game." Gomes effectively intercepted Utah's season. Because in two plays, the Cougars were in the end zone again. Detmer sent Tyler Anderson on a reverse around the right side for thirty-seven yards and then handed off to Willis for the final five yards and the TD. The eighteen-second drive, capped by Lever's PAT, jumped BYU's lead to 34–17.

McBride and his staff, driven to the brink by Richmond's three interceptions, inserted third stringer Woods into the game on the next series, and he was okay as long as he handed the ball off. When he passed it, Biegel leaped up to intercept. Two series later, Detmer and the Cougs delivered the coup de grace with a seventy-five-yard drive, topped off by an eighteen-yard TD throw to Drage with 2:33 left in the third quarter. By this time, it was not if BYU would clinch its tenth Holiday Bowl appearance, but by how much.

That was settled on the first BYU series of the fourth quarter. After Utah's Williams fumbled, with the Cougs' Giles recovering at the Y thirty-four, Detmer struck again. A twenty-five-yard pass to Drage, followed by another twenty-fiveyarder to Anderson for the TD finished off the Utes, who had essentially thrown in the towel earlier by relieving Richmond. On the next series, Woods was intercepted again by Josh Arnold, and Edwards, perhaps assuring forever his friendship with McBride, called off the bloodhounds by inserting a rookie quarterback named John Walsh, who would not attempt a single pass in the final eleven minutes.

So Detmer ended his career in Provo—oh, there would be another Holiday Bowl a month later—in relatively unspectacular fashion. He threw only thirty passes for 378 yards. But he had five TD passes, and provided Drage a career afternoon—six catches for 188 yards and three TDs, topped by the school record hookup of ninety-seven big ones. However, Detmer became the first collegian to go over 15,000 yards in a career (15,031), and he shattered the career pass efficiency record (162.7) held by ex-Cougar McMahon (156.9).

Said McBride of his latest Detmer nightmare, "We wanted to put pressure on him, but he kept breaking away—even throwing off his other foot—to make the plays go." As for BYU's defense, which forced Utah into six turnovers, McBride could only sigh, "It's a little like being in a street fight and you keep getting knocked down." The Utes could stand up for their season—7–5 overall and 4–4 in the WAC. They were a pair of field goals away from being 6–2 in the conference and 9–3 overall.

As for BYU, Edwards took a wistful look back: "The other day in practice, Norm Chow came over to me and said, 'Do you want a sobering thought? This is the last practice number fourteen will have for us.' Again, I can't say enough about Ty as a player. He is truly amazing. He is one of the great competitors I've been around."

Great? No, greatest. At the least, the most prolific collegiate passer of all time.

Detmer had one last amateur assignment before waiting four months for the NFL to come calling. One year and one day after his humbling experience against Texas A&M, he returned to The Murphy in San Diego. It wasn't as the Heisman Trophy winner—Michigan's Desmond Howard had won the 1991 version with Casey Weldon second and Detmer third—but the engineer of three WAC titles had been unable to secure a bowl win for his Cougars since rallying the Y to a 20–17 win over Colorado at the Freedom Bowl during his freshman season. BYU had been to the first eight Holiday Bowls (1978–85), winning four of them, but the Cougars' Southern California "home away from home" had turned inhospitable for Detmer and the Y in 1989 (a 50–39 loss to Penn State) and of course, the debacle versus Texas A&M. Coach Hayden Fry's seventh-ranked Iowa Hawkeyes would be a formidable opponent.

So much so that near the end of the first half BYU was down 13–0 after TD runs of thirteen and five yards by Iowa fullback Mike Saunders. But Detmer, who was twenty-nine of forty-four for 350 yards passing and two touchdowns, rallied the Cougars with a nine-yard strike to Tuipulotu as the first half ended. Then he tied it with a twenty-nine-yard throw to Anderson on the opening drive of the fourth quarter. However, the Texan who had established fifty-nine NCAA records and surpassed nearly every mark of all the great BYU QBs, couldn't pull the trigger in the final thirty seconds. His TD pass intended for tight end Byron Rex was tipped at the last second and intercepted by Hawkeye free safety Carlos James. It would be a tie for Ty. BYU finished the season ranked twenty-third while Iowa dropped to number ten.

For better (twenty-eight wins and a Heisman Trophy) or worse (the forgettable Hawaii-Texas A&M parlay of 1990), the gritty Detmer had answered the starting call for every single game (thirty-nine) from his sophomore through senior seasons. His departure led the Cougars to a five-sophomore spring practice shootout for the 1992 starting quarterback spot. The untested group included only two—John Walsh and Brock Spencer—who had seen varsity competition, a total of nine plays between them. Lamented Edwards in early March, "I wish there was a way we could manufacture [QB] experience." Amazingly, totally out of character for a coach who was computer-programmed for the annual staple "I think we can be a pretty good football team," the Provo legend admitted, "This will probably be the first time in a long time we aren't favored to win the conference." Of course, long-time Cougar faithful and WAC aficionados would tell you that Steve Young had very little experience in following McMahon, and Robbie Bosco had little experience in following Young, and . . . well, you know the rest of the story.

No such QB quandary at Utah. Not that the Utes would be favored to win the WAC. But McBride could look at his quarterback register and feel reasonably secure that Dolce, who had finished seventeenth in the nation in total offense and passed for 222 yards per game in 1991, was back for his senior season. Actually, the Utes had QBs who, between them, had amassed almost 3,400 yards passing in 1991. Mike McCoy, who had played at Long Beach State, transferred to the U after the 49ers dropped the sport. He would be immediately eligible. McBride, the eternal pessimist, was moved to say the Utes had an "established quarterback situation."

The receiving corps at both schools made the 1992 outlook more comfortable. BYU would be returning its most productive catching corps in nearly a decade. Eric Drage totaled 1,018 yards and ten TDs in 1991, and Matsuzaki had over 1,100 yards and nine TDs in three years. They would be in a corps with Nati Valdez, Bryce Doman, Tyler Anderson, and Otis Sterling. Byron Rex was back as the all-WAC tight end. Utah's Bryon Rowley was held in such high regard that he was given equal pictorial billing with the school's 1892 team portrait on the front cover of the school's one-hundredth-anniversary press guide. It didn't hurt that the 1991 all-WAC first-teamer was a preseason all-American pick and the school's career reception yardage leader (2,303 yards). McBride's unabashed assessment of Rowley: "Probably the most exciting player to ever play at Utah." Junior-college transfers Greg Hooks, Curtis Marsh, and Deron Claiborne were projected as big and fast receiving additions.

Neither school was lacking for backfield firepower. Although the Cougars lost Tuipulotu, the team's leading rusher and second leading pass receiver, Willis was projected as perhaps the most electrifying runner in school history. And Dixie Junior College transfer Kalin Hall and strapping freshman Hema Heimuli were top prospects. If bulk in the line could help them, the backs would have a heyday what with center Gary Pay, guards Evan Pilgrim and Mike Empey, and tackles Scott Brumfield and Eli Herring all weighing in at an average of 300 pounds. Utah had junior Williams back after being tabbed as the Utes' 1991 offensive player of the year following a 1,011-yard season. Seniors Steve Abrams, Charlie Brown, Brad Foster, and promising sophomore Henry Lusk gave Utah a rarity—backfield depth. Although not as huge overall as the Cougars, Utah's offensive line would have second-team all-WAC senior Mike DeHoog as the anchor with Anthony Brown, Roy Ma'afala, Russ Dailey, Tom McNitt, Ed Castillo, Mark Barton, and Lance Scott would be the mainstays.

Defensively, Utah was beating its chest over becoming the WAC's top defenders in 1991. In two seasons, McBride had transformed the 105th Division I defensive unit into the 64th best. Second-team all-WAC picks Dave Chaytors and Reggie Alston and honorable mention choices Mark Swanson and Sharrieff Shah would be the linchpins. But the guy all the chatter was about was the Colorado kid Luther Elliss, who, as a six-foot-five, 225-pound freshman, landed Ute defensive new-comer of the year honors. He was 260 now—and gaining—and he was the strongest player on the team. BYU would be as young as any Cougar team ever, but linemen Randy Brock and Lenny Gomes, linebackers Nathan Hall and Shad Hansen, and safety Derwin Gray (nine career interceptions) provided strength at each defensive plateau. Anyway, not to worry. BYU had always lived by offense with just enough defense to earn thirteen WAC championships in nineteen seasons under Edwards.

September 1 arrived and by midnight, the chant between the blue in Provo and the red in Utah had a familiar ring—the more things change, the more they stay the same. BYU unveiled Walsh who had thrown for 302 yards and three touchdowns in a 38–28 Coug win over UTEP in the Sun Bowl while Drage had had six catches for ninety-nine yards and two TDs. Hall made his rushing debut with a 120 yards and a TD.

Meanwhile, the awestruck Utes got pounded by Nebraska at Lincoln 49–22 as Dolce threw four interceptions. Granted, there was a slight degree of difference in opponents, so the scores, and the Huskers' 524 yards total offense, were somewhat

Utah's defense revival hit full stride when Anthony Davis was named all-WAC two years in a row in 1991-92.

inconsequential. Far more profound was the Utes' shocking news that Rowley, who, without logging a single catch, was lost for the season with a broken ankle. Whereas other Utah teams had gone into a season-long funk on such demoralizing news, these Utes would show the McBride character stamp.

By midnight of the season's second weekend, the teams' seasons had made a U-turn. With 65,261 fans and an ESPN-TV audience looking on in Provo, another Heisman-like performance was turned in—by the Aztecs' Marshall Faulk, who rushed for a Cougar Stadium record 299 yards while tacking on three touchdowns. Although Walsh threw for 380 yards and five touchdowns—three of them to Drage—and Hall ran for 143 yards in a 561-yard night for the Cougs, BYU had lost its home opener for the fourth time in eight years. It would get worse for the Cougars, but judging by their WAC recoveries in prior years, no one was counting them out of the conference. Even if key players began taking the ten-count in the next two weeks.

Utah played a second straight road game but enjoyed the comforts of home in Logan, where they had beaten the Aggies four straight years. Trailing 12–11 at the half, Dolce rolled up 298 of his 376 yards in the second half and threw two touchdown passes to Abrams en route to a 42–18 win. Utah picked off three Aggie passes, one of which Reggie Alston returned sixty-nine yards and another by Mark Swanson who romped to a TD. There was no reason to get excited just yet about any major Ute renaissance. The jubilation would come after a week off and then three straight games in cozy Rice Stadium.

BYU commanded football headlines in the state the next two weeks. It wasn't that the Cougars had lost two games—to UCLA at home 17–10, and to Hawaii 36–32 in Honolulu—they had lost two starting quarterbacks. In dropping back-to-back home games for the first time in the twenty-one-year career of Edwards, the Cougars fell behind the Bruins 17–0, but rallied to pull within a touchdown on David Lauder's field goal and Walsh's nineteen-yard TD pass to Drage—their sixth scoring connection in three games. With just over ten minutes to play, Walsh suffered a separation of his right shoulder. Clements replaced him and had the Cougars knocking at the goal-line door before he was intercepted by UCLA's Marvin Goodwin. BYU's ten points were the fewest since UCLA downed the Cougars 31–10 in the 1986 Freedom Bowl. There was more than points to worry about for BYU. Like, for instance, who was going to produce for them with Walsh out for the season.

Clements didn't get much of a chance to produce in Aloha Stadium. He went out with a dislocated shoulder at the 3:03 mark of the first quarter. On came sophomore Ryan Hancock, whose previous claim to collegiate fame was as a baseball pitcher. He had been WAC freshman of the year in 1991—in fact he would end up signing a pro contract with the California Angels. It was as if the Cougars never missed a beat. Hancock went twenty for thirty-three for 383 yards and two touchdowns in rallying BYU from a 29–10 deficit. A fifty-five-yard TD heave to Sterling and a twenty-seven-yarder to Rex gave the Cougars a 32–29 lead with 5:04 left. However, the Rainbows, who would, as league co-champs, represent the WAC in the Holiday Bowl, scored on a late TD from Ivin Jasper to Marlowe Lewis to win it. The Cougars were 1–3 overall and 1–2 in the WAC. There was another Beehive State team with fewer quarterback worries. And a better record.

The Utes went unbeaten at home in September, beating up on Oregon State 42–9 in their only Rice Stadium game of the month. With a week to get over the shock of losing Rowley, Utah nominated senior Sean Williams as his replacement and Dolce got along just fine with him. Dolce, going twenty-four for thirty-three for 403 yards and four touchdowns, found Williams on TD passes of thirty-six and twenty-eight yards in the first half, sandwiched around a twenty-two-yard scoring strike to Greg Hooks as Utah built a 21–0 intermission lead and cruised with 527 yards offense in all.

Utah fans began to sense something special on October 3 when their heartthrobs came from behind to topple CSU in Fort Collins 33–29. This time, it was a crunching ground game led by 143 yards from Pierre Jones and junior fullback Jamal Anderson's 86 yards and two TDs that aided the win. Yergensen's thirty-four-yard field goal and Dolce's game-winning, eight-yard pass to Sean Williams with

1:31 lifted the Utes to 3–1 overall and 1–0 in the WAC.

Dolce began to be the most talked-about QB in the league by October 10, when he engineered a 38–17 whipping of then-unbeaten Hawaii at Rice Stadium. Dolce's 19-for-34, 284-yard, two-TD outing, combined with another stellar 233-yard rushing showing (topped by 159 yards from Jones in his first start at tailback) made a shambles of the league's best defense. At 4–1 and 2–0 in the WAC, the Utes were strutting and scoreboard watching. With lower echelon WAC foes New Mexico and UTEP next up, Utah could be 4–0 and really give the Cougars something to ponder.

BYU had experienced poor starts before—in fact they had been 0–3 with Detmer a year earlier. But rarely had they been riddled by so many injuries to guys in the wheel house. At 1–3 and readying Hancock as their third starting QB in five games, the Cougars' entire season hinged on the annual USU battle for the Wagon Wheel at Provo on Friday, October 2. Any doubts Hancock was the best third-string QB in the country were dispelled when he passed for 392 yards and three touchdowns. The 30–9 BYU win, made more impressive by a defense that held the Ags to 29 yards rushing and 295 yards total offense, provided momentum for a pair of WAC wins that would regain a little in-state attention for the Cougs.

On October 10 in Provo, with a fourth straight crowd of 65,000-plus in Cougar Stadium, BYU unleashed a 579-yard offensive showing. Hall's 157 and two TDs and 129 and a TD by Willis provided the Cougs their first same-game 100-yard runners in twenty years. Hancock's 272 yards passing went almost unnoticed except for a seventy-seven-yard TD bomb to Drage.

The Cougars set the stage for a two-game foray into the real big-time of college football when they escaped Laramie with a 31–28 come-from-behind victory over Wyoming. Hancock went twenty-four for forty with 408 yards and three touchdowns in an interception-free afternoon. His favorite target again was Drage who caught nine passes for 135 yards and two TDs. It was a classic wide receiver confrontation with the Cowboys' Ryan Yarborough catching thirteen passes for 201 yards. Wyoming built a 21–7 lead before BYU reeled off twenty-four straight points, capped by the eventual game-winning twenty-three-yard TD run from Willis. The Cougars moved to 4–3 but, more importantly, jumped to 3–2 in the WAC and back into the title chase. It would be a race Utah wasn't quite ready to join.

On consecutive Saturdays against two teams who had amassed a total of seven WAC wins the previous three years, Utah scored a paltry twenty points—a 24–7 loss to New Mexico and a 20–13 home setback to UTEP (the Miners' only win in eleven games).

It was partly because the Utes suffered a costly QB injury of their own—a knee injury to Dolce in the second half of the Lobos' game in Albuquerque. Dolce, who had run for a one-yard TD, crumbled under the sixth Lobo sack of the night. In his stead, McCoy was fifteen for twenty-five for 163 yards. Utah's offensive line didn't improve much the next week, allowing five sacks of McCoy in an embarrassing loss to the Miners. The Utes coughed up three turnovers and were victimized not once, but twice, by the UTEP "fumblerooski" plays that led to two touchdowns. McCoy not only got sacked five times but threw two interceptions. Utah, not quite ready for prime time, had wasted a brilliant start and stood 4–3 and 2–2 in the WAC. And the Utes were looking for answers. Like, where in tarnation was protection from the offensive line?

While Utah was playing down to inferior competition, BYU stepped up to match talent with two icons of college football. Seeing as how they were employing a third-string quarterback who had groomed himself to fire 60-foot-6-inch fastballs and was now asked to throw 150-foot touchdowns, the Cougars emerged from the Notre Dame-Penn State, late-October sequence with reinforced national respect.

In their first-ever meeting with the Irish in South Bend, running backs Jerome Bettis (113 yards and two TDs) and Reggie Brooks (112 yards) were too much on the ground and Irish QB Rick Mirer was sharp in the passing game (twelve of seventeen for 151 yards) as BYU fell 42–16. While the Cougars couldn't stop the Notre Dame run, neither could the Irish put the clamps on the BYU passing game with Hancock finishing with 339 yards and a TD pass to Tim Nowatzke. Hancock did throw three interceptions, but that wasn't too bad considering he tossed a career-high fifty-eight passes.

Returning home on a rainy Halloween afternoon, the Cougars called on a balanced run-pass attack to upend fourteenth-ranked Penn State on the Lions' first visit ever to the Wasatch Mountains. Hall had 117 yards rushing and a TD while Hancock racked up 220 yards and threw three TD passes, one of them an eighty-yard bomb to Anderson. Kerry Collins passed for 317 yards for coach Joe Paterno, but BYU's linebackers Todd Herget and Shad Hansen had fourteen tackles each to help stymie the PSU running game. One consolation for the Nittany Lions was an audience with the Mormon Tabernacle Choir on Temple Square the next morning, the arrangements compliments of Paterno's good friend Edwards and BYU athletic director Glen Tuckett.

It would be an all-WAC finish now for BYU. They were 5–4 overall and with three wins could win a piece of a fourteenth WAC title by running the table. Including a win in The Game on November 21 in Salt Lake.

The unpredictable Utes did make it interesting. After stubbing their toes twice against the league's worst, they beat one of the best—on the road with McCoy still subbing for Dolce. Air Force was fresh off a win over San Diego State, but the Falcons were thrown a curve by the pass-happy Utes when McBride decided to keep the ball on the ground in near-blizzard conditions at the base of Pikes Peak near Colorado Springs. Keith Williams had 119 yards rushing, Jones had 84, and Anderson had 55 and a touchdown as Utah amassed 273 yards on the ground. The Falcons' vaunted wishbone was held to 220 yards as Elliss had his best day (of many to come) with ten tackles, five of them for losses.

The Ute road magic lasted just one game. The following week at Fresno, with Dolce returning to the lineup, Utah played its worst game of the year in a 41–15 loss. Dolce couldn't pass the Utes to a TD but did score on a pair of one-yard runs. An injury-ravaged Ute defense yielded 557 yards. The Utes, with a split of their last two games, could have a second consecutive winning season, a feat they hadn't accomplished for seven seasons. They were looking for more than that. Two wins—one over BYU—could land them a bowl game.

The Cougars used the Penn State victory as a springboard to their best back-to-back games of the season—a 35–0 blanking of New Mexico in Provo and a 28–7 cruise past Air Force at the Academy. In an inexplicable change of pace, the Cougars did it on the ground, piling up 265 yards against the Lobos with Willis netting 149 and three touchdowns. Hancock did toss two touchdown passes. It was BYU's first shutout since blanking New Mexico 65–0 in 1988. The Cougars kept right on marching confidently to The Game by waxing Air Force, again with a bruising ground game paced by 146 yards and two TDs by Willis. Hancock's TD pass to Drage in the first quarter set three records—BYU's forty-sixth straight game with a TD reception, an NCAA-record 222nd straight game without being shut out, and Drage's twenty-third straight game with a catch. With a 7–4 record, the Cougars were ready to clinch at least a tie for the WAC title in Salt Lake. Again.

The up-and-down Utes were up at home versus Wyoming on November 14. Dolce appeared to regain his early season form with a 27-for-40 day and 298 yards. A defense that had yielded ninety-eight points in the previous four games tightened behind the twelve-tackle performance of Blaine Berger and interceptions by Jeff Kirkman, Kareem Leary, and Sharrieff Shah. The Cowboys had just 240 yards total offense. The Ute defense, which had contributed mightily to assuring Utah a winning season (6–4 overall and 4–3 in the WAC), could only hope it had revived in time. BYU was coming to town with an offense that averaged 459 yards per game.

On the surface, the Utes had every reason to believe they could whip their worst nemesis in the sixty-eighth edition of The Game. Dolce was healthy, the Utes had a good run-pass balance, and probably as important as anything, they didn't have to contend with that Detmer fellow again. They had faced some pretty decent QBs during the year—CSU's Anthony Hill, New Mexico's Stoney Case, and Fresno's Trent Dilfer. In Hancock, they were up against a guy listed as third-string quarterback to begin the season. To top it off, the game was in Salt Lake, where Utah's two previous wins over the Cougs the last twenty years had come when BYU was in a state of flux with its quarterbacks.

On the other hand, the Cougars had toughened up their defense over the last three games, grudgingly giving up a total of twenty-four points. Except for the second-half stumble against Notre Dame, the Cougs had made a remarkable comeback from a 1–3 start. Not only were they playing for a piece of the WAC title, but there was a hint they could be a long-shot for the nationally televised (ABC) Aloha Bowl on Christmas Day if indeed they did beat the Utes and didn't win the WAC tie-breaking qualifying shuffle for the host spot in the Holiday Bowl. There was even bowl banter from the Ute camp. Obviously, a victory over the Cougars was the number-one priority since McBride, as head coach, had never beaten BYU. But even a close loss might tip the Copper Bowl scales in the Utes' favor.

For three quarters, Ute fans were more accurate in delivering their snowballs to Cougar targets than Dolce was in completing passes to Utah receivers. By halftime, the senior, in his last home appearance, had six completions in seventeen attempts for forty-four yards. By comparison, the Utes' Steve Young had seven punts. In another, far more embarrassing, comparison, that "pitcher" from BYU had 200 yards passing on a 15-of-22 effort. Oh, yes, and two touchdowns. By half, with Hancock passing at will—to most any receiver he wanted—and Willis dancing for fifty yards and a touchdown, the Cougars were romping 24–0.

The Utes almost got out of the punt-filled—three by each team—first quarter unscathed. A four-yard Willis TD run with forty-nine seconds left in the quarter and Lauder's PAT made it BYU 7–0, but there was not a lot to fret about. Shoot, there had been BYU-Utah games when the Cougars led 28–0 after one period. It was a bit disconcerting that Dolce's thirty-yard rushing total exceeded all of his other teammates—in both rushing and pass receiving, and that fifty-two yards rushing by Willis was more than Utah's entire offensive output. Still, the Cougar entourage, however small it was among the gathering of 33,348, just knew the hammer was going to fall. This BYU team had averaged thirty points a game with the second quarter its real harvest time—128 points in twelve games. Even after Lauder's forty-two-yard field goal at 12:53 of the second, Y fans anticipated more.

Now, against BYU no one prepares for trick plays, even though Edwards was weaned on single-wing contrivances like the double reverse and Statue-of-Liberty plays. So, when Rex came in motion from his tight end spot and took a handoff from Hancock on the Cougars' second series of the second quarter, everyone in the house figured it was a tight end–around play. Except Rex stopped, planted his foot and lofted a nineteen-yard pass to Drage. Rex, perhaps best known for his early-season, expletive-deleted Honolulu temper tantrum aimed at Hawaii fans (an outburst captured by ESPN cameras and audio), left college as the only 1.000 percent TD-throwing tight end in Division 1 history. His TD pass to Drage, followed by Lauder's PAT at 10:47, ballooned the lead to 17–0. Two more Young punts and a seat cushion—which, hurled onto the field by an irate Ute fan, also landed short—was Utah's response.

BYU's response was more demonstrable. In a six-minute, eighty-six-yard drive that featured two fumbles, both of which the Cougs recovered, thirteen plays and three third-down conversions, the Cougars' massive offensive front overwhelmed the Utes and helped Hancock take the team to the Utah six yard line. From there, Hancock, not to be outdone by Rex's earlier aerial prowess, rewarded his tight end with a six-yard scoring toss. Lauder's PAT spread the Coug lead to 24–0 with 1:39 left in the half and invited another fusillade of snowballs. Some of them even seemed to be aimed at the Utes.

Utah was looking for a snowdrift to hide under just after the second half opened. Receiving the kickoff, the Ute offense again stalled and Young stood near his goal line to punt for the eighth time. Cougar end Travis Hall burst through to block the punt and recovered the ball in the end zone for a touchdown. After Lauder's PAT, the Cougars could be pardoned if they were thinking "just another day at Rice Stadium." Ute fans were booing, not the Cougars. Their team was down 31–0. Snowball throwing wasn't even adequate. They were, shall we say, damn mad.

Mark A. Philbrick

Jamal Willis, one of the greatest BYU running backs ever, helped the Cougars to a 31–22 win over the Utes in 1992.

So were the Utes. By the time the third quarter ended, BYU owned a 397–174 total offense advantage and had dominated time of possession, twenty-seven minutes to eighteen. Willis had 118 yards rushing, just 56 yards shy of Utah's entire offensive total. Not only that, but the Cougars were driving and perched at the Utah twenty-four yard line with 14:49 left. Suddenly, Utah cornerback Derrick Odum stepped in front of a Hancock pass into the end zone. It was the only interception of the day by either school and it ignited the heretofore moribund Utes.

You could call it a four-and-a half-minute march to a bowl game. Even though it took nearly five precious minutes, the Utes mixed the running of Keith Williams with the suddenly accurate passing of Dolce, and on first down from the Y thirty-four. Hooks made a leaping catch in the end zone for a TD. After Dolce's two-point pass to Sean Williams, it was 31–8. Utah had endured a passel of indignities over the years, but only once (1979) had they been shut out by an Edwards-coached team. This wouldn't be the second.

Whether it was because of Hancock's season-ending injury, or Cougar fatigue, or a matter of honor, the Utes actually had a shot at victory. With 5:54 left and the Cougars trying to take time off the clock, Hancock swept to his right and was run out of bounds and into the BYU players on the sideline. Discussion still rages today on whether it was a late hit, a cheap hit, or whether Hancock's knee just gave out. Whatever the case, he was done for the day—and the season—and the Cougars had to punt. Moving seventy-six yards in just two minutes, Dolce found Joe Welch for a four-yard TD pass and hooked up with Welch for the two-point conversion. The BYU lead had been halved.

With fourth-string quarterback Tom Young at the helm—this time it was indeed Cougar relation, Steve's younger brother—BYU couldn't make a first down even though Willis went over the 1,000-yard rushing mark for the season (he had 148 this day). Starting at midfield after Brad Hunter's punt plus a personal foul on the Y, Utah again marched. Passes of seventeen yards to Anderson and fifteen and seven to Welch set the stage for Dolce's three-yard TD run with fifty-eight seconds left. BYU's Gray swatted away what seemed like a cinch two-point pass conversion to Anderson that would have made it 31–24. Utah's day and—a 6–5 regular season— was done, but not without fruit for their last-quarter labor. Dolce had amassed 347 yards passing—a whopping 213 in the final period—to Hancock's 198. Moments after McBride lauded his club by saying, "Our kids didn't lay down and die; it shows how far we've come as a football program," Copper Bowl officials elevated Utah football to a new level.

"We extend to Utah a bid to the 1992 Copper Bowl," executive director Larry Brown said to an accompanying roar of jubilation from the Ute dressing room. It had been twenty-eight years—the 1964 Liberty Bowl—since a Ute football team had heard such magical words. As for WAC tri-champion BYU, the Aloha Bowl did call. The 8–4 Cougars would be playing in Honolulu on Christmas Day.

That the Cougars, with a quarterback listed fourth on the depth chart in

September, would lead the University of Kansas 20–12 in the fourth quarter in hot and humid Hawaii, was a testament to the talent-rich school that had come to be known as Quarterback U. That the Cougars would lose 23–20 despite Young's 262-yard passing day, merely continued a postseason malaise that saw them go winless for the fourth year in a row. KU kicker Dan Eichloff booted a forty-eight-yard field goal with 2:57 left to provide the Jayhawks their come-from-behind win.

Hema Heimuli returned the opening kickoff ninety yards for a TD to which KU responded two plays later with a dipsy-doodle trick play—a seventy-four-yard pass from wide receiver Matt Gray to tight end Rodney Harris. Willis ran nine yards for a TD and Eichloff kicked a forty-two-yard field goal to leave BYU with a 14–12 halftime lead. Young's ten-yard TD pass to Sterling jumped the Cougars to a 20–12 lead, but the Jayhawks would come back to tie it on quarterback Chip Hilleary's touchdown run and subsequent two-point conversion run.

Young, who threw one other pass all year, was named BYU's most valuable player by ABC. Future San Francisco 49ers all-pro Dana Stubblefield, who sacked Young three times, was KU's MVP.

Utah was left in the highly unusual position of salvaging state football pride when they took the field against former Weber State coach Mike Price's Washington State team in Tucson. It was just the Utes' luck they would face another passing magician—another Cougar at that—in Drew Bledsoe. It was all too familiar for Utah. They looked as shell-shocked as at any time in the BYU series. Bledsoe hurled the Cougars to a 21–0 first-quarter lead before the Utes finally realized they were actually playing football in December.

Dolce fired a ten-yard pass to Sean Williams in the second quarter, and Kevin Williams ran twenty-five yards for another score to get Utah back in it. Another Bledsoe TD pass just before the half left the Utes in the throes of a 28–14 intermission deficit. Dolce, who would end his career with a 316-yard, interception-free performance, hit Henry Lusk with a forty-eight-yard TD pass in the third quarter. An eight-yard TD run by Jones pulled the Utes into a 28–28 tie. However, WSU won it 31–28 on a field goal with 5:08 left.

So, three years into McBride's tenure, the Utes had come from league doormat to stand 17–18 overall. A 6–6 season, remembered probably for the two whirlwind comebacks in the last two games, was grounds for optimism in 1993. They had all-WAC defensive linemen Luther Elliss coming back, and there was sentiment—at least in Salt Lake County—that McCoy might be the best Beehive State quarterback returning in '93. After all, Walsh and Clements would have to show they were recovered from shoulder surgery, and Hancock was pro baseball bound. Could Young really be that good after just one game?

Come, Come Ye Fans

To illustrate the difference between the Division I football programs of BYU and Utah, located some forty-five miles apart along Interstate 15, figure that two-thirds of BYU's attendance on a typical Saturday afternoon migrates south along I-15 away from the vicinity of the U and into Cougar Stadium.

Now there is much truth to the theory that the fans' Salt Lake County exodus is as much a repudiation of Ute Stadium as it is the Uteski football program. Not that either has much to be proud of in the last half-century, or in the case of Ute Stadium, the last seventy years.

A reliable source reports that in the last decade of the twentieth century there have been found beneath the splintered boards of Utah's decaying football stadium some full bottles of Lucky Lager beer, half-full mini bottles of Yukon Jack, and some dog-eared "Pud" football parlay cards. The historical society tells us those are artifacts listed in the registrar alongside Tyrannosaurus Rex. The stench would suggest the pile of dirt the stadium first covered in the twenties was the residue of the first county dump.

You get the idea just how old Ute Stadium—rescued by philanthropist Robert L. Rice and renamed Rice Stadium in 1972—really is. Why, some say LDS prophet David O. McKay played there in 1892. Actually, there are some DOM initials carved in the City Creek Canyon timbers in the corners of the stadium on the west side. Of course, there are the initials DOA carved in there, too.

So, it is no surprise that twice as many fans cram into Cougar Stadium on a typical Saturday as there are at the U. In numbers easy to understand, the average attendance at Cougar home games the last fifteen years has been 64,401, give or take a few hundred. At Utah it's been some 28,000, give or take a few thousand.

Of course, the allure at Provo is a real football team. Playing in a real stadium. Made of real metal. In real modern times. When they used nuts and bolts rather than mud and dowels.

One hundred years ago, the Cougars cavorted in pasture lands and city parks for their football kicks. Once the butt of jokes the state over and rarely one-third full, the old 10,000-seat stadium gave way to Dr. Ernie Wilkinson's dream in 1964. A new 30,000 seat stadium rose on the northwest corner of the campus.

Mark A. Philbrick

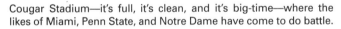

Cougar Stadium—it's full, it's clean, and it's big-time—where the likes of Miami, Penn State, and Notre Dame have come to do battle.

And the people came. As BYU's program sprinted to catch up with Utah's well-established gridiron juggernaut, the fan base increased ten times. Build it and they will come. And they did. More than 47,000 crammed into the stadium during the Tommy Hudspeth-inspired excitement of the mid-sixties. Utah hadn't seen 47,000 fans in a season.

Then, the mother of all Beehive State athletic facilities opened to the public in 1982. An expanded Cougar Stadium, the genesis of which could be traced to LaVell Edwards's guidance of the team into the national spotlight, greeted the Coug constituency.

Uteskis chuckled when the Cougs lost their home opener to The Air Force Academy in 1982. They crawled back behind their bars when BYU won the next fifteen, playing to crowds in excess of 65,000 most of the time.

Always the football pacesetter, once they realized Utah had ceded the territory, the Cougars, buoyed by unbridled enthusiasm of athletic director Glen Tuckett, pushed all the right buttons. Upgrading the schedule now that football powers would play home-and-home due to lucrative guarantees, Tuckett and Edwards worked hand-in-hand to bring the national title to Cougar Stadium in 1984.

No one in Cougardom has looked back since, while the nation has looked in.

Nationally televised games, nationally renowned opponents—Notre Dame, Penn State, UCLA, Miami, Texas A&M, and Washington to name a few—and national acclaim have been the dividends of expansion.

Come to the Taj Mahal of the Wasatch or, as media members call it, the "Provo Marriott," is the invitation to the world.

While in some corners of the world fans go to football games to eat and drink and make merry, fans flock to Cougar Stadium to watch, cheer, and relish their Cougs making mincemeat of the opposition. Going from Utah's Stadium to Cougar Stadium is like going from darkness into the light. Which is an adequate comparison of the relative strengths and weaknesses of the football programs. In Cougar Stadium, you watch victories and championships and all-Americans and a Heisman Trophy winner. At Utah's Stadium, you watch an occasional win, a championship once every Ice Age, and a consensus all-American once every coaching change or so.

In Cougar Stadium, the forward pass stokes fans' emotions to a boiling point. In Utah's stadium, off-tackle running plays leave fans just plain boiled. And while Uteskis have ballyhooed their running game, it has been the Cougars who have spawned all-American runners Eldon "The Phantom" Fortie, national rushing leader "Fleet Pete" VanValkenburg, and three-time WAC rushing leader

John Ogden.

But the demarcation line for Cougar football has been the passing revolution. So very elementary. The snap of the ball, a drop into the pocket, and an artistic heave of the ball into the air. Been going on now in Cougar Stadium for nigh on to the last third of the twentieth century.

And still they come to fill every luxury seat, wedge into row after row of battleship-gray bleacher seats. Grandmas and grandpas, babes-in-arms—generation after generation of Cougar worshippers. Blue-and-white painted wackos—all sober and all idolizing a phenomenon born of the seventies, nurtured by a home-grown legend and sustained by an old-fashioned, honest work ethic.

So Cougar fans gloat. Better, it's a wicked satisfaction that after a half century kowtowing to the Uteskis, they can smugly ask the question: When will you ever learn the nuances of the game? Better, when will you ever learn to defend eight basic pass patterns? Eight! Cougar Stadium fans will help you count—eight, that's the number of seasons the Uteskis have won eight or more games in the last half century.

Until you learn, they crow, we will rise and shout for quarterback-types like Virgil Carter, Gary Sheide, Marc Wilson, Jim McMahon, Steve Young, Robbie Bosco, Ty Detmer and Steve Sarkisian to make your life miserable—in Cougar Stadium or in Rice Stadium.

Cougar faithful will sip on their caffeine-free drinks and hot chocolate, breathe the smoke-free air, chew on chocolate-chip cookies, and go out for ice cream afterward. They'll also talk about their Cougar Stadium experiences—500-yard games, fifty-point wins, all-Americans, Hall of Famers, and coaching legends.

Build a real stadium, they tell their Uteski friends. Build a real program to compete with the big boys. Get some religion. It might help. Heaven knows it couldn't hurt. Man, it sure feels good to tweak the northern cousins. Amen.

Rice Stadium Is . . .

Rice Stadium is the ivy and history of Wrigley Field. Cougar Stadium is the concrete Kingdome.

Rice Stadium is the tradition and pageantry of Wimbledon. Cougar Stadium is the rudeness of the U.S. Open.

Rice Stadium is waiting in a giddy line with friends for hours, just to make a mad rush to the best seats in the student section two hours before game time. Cougar Stadium is arriving late and sitting in a different area code from the field.

Rice Stadium is Classic Coke (perhaps flavored from a flask of rum). Cougar Stadium is Caffeine-Free Reduced-Calorie Mr. Pibb.

Rice Stadium is eating chicken-breast sandwiches with extra tangy barbecue sauce on a hoagie roll and a bottle of Blue Ribbon at a pregame tailgate party. Cougar Stadium is smuggling in peanut-butter-and-jelly sandwiches to eat at halftime.

Rice Stadium is red coats, red caps, red mittens, red sweaters, and the occasional fanatic with his face painted red. Cougar Stadium is mostly white, about a dozen different shades of blue, and an occasional fanatic with B-Y-U stenciled on his cheeks, often spelled correctly.

Rice Stadium is The Blues Brothers theme. Cougar Stadium is "Popcorn Popping on the Apricot Tree."

Rice Stadium is staying until the last possession, knowing that the Utes are capable of scoring fifteen points in the final minute-and-a-half to pull one out. Cougar Stadium is leaving in the third quarter because it's a three-hour drive home and you have church in the morning.

Rice Stadium is a cannon firing after every score. Cougar Stadium is an annoying recording of a cat in heat being played after every pass, kick, penalty, punt, time out, or any play that doesn't lose yardage.

Rice Stadium is the world's largest block party. Cougar Stadium is the world's largest stake conference.

Rice Stadium is booing BYU's offense whenever it scores.

Cougar Stadium is booing BYU's offense whenever it punts.

Rice Stadium is the friendly confines. Cougar Stadium is the impersonal bureaucracy.

Rice Stadium is Ron McBride jogging over to shake hands with Mac's Kids. Cougar Stadium is LaVell Edwards asking directions to the sidelines.

Rice Stadium is shuttle buses to postgame victory parties at nearby taverns. Cougar Stadium is postgame prayers at midfield.

Rice Stadium is announcing the BYU score last if they're losing, just to get a big roar. Cougar Stadium is squinting your eyes to read out-of-town scores on the corporate-sponsored scoreboard.

U of U Sports Information Office

No Ute home game can begin until Ron welcomes Mac's Kids to football's friendliest venue—Rice Stadium.

Rice Stadium is parking a few blocks away and strolling over on an autumn evening. Cougar Stadium is sitting in traffic on the interstate for three hours.

Rice Stadium is standing in massive lines of people forming a tunnel to welcome the Utes onto the field. Cougar Stadium is standing in massive lines of people waiting to use the restrooms.

Rice Stadium is sitting so close to the players you can touch them. Cougar Stadium is sitting so far away that half the touchdowns are just a roar and a rumor.

Rice Stadium is a press box with its windows open so you can talk to the writers. Cougar Stadium is a glassed-in behemoth so vacuum-sealed you can't hear the game inside it.

Rice Stadium is the Rolling Stones. Cougar Stadium is Donny and Marie.

Rice Stadium is wondering who the quarterback will be next year. Cougar Stadium is demanding a new quarterback next week.

Rice Stadium is wood and peeling paint and bleachers built in the thirties. Cougar Stadium is steel and concrete and personnel-seating areas erected in the eighties.

Rice Stadium is Bubbles the Buxom Boogier. Cougar Stadium is Cosmo the Clueless Cat.

Rice Stadium is home. Cougar Stadium is hell.

CHAPTER

1993–1995
EARTHQUAKE—34 ON THE "MAC" SCALE

Nobody is quite sure who did it, nor could police pinpoint the exact time. The place was supposed to be locked up, but somehow the perpetrators sneaked a small pickup inside and apparently used ropes to do the deed. Police investigated but couldn't crack the case. Maybe it was those frat boys, they figured, or perhaps just some local rowdies. As football pranks go, it was close to the perfect crime. Because the next morning, there they sat gleaming in the Rice Stadium end zones, confounding the campus cops and taunting the vanquished enemy some forty miles south.

Somebody had pulled down Utah's goalposts.

Such was the pent-up emotion released by the Utes' 34–31 triumph over Brigham Young in November 1993, a last-minute victory that halted a one-win-a-decade pattern for Utah and perhaps signaled a startling change in the relationship between the two football programs: Parity, anyone?

Of course, it's hard to assert that a rivalry exists when only one side feels the impulse to tear down goalposts when it wins. That's not rivalry, that's jealousy, which BYU faces in almost every WAC city. Future Games will determine the extent of the Utes' competitiveness and whether the equipment and facilities can survive further victories. This particular weekend, though, was hard on goalposts.

So euphoric were the Utes and their handful of partisans after the upset in Provo, a few stormed the Cougar Stadium uprights seeking souvenirs symbolic of the destruction, much as a matador removes the ear of his defeated foe. Over our dead bodies, responded the insulted Cougar defenders with a ferocity more effective and abrupt than at any point during the previous four hours. When some of the defeated BYU players spotted the Utah celebrants climbing their posts, the offended Cougars stormed out of their locker room and across the field to accost the transgressors.

The small brawl amounted merely to a few pushes, a handful of shoves, and a barrage of angry words, and stadium security helped the team's coaches quickly quell the tantrums. But the incident, not to mention the unlikely final score, probably inspired the Rice Stadium raiders later that evening.

And it certainly provoked the most memorable taunt in the series' recent history, a postgame rant from BYU noseguard Lenny Gomes.

"Typical Utah bull**," Gomes fumed. "All those ***'s think that's all there is to life. But when I'm making fifty or sixty thousand dollars a year, they'll be pumping my gas. They're low-class losers."

The remark prompted headlines for a week, with angry rebuttals, condescending retorts, and good-natured gibes flooding the airwaves and newspaper forums. More than three years later, Gomes—and the Utes—are still reminded of the angry outburst each fall. Good thing Gomes was a senior in 1993, though, because his age spared him two more years of suffering at the hands of those gas-pumpers. The Cougars won twenty-three of thirty-six games from 1993–95, claimed a share of two WAC titles, made two bowl appearances, and climbed as high as tenth in the national rankings.

Yet an epic football earthquake jumbled the customary order of competition in Utah, where for two decades the BYU-Utah outcome was normally as predictable as the state's taste in presidential candidates. The Utes disrupted BYU's monolithic dominance by posting a 24–12 record in that span, with two postseason games and a conference title of its own, and a record rise to number nine at one point in the national media poll.

As bad as those numbers were for Gomes and the 65,000 partisans who routinely fill Cougar Stadium, much worse was Utah's fixation with the number thirty-four during those years.

Utah 34, BYU 31.

Utah 34, BYU 31. Yes, again.

Utah 34, BYU 17.

If Ron McBride is a roulette player, there is little doubt what his luckiest number is.

Yes, the goalposts may have remained standing in Cougar Stadium that fall day, but the same couldn't be said for Brigham Young's accustomed football superiority. That vanished, at least temporarily, behind the ascension of the state's modern-day underdogs from Salt Lake City.

LaVell Edwards felt like a survivor as he surveyed his team in the spring of 1993. The previous year's Cougars had been relatively successful, with an 8–5 record, a share of the school's sixteenth conference championship, and a trip to the Aloha Bowl to show for it.

Yet for the strategist behind BYU's quarterback-based offense, 1992 had seemed like one long episode of "General Hospital". His triggermen kept getting hurt at a rate too implausible to be anything but fiction, with four different quarterbacks running the show.

"It got so I was almost afraid to watch," shrugged Edwards, who nonetheless found a way to put twenty-eight or more points on the scoreboard a remarkable ten times.

But Edwards chose not to dwell on the signal-caller shuttle or fret about his quarterbacks' health. Instead, it struck him as a benefit that he now possessed three quarterbacks who had been college starters. (It would have been four, except Ryan Hancock opted in July to play professional baseball instead of Cougar football.)

"It's been a while since we had as much experience as we do this year," he deadpanned. In particular, John Walsh was back to resume the promising passing career that was interrupted by a shoulder separation in the previous season's third game.

But Edwards wasn't just talking about his quarterbacks. Another dozen starters were back from that up-and-down adventure, including a gaggle of receivers and the best one-two rushing combination in school history—halfback Jamal Willis and fireplug fullback Kalin Hall.

It was enough to convince the media members who covered the WAC. They made the Cougars an overwhelming favorite to claim the conference championship again, with twenty-one of the thirty-three voters putting BYU atop their ballot.

Yet, as intriguing as the Cougars' stash of talent was to BYU fans, there were other reasons to be excited about the 1993 football season. For one thing, there was much talk about Edwards's 191 career victories and whether he could surpass the historic 200-win plateau that season. The coach, of course, downplayed any such speculation; the idea that his team would win nine games that season, he said, was "a little bit presumptuous."

Besides, he fretted, the Cougars' fortunes would be determined unusually early in the 1993 season, too early for Edwards's taste. The schedule gave his WAC contenders no time to tune up, since all four September contests were conference games. True, they weren't against the WAC's finest; Edwards entered the season 60–8–1 lifetime against the foursome of New Mexico, Hawaii, Colorado State, and Air Force, and the expected title showdowns against Fresno State and San Diego State came in the season's second half.

Still, the coach fretted over the prospect of stumbling early against an inferior foe. A conference loss inflicted before his team had settled in could conceivably cost Edwards a fifth consecutive share of the WAC championship. "Given a choice, I'd rather play tough non-conference games first," the coach wished aloud.

But while Edwards worried about having to open the season at full boil, Cougar fans were noticeably more focused on the middle three games of the BYU season— an October gauntlet as challenging as any trio of opponents ever to appear on a

Cougar schedule. A visit to the Rose Bowl to face UCLA would attract national attention, and Fresno State's homecoming appearance in Provo figured to decide the conference championship, or so the preseason polls predicted.

Sandwiched in between was perhaps the most-anticipated football visitor ever to land in Utah, and certainly the biggest since Miami dropped by to endorse Ty Detmer's Heisman candidacy three years earlier. Notre Dame, college football's flagship franchise, would make its first appearance in the Wasatch Mountains, a bow from the most tradition-laden football power in America to its upstart imitator out West.

True to their nature, fans couldn't help looking ahead to the mid-October church-school showdown. True to his nature, Edwards wouldn't even consider it. "That's a long way off. We've got a lot of work to do before then," he shrugged.

Work was Ron McBride's theme at Utah as well, especially since he had proven to his squad how big the payoff could be. In McBride's first three seasons, the team had reached a new goal each year. In year one, the Utes became more physical and more organized, sowing much optimism despite a 4–7 record. Year two produced a winning record at 7–5, and McBride's third season ended with Utah's first bowl appearance in twenty-eight years and a 6–6 mark.

The next logical step was contending for a conference championship, a lofty goal at a school that had exactly one Western Athletic Conference title to its credit, and that one nearly three decades old. Could Utah keep climbing that football ladder? The WAC media didn't seem to think so, picking the Utes sixth in its preseason poll. And even McBride didn't seem to know. "We've got the talent, but there are so many things that go into winning a title—schedule, luck, timing, injuries," the coach said. "This could be an excellent team . . . but I don't like to make any predictions."

McBride figured defense would determine Utah's fate, since the offense was unusually well stocked with veterans. Five running backs with more than 300 career yards—tailbacks Keith Williams, Pierre Jones, and Charlie Brown, and fullbacks Jamal Anderson and Brad Foster—manned the backfield and offered amazing versatility. Plus, senior Bryan Rowley's fractured ankle, which cost him all but one quarter of the 1992 season, had healed, allowing the former second-team all-American (sixty catches for 1,011 yards and eleven touchdowns) to rejoin flanker Greg Hooks and slotback Henry Lusk in the receiving corps.

The offensive line was solid, too, leaving quarterback Mike McCoy as the offense's unproven commodity. But McBride and his staff believed McCoy was a question mark on paper only, and that his mostly unimpressive three-game debut as emergency starter during Frank Dolce's injury the previous year was not a true indication of his ability. That confidence was buoyed by McCoy's strong showing in spring ball and fall camp. "Mike is a talented guy, and he's really starting to show it," said a relieved offensive coordinator Rick Rasnick.

The defense featured only four returning starters, however, making McBride sweat a little. And like Edwards, McBride fretted over his schedule, since Utah's twelve-game slate included no off weeks, physical non-conference teams to open the season (Arizona State, Utah State, and Kansas), and a four-week stretch of WAC powers San Diego State, Hawaii, Air Force, and Brigham Young to end it, when the Utes were liable to be tired or hurt.

"We just play the games they tell us to, can't do anything about that," down-played McBride. Still, his concern showed. "It's absolutely critical that we stay healthy."

Determined to make the best of a difficult challenge, McBride tried selling his team on the notion that beating Arizona State in the season opener would be a ter-rific way to launch a successful season. "It's a great opportunity to get some momentum going right away," he decided. The momentum lasted for exactly two seconds.

Keith Williams settled under the game's opening kickoff, hesitated in the 103-degree heat, took an uncertain step, and then dropped to one knee to down the ball. Trouble was, he was standing on the two yard line at the time.

"The kick took so long to come down . . . it just hung there and hung there and hung there," the embarrassed tailback said. "I was backing up and by the time it came down I was sure I was in the end zone. I couldn't believe I wasn't."

Unfortunately for the Utes, their evening was about to get even worse. The vet-eran offensive line was helpless against a Sun Devils onslaught led by defensive end Shante Carver, and McCoy spent the few minutes Utah owned the ball running for his life. He got off just nine passes in the first half and completed only one. When the Utes received one of their few breaks, a blocked punt that defensive end Bronzell Miller recovered at the ASU nine, McCoy tried to thread a pass into the middle of the Sun Devil defense. Big mistake. The pass bounced off wideout Greg Hooks's shoulder and into the hands of ASU linebacker Dan Lucas, who broke a tackle and rumbled forty-nine yards downfield. End of threat.

That wasn't the Sun Devils' only lucky bounce, either. Sophomore tailback Mario Bates bounced off a would-be tackler on fourth-and-one on Arizona State's first possession, got outside and ran thirty-five yards into the end zone. On the next ASU possession, the Sun Devils drove to Utah's eight when quarterback Grady Benton tossed to Carlos Artis. The ball slipped through the ASU receiver's hands and into the end zone—where another Sun Devil, Clyde McCoy, grabbed it for another touchdown. It added up to a humiliating 38–0 pasting that could have been even worse had ASU not killed the clock in the fourth quarter. Utah managed only 256 yards of offense, and a shell-shocked McBride was stuck for answers. "Nobody was more surprised than me how we played," he said. "I expected more out of this football team."

Brigham Young's coach didn't know what to expect in his team's opener, so the Cougars' 34–31 comeback victory wasn't a big surprise. The Cougars were seventeen-point favorites against a New Mexico team it had beaten twelve straight times. But "it's more than just rhetoric—you have no way of knowing what's going to happen in an opening-night game," Edwards said. "I told the players it was one of the all-time gut checks."

Especially since the Cougars faced a hostile crowd of 33,659, the Lobos' first football sellout in their history. And if the atmosphere didn't affect the Cougars, injuries did. A training-camp ankle injury kept Kalin Hall out of the lineup, and Jamal Willis left the game with an ankle sprain of his own in the first quarter. That left BYU's offense in the hands of sophomore fullback Hema Heimuli, quarterback John Walsh, and receiver Bryce Doman.

The trio was enough to overcome Stoney Case and a surprisingly efficient New Mexico offense. Heimuli picked up seventy yards on thirteen rushes, Doman scored three touchdowns, one on a fumble recovery in the end zone, and Walsh threw for 384 yards and four touchdowns. The biggest was a fifty-two-yard bomb to Tim Nowatzke in the fourth quarter, a score that turned a four-point BYU deficit into a 34–31 lead. "That's what we do at BYU. We make plays," Walsh said.

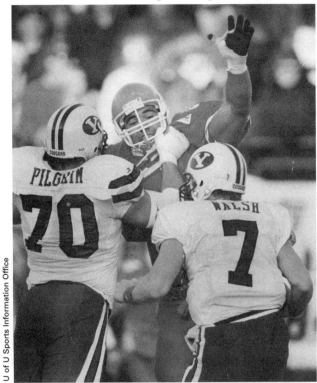

All-American defensive tackle Luther Elliss was kept away from BYU quarterback John Walsh by guard Evan Pilgrim for most of their 1994 matchup. But Elliss recovered Walsh's fumble late in the game to clinch Utah's second 34–31 victory.

U of U Sports Information Office

Still, the Cougars had to fend off a late New Mexico drive that brought them to the BYU twenty-three yard line with 1:23 to play. After three incomplete passes New Mexico's Nathan Vail tried a forty-yard field goal to tie the game. The kick sailed high above the left goalpost, and the Lobos believed it had gone through. So did Edwards: "It looked pretty close to me," he said. But the officials ruled the kick had drifted just outside the bar, and BYU's victory was secure.

The Cougars needed another fourth-quarter comeback and another missed field goal by the opposition a week later in their home opener against Hawaii. The BYU defense was confused by the Rainbows' option offense, and Hawaii ran up 454 rushing yards en route to a 38–31 lead with six minutes left.

Worse, BYU was staring at a fourth-and-ten near midfield, a play that could hand over the upset to the thirteen-point underdog Rainbows. But Walsh found Tyler Anderson ahead of a Hawaii safety, and zipped a dart into his arms for the game-tying score. The Rainbows then killed most of the clock driving to the Cougar five but couldn't reach the end zone and set up instead for a chip-shot twenty-one-yard field goal. But the kick bounced off the left upright with thirty-nine seconds left, and BYU had a chance to turn the tables.

Two plays later, Eric Drage slanted across the middle, caught a Walsh pass, and raced fifty-eight yards downfield. Kicker Joe Herrick trotted out, booted a forty-yard field goal, and the Cougars had escaped again.

BYU was 2–0, ranked nineteenth in the nation and already in first place in the WAC. Yet the Cougars knew their pair of three-point Houdini jobs had proven they weren't ready for the meat of the schedule. "We're way off. We're nowhere close to where we need to be," groused noseguard Lenny Gomes. The defense especially was hurting, having allowed sixty-nine points and 1,032 yards—ranking the Cougars 100th in the nation. "We haven't even slowed anybody down," said defensive tackle Randy Brock.

That's why the following two weeks were so encouraging to the Cougar faithful. First, BYU subdued Colorado State in a Fort Collins sleetstorm 27–22, thanks to seventeen first-quarter points and a late drive that ran out the clock. The Rams managed only 276 yards of offense, and only an eighty-four-yard interception return by CSU's Andre Strode made the game close.

Air Force had no such luck a week later in Cougar Stadium, managing only a first-quarter field goal in a 30–3 loss. The Falcons' wishbone offense, which often dazzles WAC defenses, couldn't match Hawaii's success of two weeks earlier, gaining just 244 yards. Meanwhile, the Cougars spent much of the afternoon celebrating records and recoveries. The backfield tandem finally performed as advertised: Jamal Willis rushed for ninety-eight yards on just eleven carries, and Kalin Hall added eighty-seven yards and a touchdown in eight attempts. And with a six-yard corner route in the second quarter, Eric Drage became BYU's career leader in touchdown catches with twenty-six. He added another TD, a forty-nine-yarder about five minutes later, then added the career-reception-yardage record with a four-yard catch in the third quarter, giving him 2,637.

That closed a difficult but rewarding first month for BYU, a stretch that put the Cougars in control of the WAC race at 4–0 and made them optimistic about their chances against some nationally ranked non-conference opposition. "We've fixed our problems," assured Walsh. "It hasn't always looked like it, but we're an awfully good football team now."

Meanwhile, the Utes by that time had sent just as many mixed signals about their ability, but they had nowhere near as much to show for it. As bad as McBride's team had looked in Tempe, it seemed unbeatable two weeks later against Kansas, with an encouraging, if difficult, victory over Utah State in between. But just when Utah fans were beginning to believe in the team's potential, three straight embarrassing losses to Wyoming, Idaho, and New Mexico demoralized them again.

"Mentally, we're obviously not a good football team," McBride fumed as the season began slipping away. "There's not much I can do if they don't want to execute."

That wasn't a problem when Utah State's Aggies visited Rice Stadium. Sure, USU quarterback Anthony Calvillo was an annoyance, since he threw eighty-yard and sixty-six-yard touchdown passes to keep the game close. But Utah emerged with the 31–29 victory thanks to Bryan Rowley, who caught seven passes, three for touchdowns, and Derek Whiddon, who recovered a fumbled punt on the Aggies' twenty-seven yard line.

The following week in Lawrence, Kansas, the Utes played like they belonged in the Big Eight, outclassing Kansas 41–16 with a near-perfect first quarter. In rolling to a 21–0 lead, Utah outgained the Jayhawks 218–4 and picked up fifteen first downs to KU's none; by halftime, the score was 31–3.

It looked like that roll would continue seven days later in Laramie, when Keith Williams atoned for his opening-night kick-returning gaffe by racing ninety-nine yards for a game-opening touchdown. But, as though they had caught a virus on the high plains, suddenly the Utes seemed to lose all football ability. Williams' footrace was the only touchdown Utah would manage the entire day in a penalty-filled 28–12 loss to Wyoming.

Relief figured to be on the way in the shape of a I-AA program, the Big Sky Conference's Idaho Vandals. McBride knew differently, fretting all week about the no-win prospect of playing down in class. While his team grew confident about playing a Big Sky team at home, the Vandals could approach the game like their own Super Bowl, their one shot at getting some attention. Costing McBride even more sleep was the Vandal offense, which came in after a week off, a breather earned by their consecutive point totals of thirty-eight, sixty-six, and fifty-six points.

Sure enough, Idaho quarterback Doug Nussmeier picked the Utes apart, piling up 416 yards of offense, including 99 from battering-ram fullback Sherriden May. A vocal contingent of Vandal fans whooped it up all night at Utah's expense, especially on third downs. Idaho converted nine of thirteen en route to the 28–17 decision.

It wasn't easy to find bright spots, but Jamal Anderson was one. The senior running back bulled through Idaho's defense for 104 yards, his first 100-yard game. But despite his eight-yards-per-carry average, Anderson was rarely given the ball inside the twenty yard line, and it was costing Utah and aggravating fans. The Utes rolled up 408 yards of offense, yet extended their frustrating streak of quarters without a touchdown to seven before finally converting a meaningless one late in the game. "We've kind of hit rock bottom here," mumbled a shell-shocked McBride.

Maybe not. Another top quarterback—New Mexico's Stoney Case—duplicated the torture a week later, tossing four touchdowns and running for another before pulling out a back-and-forth 42–35 offensive showcase. By the fourth quarter, the Utes' fatigued and injury-ravaged defense simply couldn't stop Case and the Lobos, who scored three TDs and netted nine or more yards on fourteen different plays in the period.

It got so bad, McBride had to change his offensive strategy. With the scored tied 35–35, Utah moved the ball to its own forty-three, but faced a fourth-and-one situation with four minutes left. Under normal circumstances, the Utes would have punted and hoped to pin the Lobos deep in their own territory. But McBride had so little confidence left in the defense, he chose instead to try Harold Lusk at quarterback and run an option play around the left side. It didn't work; Lusk was stopped for a one-yard loss and the Lobos were in the end zone for the game-winning score two minutes later. "They were just marching right down the field," McBride complained. "We couldn't stop anything they did."

It didn't help that an amazing rash of injuries had reduced his defense to a patchwork of walk-ons and converted offensive players. Six of Utah's opening-night starters were out with various ailments, including the top five defensive backs. Sharrieff Shah, the two-time honorable mention all-WAC defender, had to end his career after just three games of his senior season, thanks to a neck injury.

So, by early October, Utah stood 2–4 and was on a downward slide, in danger of falling apart and frustrated by a series of games they felt they should have won. The Cougars, meanwhile, were 4–0, eager for a shot at some national exposure and energized by a series of games they knew they had somehow pulled out with grit and determination.

Who could explain, then, why both programs suddenly pivoted and went in the opposite direction? Certainly Utah was better than its record made it appear, and the Cougars probably weren't as good as their unblemished mark suggested. Still, neither suspicion led anybody to expect the Utes to plow through their remaining six regular-season games at 5–1, and the Cougars to inexplicably stumble to a 2–5 finish.

Certainly BYU fans didn't expect the 68–14 humiliation inflicted in the Rose Bowl by UCLA, a drubbing that snuffed any hopes of moving higher than nineteenth in the national rankings. It was a homecoming for Cougar quarterback John Walsh, a Southern California schoolboy, but an awfully rude welcome. Walsh was sacked ten times, fumbled twice, threw three interceptions and watched as two of them were returned for touchdowns. It was the worst loss in Cougar history, the most points ever surrendered by BYU and the team's most lopsided first half (40–7). At least it was a road game. The record for worst BYU loss ever in renovated Cougar Stadium didn't come until the following week.

If nothing else, the disaster gave BYU a benchmark to compare Notre Dame to. Unfortunately for the Cougars, the third-ranked Irish rose to the occasion with a 45–20 battering that made the stadium record crowd of 66,247 appreciate the hospitable WAC a whole lot more. "They didn't disappoint a bit," admired Edwards after watching Notre Dame hammer his defense for 525 yards, 307 of them on the ground, score on its first four possessions, and lead 31–7 at halftime. BYU managed just 235 yards and lost Walsh to a knee injury early in the game. Tom Young and Steve Clements did well in mop-up roles, but the disappointed Cougars knew they were outclassed.

They didn't expect the blowout hangover to last another week, but Fresno State shocked Cougar Stadium with a 48–45 upset that may have been the biggest win in Bulldog history. Walsh limped off the bench late in the first half to spark a BYU rally after his understudies failed to impress, but the Cougars had no answer for FSU quarterback Trent Dilfer, who kept showing off amazing marksmanship with four touchdown passes. Dilfer and the Bulldogs built a 34–17 lead, then held off BYU despite Walsh's five TD passes. "We got it going. We were a real steamroller," said Eric Drage, who caught ten passes for 232 yards. "Unfortunately, they had a bigger steamroller."

The Cougars didn't realize Utah State had a steamroller, too, but the Aggies used several the following Saturday—including one that broke five of Drage's ribs and put him on the shelf for a month. The biggest one, though, was a quarterback named Anthony Calvillo, who engineered a 58–56 stunner over the disbelieving Cougars. With his accurate arm and elusive running ability, Calvillo accounted for 537 of USU's 654 yards of offense himself. More importantly, he kept the Aggies poised and focused as BYU itself kept scoring. Utah State hadn't beaten BYU in eleven years, hadn't even come within three touchdowns in a decade, but Calvillo kept connecting on long passes and holding off the Cougars. Still, Tyler Anderson returned a kickoff 100 yards for a score, and Jamal Willis made an incredible one-handed catch for a seventy-two-yard TD. And when BYU rallied to within 51–49 after once trailing 44–28, and then recovered an onside kick, it seemed like only a matter of time till the Aggies folded. But a penalty nullified the kick, and Calvillo directed one more scoring drive to kill BYU's chances. Walsh broke Ty Detmer's school record by passing for 619 yards, but he hardly cared. BYU's record was a disappointing 4–4, and Walsh and his teammates were in shock.

October 1993 had become the worst month of Edwards's long career, with four losses, the school's longest skid in twenty years, and 219 points and 2,314 yards allowed. "It's been a long time since we've been in this kind of situation. Certainly it's been very hard," conceded Edwards. "The key now is what we do to turn it around."

What they did was go back to the formula that had worked in September—get a lead and some luck. It worked in San Diego, where the Cougars escaped with a 45–44 season-salvaging victory. BYU allowed a 45–31 fourth-quarter lead to slip away, thanks especially to Aztec linebacker Shawn Smith's interception with three minutes to go. SDSU quarterback Tim Gutierrez tossed an eight-yard touchdown pass five plays later, and the Aztecs were within one. They decided to go for two points and the victory, but defensive end Randy Brock nearly sacked Gutierrez, who scrambled away and then fumbled. He recovered the ball but was stopped short of the goal. Suddenly, the Cougars had righted themselves and stayed in the WAC race. They were shaky but alive as they awaited Utah's arrival in Provo.

The Utes by then were a totally different team as well, far more competent and confident than the bunch that stumbled through the season's first half. Who would ever imagine that a victory over perennial doormat UTEP could be such effective tonic? That's what sparked Utah's revival, however, a 45–29 beating of the Miners behind increasingly effective fullback Jamal Anderson, who collected 117 yards on just thirteen carries. Bryan Rowley had 101 yards on six catches, one a historic one. Early in the second quarter, as Mike McCoy scrambled out of the way of UTEP linebacker Barron Wortham, he spotted Rowley alone in the right corner of the end zone. One nifty fifteen-yard pass later, and Rowley was in the record book.

Far more important to the Utes, however, was putting themselves back in the win column. "Today we showed some life," said a relieved McBride.

He wasn't so sure a week later, when Colorado State, featuring the WAC's least-effective offense, took a 21–10 lead by reeling off seventy-plus-yard drives on each of its first three possessions. After the third score, the coach called his defense together and let them have it. "There was some screaming," said tackle Blaine Berger. It worked. The Rams' remaining six series that day ended with two punts, two Ernest Boyd interceptions, and two fumbles. McCoy, meanwhile, was sensational, throwing for 377 yards, 132 of them to Deron Claiborne, and directing the 38–21 win. So effective was McCoy's offense that Utah never punted.

The scoring machine kept rolling a week later when San Diego State visited, but the defense went back into its funk. The two teams traded scores on eight consecutive possessions in the second half, until DeAndre Maxwell caught a pop-up in the corner with a minute to go, putting the Aztecs ahead 41–38. But Utah, already enjoying stellar days from Anderson (158 yards and three touchdowns), McCoy (389 passing yards), and slotback Henry Lusk (166 yards including an 87-yard TD romp), was hardly dead. McCoy marched into the huddle and announced to his teammates that they were going to win. He connected with Lusk for twenty-two yards, then to Claiborne along the sideline for eleven more. Finally, with fourteen seconds remaining and the ball at SDSU's seventeen yard line, McCoy called a slant pass to Greg Hooks. As they walked to the line of scrimmage, both quarterback and receiver realized the Aztecs were putting only one defender on Hooks. They looked at each other and smiled, then connected over the middle for the game-winning touchdown. Utah 45, San Diego State 41, and the Utes were on a three-game roll.

They were also running out of gas, and defensive backs. Utah traveled to Hawaii the following week, with running backs, kickers, and linebackers working out in the secondary, where the injury toll had reached eight. By the second half in Honolulu, the Rainbows had figured out how to take advantage of Utah's inexperienced secondary, and Hawaii rattled off twenty-seven points for a 41–30 momentum-halting win. Too bad, since McCoy exploded for 470 passing yards by hitting eight different receivers.

McCoy repeated the performance with 459 yards seven days later, and this time it was enough for a win, 41–24 over Air Force. It didn't hurt that Jamal Anderson capped his Rice Stadium career with another bravura performance—145 yards and three touchdowns on the ground with another fifty yards and a score through the air. It was a standard performance for the offensive stars; far more surprising was the creditable job that running back Keith Williams did as a converted cornerback, making nine unassisted tackles and recovering an AFA fumble. The defense as a whole stiffened after allowing the Falcons' wishbone offense to execute a pair of extended scoring drives. "We were at the edge of falling into a pit," said defensive tackle Blaine Berger. "We get so frustrated trying to figure out answers. We couldn't let it happen again, so we walked out there and something clicked. This time there were answers. We reined in the horses."

That left Utah at a surprising 6–5, the first time in more than forty years the Utes had won six games in three consecutive seasons. But it was hardly enough for McBride's recharged troops. The Copper and Freedom Bowls had sent word that a 7–5 Utah team might earn an invitation to the postseason. The Cougars, meanwhile, were 5–1 in conference and still a title contender. Their midseason follies behind them, Edwards's gang believed beating Utah would restore the luster on a tarnished season.

Certainly history was on BYU's side, since the Utes hadn't escaped Provo with a victory since 1971, before Edwards took over as head coach. And despite its 5–4 record, BYU was red-hot offensively, with 146 points and fifteen passing touch-downs in its previous three games. With Utah still taking volunteers in its secondary, the idea that the Cougars would amass anything fewer than forty-five or so points seemed far-fetched.

Of course, the Utes knew a little bit about moving the ball too, and they showed it right from the start. On the game's fourth play, Anderson took a screen pass and turned upfield through an overmatched BYU secondary; by the time he was finally gang-tackled, he had gained forty-seven yards to the BYU six. Two plays later, Bryan Rowley broke Utah's career touchdown-reception record by catching a four-yard floater for his twenty-fifth score.

The Cougars responded by marching inside Utah's twenty but had to settle for a Joe Herrick field goal. Both teams then mounted long drives—the Utes capped an eighty-yard effort with another pass to Anderson, and the Cougars reached the end zone on a four-yard bullet to Bryce Doman—but were stymied on other scoring opportunities. Walsh threw interceptions into the gimpy Utah secondary (he had a career-worst five on that day), where cornerbacks Mark Swanson and Ernest Boyd were playing in pain. Both had been declared out for the season, Swanson with a shoulder injury and Boyd after knee surgery, but neither could stand to miss his shot at the Cougars. Their return allowed freshman Harold Lusk to move to safety, a position he would hold for the next three seasons.

The Utes, meanwhile, were moving the ball with ease—by halftime, Anderson had 86 rushing yards and McCoy had 270 through the air—but bad luck was keeping points off the board. In one case, the Utes removed three points themselves, when Chris Yergensen booted a 36-yard field goal, but BYU was flagged for being offsides. The Utes accepted the penalty, took the ball on BYU's thirteen yard line, and tried a plunge into the line on fourth-and-one. Anderson was stood up by the center of the Cougar line, and the Cougars took over. On Utah's next drive, Pierre Jones sprinted around the left side for a first down inside BYU's ten, but a holding penalty moved the Utes back and they had to settle for a field goal.

With less than a minute to go before halftime, Utah was handed an opportunity by its defense: John Walsh was sacked and on the following play hurried a pass that was picked-off by Lusk. McCoy threw three quick passes to move the Utes to BYU's twenty but then was sacked himself and fumbled the ball, away. Freshman Andrew Nash fell on the ball and the half ended with Utah in front 17–10.

Utah's missed opportunities loomed critical in the second half, when BYU turned to its running game and tied the score on a Walsh one-yard sneak. Utah countered by pulling off a trick play when Bryan Rowley, handed the ball on a reverse, tossed a strike to Deron Claiborne twenty-eight yards downfield. But when the drive stalled, Yergensen missed a chip-shot field goal—his second miss of the day.

The teams traded interceptions to close out the third quarter and entered the final period tied. But only briefly. From the shotgun at his own sixteen, McCoy recognized BYU's blitz as he called signals. He called an audible for more protection and braced himself for the onslaught. When the snap came, and BYU's safeties with it, McCoy didn't have time to even grip the ball correctly. He just shoveled the pass forward in the direction of wideout Curtis Marsh, an underachiever who had more drops than catches his junior season. "I saw there was no free safety in the middle, so I just caught it and threw it," said McCoy. "We had five blockers and they had six guys coming, so I had to get rid of it." Marsh caught the ball in stride, cut left to the sideline, and raced untouched to the end zone for a dramatic touchdown that silenced the 65,000 Cougar fans.

Yergensen, who had already missed chip-shot field goals wide right and wide left, drilled the PAT into the crossbar, a significant omen for a kicker who was still frequently reminded of his Copper Bowl letdown. And when Tim Nowatzke returned the kickoff forty yards to the Cougar forty-eight, BYU seized the opening. Nine plays later, Kalin Hall bulled four yards into the end zone, and BYU had its first lead at 24–23.

Suddenly, both offenses were in full stride, the mistakes eliminated and the defenses in full retreat. Utah gained eight yards or more on four of its next five plays and ate up nearly six minutes with an eighty-yard drive capped by a four-yard pitchout to Jamal Anderson. The Utes added a two-point conversion, then watched as Walsh threw completions of fourteen, nineteen, and thirty yards. In less than ninety seconds, the game was tied again, thanks to another Walsh one-yard plunge.

Mixing short passes and Anderson runs, Utah headed back downfield, hoping to run off the game's final four minutes and set up a decisive score. The Utes picked up three first downs, but the Cougar pass coverage finally stiffened at its own thirty-seven. McCoy tried three different receivers running three different routes, but none connected. With thirty seconds left, McBride had no choice but to turn to his much-maligned kicker, who had never connected from such a distance. Yergensen aimed at the right upright, figuring his boot would hook left.

It did. The kick split the uprights with plenty to spare, and Utah's sideline erupted, enveloping Yergensen with hugs of celebration for a change, not consolation. A twenty-two-year drought ended with one memorable field goal.

Walsh tried to rally the distraught Cougars, but three straight passes fell incomplete, and Mark Swanson intercepted BYU's final desperation heave, sparking a wild victory party by the visitors. McBride was mobbed by his players and tackled by jubilant fans. The bash turned ugly for a few minutes when Cougar players, headed to their locker room on the other side of the field, noticed some Utes trying to pull down the goalposts. They put their helmets back on and rushed over to prevent such an insult on their home field. There was some shoving and woofing, but order was soon restored because the Utes wanted to bask in their achievement, not fight over it.

The Cougars were enraged nonetheless; even the usually taciturn Edwards was annoyed. "I don't think I've ever seen that, tearing down somebody else's goalposts," he said. "Beyond that, I'm not going to comment." The players were less reserved. "That was the worst exhibition by a winning team I've ever seen in my life," fumed receiver Bryce Doman. "It'll be good motivation for next year, I'll tell you that."

The Utes said they were merely caught up in the euphoria of such a meaningful victory. "We were just excited. That's over twenty years of frustration," said Bryan Rowley, who exclaimed that he was glad he had broken his leg a year earlier just so he would still be around to enjoy the moment. "To beat the Y down here, it's the greatest feeling ever."

Same thing for tight end Kurt Haws, once recruited by BYU but left without a scholarship when he returned from an LDS Church mission, and Taylorsville native Lance Scott, who developed a hatred for the Cougars as a child. "I accomplished a lot of things in my life today, a lot of things I've dreamed of," Scott said.

McBride went even further. "This is the biggest win of my life. This is our finest hour," he said in a hoarse voice. "I don't condone tearing down the goalposts at an opposing field, but I can't describe the emotions of something like this. It's unbelievable." The coach said he had built up some long-standing animosity toward the Brigham Young program over the years, beginning in 1977, his first year as a Ute assistant. The Cougars routed Utah 38–8 and BYU quarterback Marc Wilson reentered the game late to set an NCAA passing record. "That's my first recollection of BYU," he said. "I remember all those little things; they stick with you. They've been building up for a lot of years."

The Cougars had to regroup quickly, because they had an unusual post-Utah regular-season game remaining with 1–10 UTEP. And because of a series of upsets around the conference, BYU still could go to the Holiday Bowl as WAC co-champion with a victory. That made it much easier to focus, and sure enough, the Cougars stomped the Miners 47–16.

Despite a 6–5 record, their worst in twenty years, BYU had tied Fresno State and Wyoming for the WAC title, and the tie-breaker worked in their favor. That was all that mattered to Edwards. "A month ago, I told the players they weren't going to remember the games we lost, just the championship we won," the coach said after getting the news that his team would face 9–1–1 Ohio State in the Holiday Bowl.

The Utes got some welcome news too when the Freedom Bowl invited them to make their second straight postseason appearance, against 7–5 Southern Cal. As excited as Utah was about the matchup, the Trojans were equally unenthused. They had lost to Fresno State in the previous season's Freedom Bowl, and their athletic director complained that "playing a WAC team is a no-win proposition for us."

Especially one that had turned itself around so completely at midseason. From its 2–4 low point, the Utes suddenly became unstoppable. After averaging just 22.7 points in the first half of the season, the Utes never scored fewer than 30 in their next six games. And after gaining 450 yards just once in the first six games, they averaged 581 in their final six. "What I love about this team is how they took adversity and made something out of it. That's what I'll always remember," said McBride.

They ran into adversity early on in the Freedom Bowl, a game that resembled their season in miniature. A terrific second half nearly offset the Utes' first-half nightmare—how's that for an eerie parallel?—but Utah couldn't quite catch the Trojans after spotting them twenty-eight points. USC receiver Johnnie Morton earned the game's MVP honors with a seven-catch, two-touchdown half. But after their fourth quick score early in the second quarter, the Trojans could no longer reach the end zone. Utah realized the USC passing attack was similar to a typical WAC offense and made adjustments. "Once we realized we were as good as they are, we started playing football," said McBride.

First, Mike McCoy hit Henry Lusk with a short pass and watched him break three tackles for a fifty-nine-yard score. On its next series, Utah let Jamal Anderson handle matters, first with a twenty-yard reception and then a thirty-four-yard burst to the end zone on a pitchout. In the fourth quarter, Utah converted a fourth-and-ten with a pass to Lusk and reached the end zone for the third time. But the Trojans ran out the clock to protect their difficult victory. "I was impressed they could come back like that," said USC coach John Robinson. "A lot of teams would have quit."

There was no quit in the Cougars down the coast in a Holiday Bowl played at the same time as the Freedom Bowl. Trouble was, there was no execution when it mattered most, either. BYU drove deep into Buckeye territory three times in the fourth quarter but couldn't summon its Holiday Bowl magic this time. Tailback Raymont Harris was carrying the eleventh-ranked Buckeyes, bulldozing his way to a 235-yard, three-touchdown night. The Cougars rallied to 21–21 by halftime, but a scoreless second half doomed them to a bowl loss by the same 28–21 score that Utah suffered just 100 miles to the north.

Even the Cougars couldn't believe they had lost after John Walsh hit Eric Drage with a fifty-two-yard bomb in the final minute, moving the ball to OSU's six yard line. But four straight incompletions ended the threat and frustrated the BYU underdogs. "We played better, but they scored more points," said noseguard Lenny Gomes. "If we execute at crucial times, we win."

"We're probably the best 6–6 team in the country," said guard Evan Pilgrim, looking for a positive spin. "But I guess that's not saying much."

There was plenty of anticipation in Salt Lake City and Provo as the 1994 football season approached, but there was a growing apprehension too. Both teams figured they had enough talent to rule the WAC, but neither was certain that talent would be enough.

The doubts were especially acute at Cougar Stadium, where LaVell Edwards's squad was coming off its worst season in twenty years. As long as Brigham Young was dominating the WAC, nobody doubted Edwards's coaching ability. But a season that included several embarrassing losses sparked a host of cheap-seat whispers and talk-show rumblings: Is the coach getting too old? Is BYU's football program slipping? "That's ridiculous," snapped assistant coach Norm Chow on one radio-show appearance. "We played some good teams and had some difficult injuries. It has nothing to do with the coach's age."

Edwards was taking steps to shore up his team's generous defense by recruiting nineteen players to that side of the ball. And the coaching staff was excited about John Walsh's junior season, when he was expected to carve out a permanent place in the school's pantheon of quarterbacks. "He's as good as any of them," Chow said, "and he has a chance to be better than a lot of them." The local and national media seemed to buy it, making the Cougars the preseason favorite in the WAC. The *USA Today* coaches' poll put BYU at twentieth in the nation.

Up north, fans were buzzing over another impressive ranking: *Sports Illustrated* made Utah the twentieth-ranked team in its preseason top twenty-five, citing its arsenal of offensive weapons and its veteran defensive line. "I don't think I've ever seen expectations as high among the fans," said assistant coach Fred Graves.

That sort of talk made Ron McBride nervous. "Publicity is like poison. If you swallow it, you're in trouble," the coach preached to his team. "It looks like we've got talent, but who knows?" As if to prove his point, the Utes' luck turned bad just ten days before opening night, when do-everything senior Henry Lusk took a hit just under his shoulder pads during Utah's final scrimmage and broke his left shoulder blade. The collision left a scary dent in his pads and a scarier void in Utah's offense.

Lusk, who "cried and cried when doctors told me the news," was the Utes' best and most versatile athlete, and the focal point of the team's offense. The team's Freedom Bowl MVP the previous December, Lusk played fullback, slotback, and tight end at various times and was Utah's kickoff returner as well.

"It's a huge blow," said quarterback Mike McCoy, who lost one of his most reliable receivers. "He is a guy who never gets brought down by the first hit."

But neither were the Utes. After dedicating the season to their fallen teammate, they proceeded to march through the first month unblemished—seemingly untested. No September opponent could crack 100 rushing yards or 300 total yards. Utah set the tone by stuffing Utah State 32–17 in the season opener, allowing the Aggies only six first downs and thirty-nine rushing yards.

That was followed by a Rice Stadium revenge game against Idaho State. With the memory of the previous year's humiliating loss to Idaho made fresh in their minds by McBride, the Utes didn't even give the Bengals time to point out that they weren't the Vandals before suffering a 66–0 thrashing. It was vengeance for assistant coach Kyle Whittingham, too, since he had been Idaho State's defensive coordinator the previous year before being demoted by ISU head man Brian McNeeley. The Utes threw just six second-half passes, yet still scored forty-five points on the undermanned Bengals, including three touchdowns by freshman tailback Juan Johnson.

He kept it up the following week in Oregon, scoring on the opening drive to spark a 34–16 victory over the Ducks, an accomplishment eventually made much more dazzling when Oregon went on to become Pac–10 champions and Rose Bowl winners.

Utah followed up with a 41–7 thrashing of the WAC's best offensive squad, the Wyoming Cowboys, who managed just 217 yards, less than half their average. By the time Utah's first weekend off rolled around, McBride's crew was 4–0, ranked twenty-fifth in the national media poll—the Utes' first appearance in the national rankings since 1947—and had begun to allay the coach's preseason worries. Well, not entirely. "BYU already has three conference wins," McBride fretted in early October. "And who's going to beat Colorado State?"

Indeed, those three teams looked like the class of the league after the first month, especially after the BYU-CSU showdown in Cougar Stadium. The Cougars had opened with a pair of difficult road victories, 13–12 in Hawaii and 45–21 at Air Force, leaving Edwards with 199 career victories as he prepared for BYU's home opener.

He knew he was fortunate to be 2–0, especially after an error-filled evening in Honolulu, where the Rainbows blocked two field goals, sacked Walsh six times, and shut out BYU in the first half. But the Cougar defense, the same one that allowed WAC offenses to run wild the previous year, stuffed the Hawaii option attack, allowing just eighty-one yards in thirty-one carries. "We wanted to send a little message to the WAC," said defensive tackle Mike Ulufale. "We've got a defense this year."

They convinced the Falcons the following week, blanking Air Force in the second half while freeing halfback Jamal Willis for 151 yards and three touchdowns.

That got Cougar fans ready to celebrate Edwards's milestone; indeed, the programs for BYU's home opener slated the game as the coach's 200th victory. Which didn't sit well with the Colorado State Rams, who harassed Walsh into four interceptions, four sacks, and a fumble—and a 28–21 upset. "That insult in the program, we took that to heart," said CSU defensive end Sean Moran. "Maybe he can get it next week."

He did, though it wasn't easy. The Cougars bounced back with one of those games that makes the WAC famous, finally earning a 49–47 victory that featured forty-one fourth-quarter points. Willis again was the star, rushing for 204 yards, including a fourteen-yard fourth-down effort that killed New Mexico's comeback. The Lobos had scored two touchdowns within sixty-five seconds by pouncing on an onside kick, but couldn't pull it off twice. "It's sheer relief," said Edwards after his players doused him with Gatorade in celebration of the fourteenth coach to attain the 200-win plateau. "It's something I tried to keep out of my mind, but obviously it's a special moment."

The veteran coach had no time to savor it, though, since Utah State came to visit just six days later. But the defense that had allowed the Aggies fifty-eight points the previous year, this time stuffed USU's young offense, holding the Ags to just two field goals in a 34–6 victory. And the Cougars extended their record to 5–1, and 4–1 in the WAC, by winning their first game ever at Fresno State 32–30. It was another scary game for BYU, since the Bulldogs pulled a reverse pass for a sixty-eight-yard score on the game's first play, then added another long score on their next possession. But Walsh hit Tim Nowatzke with a fifty-eight-yard bomb on his first pass and later added a sixty-eight-yard score of his own on a short pass to tight end Itula Mili.

The afternoon was a success for the Cougars but had one shadow: on the other side of the country, Notre Dame, BYU's next opponent, was losing to Boston College, a result that worried defensive end Randy Brock. "Man, they're gonna be mad," he fretted.

If that was true, the seventeenth-ranked Irish were flat-out furious after the following Saturday's game with BYU, a fifteen-point underdog. But more likely, they were just humbled after being thoroughly beaten by the Cougars 21–14. "It's like a nightmare. It's devastating," said Notre Dame assistant Bob Davie, now the Fighting Irish head coach.

But for the Cougars, winning in front of the legendary Touchdown Jesus was quite the opposite. "There's nothing sweeter than this," said Tim Nowatzke, who grew up just forty miles from South Bend.

It started badly for BYU, which allowed a forty-one-yard touchdown run by Randy Kinder on Notre Dame's first drive, then fumbled away the kickoff on its own eleven yard line. But the Cougars' defensive line held, and Steve Schroffner missed the first of three field-goal tries, completely changing the character of the game. In the third quarter, the Irish drove to the BYU three but failed to score.

"Having success inside the twenty is a matter of toughness," said Irish running back Marc Edwards. "We were just out-toughed."

Walsh, meanwhile, ran BYU's offense with more confidence than he had all season, and Willis ran for both of the Cougar touchdowns, on a nineteen-yard romp after catching a pass and on a one-yard plunge. "That's why we come to BYU, to play and beat teams like this," Walsh said. "This is the biggest win of my career, and one of the biggest ever at BYU. We didn't come here to be in awe of anybody."

Of course, neither was UTEP one week later. The Miners took a 14–7 first-quarter lead, then rallied with fourteen fourth-quarter points to frighten the Cougars before losing 34–28. The difference was Willis, who ran for 136 yards and became BYU's all-time leading rusher by surpassing Lakei Heimuli's 2,710-yard career total. "What a clutch player he is," admired Notre Dame coach Lou Holtz. "Looking around the country, it would be hard to find a better back or a more versatile runner."

His fortunes mirrored, or perhaps dictated, his team's fortunes in a pair of non-conference games the following two weeks. Willis gained just 44 yards in a 36–15 home loss to Arizona State (though he did add a 70-yard touchdown on a lateral from Chad Lewis), then burst for 137 in a 24–10 yawner over Northeast Louisiana.

It was backfield mate Hema Heimuli's turn against San Diego State; the junior running back scored twice and picked up 115 yards in a 35–28 shootout victory featured on ESPN's "Thursday Night Football." Walsh was the real star, though, passing for 392 yards and matching Aztec quarterback Billy Blanton touchdown drive for touchdown drive. "His poise is what kept us going," credited Edwards after BYU improved to 9–2 and 6–1 in the WAC. "He wouldn't let us lose."

Thanks to another quarterback, there wasn't much losing going on in Salt Lake City either. The Utes reeled off victories over San Diego State 38–22 and Hawaii 14–3 by unleashing its offense and snuffing the opposition's. Mike McCoy passed for 361 yards and three touchdowns in San Diego, while defensive end Bronzell Miller hounded the Aztecs with three sacks and two fumble recoveries. On a rain-slickened Rice Stadium turf a week later, Utah and Hawaii remained scoreless through three quarters despite the Utes' 402 yards of offense; the defense forced the Rainbows to punt away their first eight possessions. Two late touchdowns improved Utah to 6–0 for the first time since 1953.

It also set up one of the biggest games in WAC history, between the eighteenth-ranked Utes and the twelfth-rated Colorado State Rams, also unbeaten at 7–0. The strength of the teams drew national attention to Fort Collins, with stories in the *New York Times, USA Today,* and *Sports Illustrated.* ABC decided to broadcast the game regionally.

The network got its money's worth. The WAC showdown featured sixty second-half points, five blocked kicks, and two interceptions returned for touchdowns.

CSU was able to move the ball better than any Ute opponent, racking up 460 yards. But five turnovers undid the Rams' efforts.

Midway through the fourth quarter, the game was tied 31–31. The Utes responded with a long drive that reached the end zone on McCoy's eight-yard alley-oop pass to Curtis Marsh. The Rams countered by driving sixty-eight yards to the Utah twelve with forty-four seconds remaining. But on fourth down, CSU quarterback Anthoney Hall rolled left and lofted a pass into the end zone. Utah safety Harold Lusk cut in front of CSU receiver Matt Phillips, intercepted the pass and sprinted 100 yards down the sideline for a game-clinching touchdown: 45–31.

"The pressure was incredible. Unbelievable," said a breathless McBride afterwards. "That victory was about as big as it gets in this lifetime."

"I was just hoping we'd get the ball last," laughed McCoy.

From there, Utah easily outclassed UTEP 52–7 on four Charlie Brown touchdowns and, at 8–0, moved into the top ten for the first time in school history.

Suddenly, the bad luck McBride had been expecting all season struck. With the WAC championship within their sights, the Utes jumped to a 14–0 lead over New Mexico, and went into halftime up 21–11 on the Lobos. But despite their 417 total yards, the Utes never scored again, and the defense allowed New Mexico to rally behind elusive quarterback Stoney Case. A Nathan Vail field goal with thirty-two seconds left broke hundreds of hearts in Utah and caused the Albuquerque fans to tear down their goalposts after the 23–21 upset.

The posts came down again a week later in Colorado Springs, after Air Force inflicted a similar 40–33 defeat on the suddenly reeling Utes, who this time blew a 17–0 lead. It left Utah, 8–2 and 5–2 in conference, with only slim hopes of a WAC title heading into their finale with BYU.

But as disappointed as the Utes were over squandering their perfect season, it wasn't hard to get up for The Game. Both teams were ranked in the top twenty, both still had bowl hopes—and it was Utah and BYU, after all. To show how much it meant to them, several Ute offensive linemen had the Utah logo tattooed on their arms.

The game was one of the most entertaining of the entire series, a true classic featuring six lead changes, four in the fourth quarter, and numerous big plays. The first one came ten minutes into it, when Curtis Marsh caught a slant pass and jetted past the BYU secondary, finally diving for the end zone flag for a fifty-seven-yard score.

Down 10–0, BYU struck quickly in the second quarter, scoring seventeen points in less than five minutes, one touchdown on a thirty-one-yard strike from John Walsh to Bryce Doman. Back came the Utes, who added a field goal and one final scoring drive, capped by a fifteen-yard pass to Deron Claiborne with fifteen seconds left before halftime. The Cougars regained the lead early in the third quarter on a short pass to Tim Nowatzke, and when the Utes went scoreless in the period, the Rice Stadium crowd feared a repeat of the previous two weeks' collapses.

But a great Utah punt and a bad one by BYU gave Utah terrific field position at the BYU seventeen, and it took just two plays for McCoy to find Claiborne with a short touchdown that gave the Utes a 27–24 lead with six minutes remaining. Walsh responded with what he hoped was the game-winning, eighty-yard drive, culminating in a perfectly thrown twenty-seven-yard pass to Mike Johnston that put BYU ahead again.

One problem: "We left them too much time," said offensive guard Evan Pilgrim of the 2:15 left. Sure enough, with the crowd chanting "Thirty-four thirty-one, thirty-four thirty-one," the score of the previous year's game, freshman speedster Cal Beck busted the kickoff down the right sideline—right in front of the Cougar bench—sixty-seven yards to the BYU thirty-two. "I didn't even realize how far I had gone until my teammates ran up and started jumping on me," Beck said.

After two running plays, McCoy looked for a receiver but found only tailback Charlie Brown uncovered in the left flat. McCoy tossed him the ball, then watched in amazement as Brown broke a couple of tackles and bounced into the end zone for the game-winning score.

Still, the Cougars had a minute left to work with, and Walsh completed two quick passes to move BYU to Utah's thirty-four. Edwards and his fellow coaches began debating whether kicking a field goal for a tie was good enough, or if they should go for the touchdown. But with seventeen seconds left, the decision became moot when Utah defensive end Bronzell Miller bowled over his blocker and blind-sided Walsh. Luther Elliss fell on the ball, and Utah had its second straight 34–31 win over BYU, unleashing pandemonium on the field. The goalposts came down—this time without protest from the Cougars—and Utah fans swarmed the field and their team.

"It doesn't get any better than this," yelled McBride as he hugged dozens of fans. "I don't think anyone in the state of Utah could want a better game than that."

They did in the morgue-quiet Cougar locker room. "It's the same damn story. I can handle losing to just about anybody but Utah," said Randy Brock. "This is really tough to swallow."

LaVell Edwards called it one of the worst defeats of his career. "It ranks right up there. To have a chance to win it and then not get it done, that makes it tough," the coach said.

"I'd almost trade this for the win over Notre Dame," said center Jim Edwards. "This was our most important game of the season. That's the reason we worked so hard all year—to beat Utah."

Instead, the Cougars had to settle for a 9–3 record and a second-place finish in the WAC (tied with Utah at 6–2, behind Colorado State's 7–1), which earned them a trip to the Copper Bowl to face Oklahoma. The Utes were invited to Anaheim for the second straight year and drew Arizona in the Freedom Bowl.

BYU took a five-year bowl-game losing streak to Tucson but received some good fortune when Oklahoma made coach Gary Gibbs a lame duck by firing him three weeks before the bowl game. The Sooners came into Arizona Stadium unfocused, a severe disadvantage against a Cougar team begging to take out its frustrations on somebody.

Right from the night's opening drive, when Walsh marched the Cougars seventy-seven yards in nine plays, BYU showed it meant business. Thanks to touchdown grabs by Bryce Doman and Mike Johnston, and a defense that never allowed the Sooners to cross midfield in the first half, the Cougars rolled to a 17–0 halftime advantage.

Walsh continued to apply the pressure in the second half, finishing one of his greatest games as Cougar QB with 451 yards and four touchdowns, engineering the 31–6 triumph. It turned out to be Walsh's good-bye to BYU; a month later, he announced he was skipping his senior season to turn pro.

For one night, though, he could bask in the acclaim that BYU quarterbacks have become accustomed to. "John was on fire, that's all you can say," said Johnston, marveling that Walsh completed ten of his first eleven passes. "He showed what kind of quarterback he is." And the Cougars showed what kind of team they were, finishing a season full of photo-finishes at 10–3, an emphatic answer to the whispers that Edwards and his program were slipping.

The Utes, meanwhile, were finishing the greatest season in school history with another first for McBride: a bowl victory. More impressive, it came while Utah's normally potent offense was getting stuffed by Arizona's renowned Desert Swarm defense. The Utes managed just seventy-five total yards, only six on the ground—yet upset the Wildcats 16–13.

They did it with defense, and a little luck. Tied 7–7 after three quarters, the Utes, who allowed Arizona to convert just three of thirteen third-down plays, gave up a field goal and then handed the Wildcats a huge opportunity when a McCoy pass was intercepted and returned to Utah's twenty yard line. Four plays later, the Wildcats had first-and-goal at Utah's two. But twice quarterback Dan Wilson found receivers wide open in the end zone—and twice the Arizona wideouts dropped easy passes. When the Wildcats settled for another field goal, and a 13–7 lead, the Utes had their first crucial break.

They got another one when their next drive stalled. Jason Jones's punt rolled to Arizona's one yard line, where Utah smothered it. When the Wildcats couldn't move the ball, they chose to take an intentional safety rather than risk a blocked punt. "A smart play," said McBride, but events soon proved him wrong.

Hadn't the Wildcats seen films of Cal Beck's crucial kick return against BYU?

Apparently not, because they sailed the free kick right into the freshman's arms, then let him break into the clear at midfield and race to Arizona's five yard line. With four minutes left, the Utes had a Grand Canyon-sized opportunity.

They nearly blew it. Scrambling away from an intense pass rush, McCoy threw three passes incomplete. On fourth down, the Wildcats again harassed Utah's quarterback, and defensive tackle Jim Osborne finally brought McCoy down near the right sideline. But just before being pulled to the turf, McCoy lofted a floater to the back of the end zone—and into Kevin Dyson's arms. Touchdown, Utah.

"That's the thing about this team, they keep playing and playing and something happens," said a jubilant McBride. "Mike (McCoy) made a fantastic play. I don't know how he did it, but that's the kind of player he is."

Utah's 10–2 finish convinced the nation's football pollsters, who made Utah the tenth-ranked team in their final ratings. The coaches made the Utes number eight. There was no mystery why, according to McBride. "This is the best defense I've ever coached, by far," the coach said. Led by Luther Elliss, the WAC's Defensive Player of the Year and a consensus all-American, Utah's defense led the conference in every category and finished in the top twenty in the NCAA as well, including ninth in rushing defense. "The whole team is so dedicated. They proved what hard work can accomplish," said McBride.

As great as their 1994 seasons were, both Utah and BYU could take plenty of motivation into 1995 from them—namely, a conference title.

Despite ten-win seasons, despite national rankings, and despite impressive bowl victories, both squads had to live with an annoying label: second place. That, more than anything, drove McBride, who had never won a WAC championship, and Edwards, who had won five in a row before 1994. "We left something undone and we know it," said Utah's McBride. "All those seniors aren't around to get the job done, but we have the players who can."

One in particular was Henry Lusk. The senior slotback assumed his college career had ended when his shoulder blade was broken a year earlier. But Lusk successfully petitioned the NCAA for a medical exemption, and the college football decision-makers agreed.

That didn't solve McBride's biggest puzzle, however; he still needed to choose a new quarterback to replace Mike McCoy. Brandon Jones, McCoy's backup the previous season, and walk-on Mike Fouts, nephew of the Hall of Fame quarterback Dan Fouts, made the decision difficult with up-and-down play during drills. McBride, offensive coordinator Fred Graves, and quarterback coach Tommy Lee waited until the week before Utah's season opener to pick Jones as their man.

No such uncertainty existed in Provo, where Steve Sarkisian transferred to BYU from El Camino Junior College as football's most-sought JC player. The Cougars

Rick Egan/THE SALT LAKE TRIBUNE

BYU players stepped in to prevent the Utes from tearing down the goalposts in 1993, but there was nobody to stop the delirious Utes and their fans from celebrating at Rice Stadium in 1994.

convinced Sarkisian, a non-Mormon, to move to Provo largely by assuring him of the first shot at a starting job.

Not that it took long for him to convince any skeptics. Sarkisian threw a handful of touchdown passes in BYU's spring game and sold his teammates and coaches. "He's got a great arm and is very mobile. I'm excited for him," said assistant coach Norm Chow.

The secret, said Sarkisian, was convincing himself that BYU's offense isn't the harder-than-trigonometry complexity he first believed. "I was trying to think so hard, it drove me crazy. Usually a coach will put in two plays a day and we run them; here, it was 'We're putting in these ten plays.' Then I realized these are the same plays we ran at El Camino. Everyone runs the same plays," Sarkisian said.

"The difference is, everything is so precise. We run routes, and we run them exactly like we're supposed to, and we put the ball exactly where it's supposed to go, and we do it over and over. It's really a pinpoint thing."

At least it is during practice. In the season opener, however, Sarkisian discovered that football is a little different with a motivated defense taking shots at you. The new quarterback threw for 346 yards but was intercepted twice, sacked four times, and spent much of the day scrambling away from pressures real and imagined. For the second straight season, BYU opened with a scoreless first half, but this time the

Cougars couldn't right themselves. Air Force avenged a dozen straight losses to BYU with a convincing 38–12 thrashing.

"I needed to step up in the pocket more than I did. I got antsy and stepped out instead of just sliding up," Sarkisian said.

"We looked like we were running in buckets of sand," assessed Edwards after his running game was humbled by a minus-twenty-nine-yard effort.

Sarkisian improved noticeably in his home debut a week later, but so did the quality of opposition. Twelfth-ranked UCLA had startled Miami 31–8 a week earlier, so the Bruins were confident enough to wait for BYU mistakes, then pounce. When it happened, UCLA turned a 9–3 struggle into a 23–9 scrimmage. Looking mostly for his tight ends and H-backs, Sarkisian threw for 305 yards. But he was stripped of the ball by UCLA linebacker Donnie Edwards deep in his own territory in the third quarter, and the Bruins recovered on BYU's one, then quickly scored. A couple of plays later, Sarkisian was intercepted, and UCLA added an easy thirty-yard drive for another touchdown.

"We were moving the ball both times," moaned Edwards after watching his team fall to 0–2 for just the second time in twenty years.

In Salt Lake, McBride was suffering through a new quarterback's growing pains too. The Utes opened 0–2 for the first time since 1986 by losing home games to Pac–10 opponents Oregon and Stanford by identical 27–20 scores. The Utes displayed little offense in either game under Brandon Jones, who narrowly won the starting job. Against the Ducks, Utah collected just sixty-three second-half yards; their two touchdowns were scored on a seventy-one-yard scramble by punter Dan Pulsipher after his protection broke down, and a ninety-seven-yard interception return by freshman safety Brandon Dart. "Our offense was obviously nonexistent," McBride complained.

Same thing in week two, when Jones completed just eight of nineteen passes for 109 yards, nearly half of them on a short pass that new receiver Rocky Henry turned into a forty-four-yard gain. The Utes rallied on two big plays: Harold Lusk intercepted a pass and returned it to the Cardinal four, and Cal Beck blocked a Stanford punt.

In the fourth quarter, McBride turned to Mike Fouts, who nearly pulled out a game-winning drive. But when he arrived at Stanford's three yard line, Fouts tried a dump pass to a well-covered Henry Lusk. The toss was picked off at the goal-line, and the Cardinal win was secure.

Fouts had been unimpressive until his final drive, completing only four of thirteen passes. But he had provided enough energy to convince McBride, who made Fouts his starter a week later, a job the quarterback never relinquished in two seasons.

He certainly had an auspicious debut, throwing four touchdown passes and regularly escaping pressure to make big plays and direct Utah's 36–9 bombing of New Mexico. "Fouts was awesome. He made a lot of plays," said McBride after his offense rolled up 508 yards, more than its combined total from its first two games.

So what's better than "awesome"? Whatever it is, that's what Fouts was a week later, when he directed a fourth-quarter comeback that stunned Fresno State and handed the Bulldogs their first loss 25–21. After a floundering start that left Utah down 21–10 after three quarters, Fouts directed a drive that arrived at the end zone (on freshman battering ram Chris Fuamatu-Ma'afala's three-yard run) with just 2:09 left. The Utah defense held Fresno State three-and-out, and with just forty-seven seconds remaining, Fouts found Rocky Henry streaking toward the goal line and hit him with a thirty-four-yard game-winning pass. "He looked like a ten-year veteran in that fourth quarter," McBride said. "He looked like Dan Fouts out there."

That figures, since Fuamatu-Ma'afala looked like a Hawaiian Earl Campbell as September closed with a 34–21 win at Texas-El Paso. The 270-pound teenager had 130 yards, including 78 in a fourth quarter where would-be tacklers looked more like bowling pins. On one drive, Fuamatu-Ma'afala carried the ball on all four plays: gains of five, thirteen, twenty-five, and fourteen yards for a touchdown.

The win left Utah 3–2 and at 3–0 atop the WAC, but McBride was uneasy. All five games were filled with mistakes and turnovers. "We're playing terrible, terrible," McBride said. "We can't keep playing like this and expect to win." As if on cue, San Diego State and Colorado State took advantage the following two weeks in Rice Stadium, pulling out narrow victories (24–21 for the Aztecs and 19–14 for the Rams) thanks in large part to Utah turnovers (seven in the two games).

That San Diego State-Colorado State tandem of games hadn't been nearly as hard on the Cougars in September, mostly because it was the Aztecs and Rams making the fatal mistakes against BYU. San Diego State's biggest error, one that BYU opponents quickly learned to avoid, was kicking the ball to James Dye, a speedy transfer from Utah State. Four minutes into the game at Cougar Stadium, Aztec punter Neal Prefontaine got off what he believed was a pretty nice kick. But Dye settled under it fifty-three yards downfield, broke three tackles, and flashed into the middle of the field for an eighty-four-yard touchdown romp.

That was the Cougars' only touchdown in the first three quarters, and they entered the final period trailing 12–10. Because of a laundry mistake, the Cougars were wearing all blue uniforms for the first time ever, and concern was growing that the break with tradition had hexed the home team. But an eighty-yard drive restored order, and cornerback Tim McTyer added a sixty-yard interception return to insure BYU's 31–19 win.

Colorado State's biggest mistake was trying to run on the Cougars' defensive front; the Rams gained only fourteen yards on the ground. The Cougars, even playing without tight end Itula Mili and defensive tackle Mike Ulufale, who had been suspended four games for honor-code violations, dominated the defending conference champions, holding the ball nearly thirty-eight minutes and scoring twenty-eight straight points en route to a 28–21 win that moved BYU within a game of first-place Utah.

Maybe the Cougars were saving up their mistakes for Arizona State, because they committed enough infractions (109 yards of penalties) and ill-timed turnovers (five) to turn what looked like an impressive road victory into a stunning 29–21 loss in Tempe, Arizona. When Mike Johnston caught a twenty-three-yard touchdown pass in the third quarter, BYU had a 21–13 advantage and plenty of momentum. The Sun Devils fought back, marching to BYU's one, but ASU tailback Terry Battle was stonewalled by linebacker Stan Raass on fourth down, seemingly dooming the Devils. Instead, Sarkisian fumbled the ball on the next play; ASU quickly scored to pull within two points at 21–19. The Sun Devils' next possession went nowhere, but a roughing-the-punter penalty on nickelback Ben Cook kept their drive alive so quarterback Jake Plummer could throw a forty-seven-yard pass off BYU safety Eddie Sampson's helmet, setting up the go-ahead score. A last-ditch drive resulted only in an interception and a clinching score for ASU. "It was a major disappointment," said Edwards. "We played well enough to win, but we shot ourselves in the foot so many times."

Still, the Cougars could console themselves with the fact that it didn't count in the WAC standings, where BYU had moved in front of Utah and held the inside track to a title—as usual. What was odd was how they were doing it: by scoring with defense and special teams, and just enough offense to win. Case in point was against Wyoming, when three field goals, a ninety-yard punt return by Dye, and just one touchdown drive was too much for the Cowboys. "We're just not very good," said assistant coach Norm Chow. "We're very ordinary at the skill level." Yet the Cougars were 3–1 and in first place in the WAC.

The offense must have been offended by Chow's remarks, because BYU suddenly became a yardage machine, rolling up more than 480 yards each of the next three weeks in consecutive blowouts of Hawaii 45–7, Tulsa 45–35, and New Mexico 31–14. Heading into The Game with Utah, the Cougars stood 6–3 and extremely confident.

But the Utes, too, had turned their season around, and they could pinpoint the precise moment when it had happened. With 1:49 left in their Rice Stadium match with Air Force, trailing the Falcons 21–7, the Utes suddenly grabbed their own mediocrity by the throat. The result was an absurd, inconceivable, preposterous 22–21 victory that required merely a resolute defensive effort, a series of wildly propitious bounces, and the sudden, improbable resuscitation of an offense in hibernation. Oh, and fifteen points in the final forty-one seconds.

"We were dead in the fourth quarter. . . . We were done. This is storybook stuff," said a dazed Ron McBride after Kevin Dyson's forty-five-yard touchdown catch capped the blitzkrieg rally that was immortalized the following fall in *Sports Illustrated.* "You've gotta believe. While there's life and breath, there's still a chance."

The coach would have gotten an argument when Mike Fouts was blindsided and fumbled the ball away with 6:11 left. Air Force ran the clock down to 1:49 before punting. Suddenly, the Utes' offense awoke with a start and a ferocity. Fouts completed three huge passes, one a fifty-four-yard bomb to Terence Keehan and another a seventeen-yard touchdown to Rocky Henry. The Utes added a two-point conversion using its scattered-line "Duck" formation, and then Dan Pulsipher drilled a perfect onside kick into the ribs of AFA fullback Nakia Addison, who couldn't handle the knuckleball. Artis Jackson smothered the ball for Utah. In the huddle, Fouts told Kevin Dyson to "get on your horse," and Dyson responded by getting seven yards in front of cornerback Kelvin King. Fouts hit Dyson in stride for a forty-five-yard touchdown, Rice Stadium exploded, and the Falcons were left choked up in tears over their blown title hopes.

No such problem for Utah, which dominated Utah State 40–20, thanks to Fuamatu-Ma'afala's 180-yard performance, and then handled Wyoming 30–24, thanks to an offense that held the ball for nearly forty-five minutes.

Utah's three-game winning streak left the Utes at 5–2 in the WAC, tied with San Diego State and Colorado State and behind only BYU at 5–1. That set up a historic day for the bitter rivals, the first time in WAC history that the winner of the Wasatch Front grudge match was assured a share of the conference title. That, both sides contended, was more important than any silly little rivalry.

Or so they said. But the Cougars had been grumbling about Utah's back-to-back 34–31 victories all year, especially over what they perceived as Ute fans'—and some players'—eagerness to gloat. "They're a classless bunch all around," one player loudly reminded his teammates at BYU's final practice, describing the scene two years previous when Utah players tried to tear down the Cougar Stadium goalposts.

And for their part, the Utes resented BYU's insistence that Utah's breakthrough wins had been flukes, pulled out with lucky last-minute plays. "They said we couldn't do it again, but we did. But now they still say it," groused safety Harold Lusk. "When will they be convinced?"

Sarkisian, new to the rivalry, was convinced right from the first series. The BYU quarterback completed his first pass for twenty-one yards, on an out pattern to Tom Baldwin, but spent the next three plays scrambling away from a fired-up Ute pass rush. Finally, he threw deep, but Henry Lusk stepped up and intercepted at the twelve. "They were quicker than I expected," Sarkisian credited. "I ran a lot."

Utah moved sixty-five yards and ran thirteen plays but ended up punting, as did the Cougars. The Utes ended the first quarter by marching into BYU territory on nine plays, most of them handoffs to Fuamatu-Ma'afala. On the first play of the second quarter, the freshman put on one of his bowling-ball displays, bounding through the line and into the end zone thirty-two yards away for a touchdown.

The drive surprised the Cougars, who had expected their size to slow the fabulous freshman. But Fuamatu-Ma'afala often seemed barely to notice. "There's no question he had a major impact," Edwards shrugged. "We thought we could neutralize him."

A celebration penalty gave BYU the ensuing kickoff at midfield, and the Cougars ran six quick plays before posting a Bill Hansen field goal. Utah responded with a field-goal drive of its own, but with a difference. While BYU's drive took just two minutes, the Utes held the ball five and a half minutes. Same thing when the Cougars got the ball back—Sarkisian was intercepted by Armond Boglin on the third play, then Fouts kept the ball more than three minutes before Pulsipher chalked up another field goal to make the halftime score 13–3 Utah.

"Once we put the doubts in their minds, we wanted to finish them off quick," said McBride. "Opening the second half with a score was big." Indeed, the Utes moved seventy-nine yards in eleven plays, mixing up Fuamatu-Ma'afala gallops with Fouts laser passes, until the quarterback found Keehan streaking down the right sideline for a twenty-seven-yard score.

BYU moved just seventeen yards before punting away its next possession, and the Utes, now on an unstoppable roll, marched sixty-one yards for another touchdown, this time a four-yard dump pass to Henry Lusk. With a minute left in the third quarter, it was 27–3 Utah, and the Cougars were goners.

The Utes were dominating the line of scrimmage, running up 445 yards and hogging the ball for a stupefying 40:47. Defensively, Utah shut off BYU's running attack, allowing only 50 yards on the ground. For the first time in years, the Cougars were not the superior team physically. "That was a big surprise," Edwards conceded. "That was where I thought we would step up. But they just ran over us."

The Utes tacked on a fourth-quarter touchdown, mostly because on fourth-and-twelve, Fouts hit Dyson with a thirty-one-yard gain. Fuamatu-Ma'afala punched in the six-yard score two plays later. Appropriate, since the two Ute newcomers had had a tremendous effect on the contest. Fuamatu-Ma'afala finished with 108 yards on twenty-four carries. And Fouts, clearly the better JC quarterback on this day, completed twenty-one of thirty-one passes for 275 yards.

The Cougars added two late scores, including an eighteen-yard pass to Hema Heimuli in the final seconds, to make the final a respectable 34–17. But the game was never that close, and the Utes, by now used to beating BYU, barely celebrated the moment. They loped off the field, more jubilant over their first conference co-championship in thirty years than the beating they inflicted on their rival.

"I never thought it would be like this," said Henry Lusk of the lopsided win. "I

Rick Egan/THE SALT LAKE TRIBUNE

By the end of Utah's third straight victory over BYU, Cougar fans Shane Nielsen, Lance Greener, and Danny Fugais had lost a lot of their enthusiasm.

said all along it would be a dogfight. This just showed who really wanted it." The Utes converted an astonishing fifteen of twenty-two third downs and were three for three on fourth down.

"I can't describe the horror I feel," said Cougar Hema Heimuli.

The Utes were able to relax and contemplate their bowl chances after finishing with four straight wins, a 7–4 record, and a portion of the title. But the Cougars had to regroup for one more game, a visit to Fresno State, that could still earn BYU a share of the WAC title.

Sarkisian, upset over his four-interception performance against Utah, made sure of it. The quarterback set an NCAA record by completing 91.2 percent of his passes, thirty-one of thirty-four, for 399 yards and three touchdowns. He also ran for another score in the Cougars' 45–28 rout of the Bulldogs. FSU coach Jim Sweeney had tried to recruit Sarkisian but said this passing machine was far superior to the JC quarterback he remembered. "Sarkisian is awesome. He does so much more now," Sweeney marveled.

Sweeney's Bulldogs provided the motivation, too. FSU linebacker Chris Love once hopped offsides and leveled Sarkisian, who was still calling signals. "I got a little pissed off when that guy hit me," said Sarkisian. "I guess I play better that way."

The victory also left BYU at 6–2 in the conference, 7–4 overall, and in a four-way tie with Utah, Colorado State, and Air Force. Under the WAC's tie-breaking rules, CSU received the automatic invitation to the Holiday Bowl. The Copper Bowl soon decided on Air Force over Utah, in what executive director Larry Brown called "an agonizing decision."

That left Utah and Brigham Young, both teams having finished the season impressively, with nowhere to go. Snubbed by the bowls, their seasons were abruptly and unceremoniously ended.

To the Utes and Ron McBride, still celebrating their title, it was a bitter disappointment. "We were the best team in the conference at the end," emphasized McBride, itching to hold some extra bowl practices. Still, he said, "there wasn't anybody sitting around feeling sorry for ourselves, that's for sure."

Same with Edwards and the Cougars, even though a December at home meant their streak of seventeen straight bowl games was ended. "We'll just have to start another streak," harumphed the coach. He cheered himself with the co-championship, his seventeenth as coach. "From that standpoint, I feel pretty good about the season."

But one thing nagged at Edwards, kept barging into his thoughts every day: He had lost to Utah. Again. And again. "It's so hard to explain," winced LaVell Edwards. "Hard to live with, too."

The Biggest Game

This is tough. Like when you've gone into the candy shop and are confronted with caramel squares, lemon drops, red-hots, orange slices, Tootsie Rolls, M&Ms, gummy-bears, and licorice bits. Which scintillating BYU win over Utah do I choose?

In fact there is even a loss to consider—the 1953 nationally televised game when, after BYU lost 33–32 in Ute Stadium, the losing Cougar players carried coach Chick Atkinson off the field on their shoulders.

Or, there was the 1958 game in which the Cougars, with quarterback Wayne Startin passing and tailback Weldon Jackson running, rallied to whip the Uteskis 14–7 in Salt Lake City to snap an eleven-game losing streak in the rivalry and earn BYU only its second rivalry win of all time.

Or, there was 1965 when the Cougars unleashed Virgil Carter, who passed the defending Liberty Bowl-champion Uteskis into submission 25–20 and set the stage for BYU's first championship in forty-one years of football.

Or, there was 1972 when a forty-two-year-old rookie head coach named LaVell Edwards brought his underdog Cougars into Ute Stadium where Pete VanValkenburg, who grew up in the shadow of the Ute goalposts at Hillcrest High, ran for a school record thirty-seven times in the Cougars' 16–7 win. The triumph denied the Uteskis a piece of the WAC title. Plus, the win launched BYU into an era of unparalleled success and sent Utah on a downward spiral that, except for an occasional win over the Cougars, would last for two decades.

Or, it could be any one of the three "retribution" BYU victories—1979, 1989, and 1996.

After coughing up a 22–7 third-quarter lead and losing 23–22 to the Uteskis at Rice Stadium in 1978, the Cougars stomped on their northern rivals 27–0 the next year in Cougar Stadium. If 27–0 seemed bad, what about 1989, just a year after the Scott Mitchell-led Uteskis broke a nine-year victory drought over the Cougs with a 57–28 win? Ty Detmer's four TD passes in the first half led to a 49–0 BYU

lead, and the Cougars embarrassed the Uteskis 70–31, with the highest winning point total in the history of the rivalry.

Then there was 1996. After three straight losses to the Uteskis, the first time in thirty years they had suffered such in-state humiliation, BYU turned Utah inside-out with a ferocious running game led by Brian McKenzie and Ronney Jenkins. Passing? All-WAC quarterback Steve Sarkisian threw twelve times (no touchdowns) in the 37–17 win that, by Utah County standards, was the ultimate insult to the Utes, who had been the preseason pick to win not only the WAC Mountain Division title but the overall WAC crown.

But The Game that will stand the test of time, the one with national championship ramifications, and the one which the Cougars needed to retain hopes for the school's only unbeaten season, unfolded on November 17, 1984, in Salt Lake City.

It wasn't that coach LaVell Edwards's Cougars absolutely needed another victory over the Uteskis for in-state bragging rights—BYU had won five in a row over Utah, eleven out of twelve during the Edwards Era. In 1983, Steve Young had humiliated the Uteskis with a six-touchdown passing blitz and a 55–7 win in Provo. It was the revenge motive and the fact that BYU had a new quarterback in Robbie Bosco that fueled the Uteskis' upset hopes. Those factors, plus the fact that the Cougars would surely be feeling the pressure of a 10–0 record and a number-three national ranking.

And there was pressure. BYU turned the ball over five times. Bosco was intercepted, he fumbled, was sacked three times, and, by his standards, had an off day with twenty-seven for forty-four in passing for 367 yards. Still the statistics would show BYU with 521 yards offense, with running back Hema Heimuli piling up 117 of the Cougars' 154 yards rushing.

Fifteen of the twenty-five WAC first-team selections participated in the game on an unseasonably warm late-autumn afternoon. On offense, BYU boasted wide receiver Glen Kozlowski, tight end David Mills, guard Craig

Mark A. Philbrick

BYU's Kyle Morrell upends Eddie Johnson as Cary Whittingham moves up to help cover the play. With this win in 1984, BYU jumped to number one in the nation. They went on to an unde-feated season and ended the year as national champs.

Garrick, center Trevor Matich, and Bosco, while Utah had wideout Danny Huey, guard Carlton Walker, and running back Eddie Johnson. Defensively, the Cougars had tackle Jim Herrmann, linebacker Marv Allen, and safety Kyle Morrell, while Utah sported linemen Filipo Mokofisi and Peter Owens, linebacker Mark Blosch, and return specialist Erroll Tucker.

Eleven Cougars who played in The Game would find themselves in the NFL eventually. Three of them—Matich, linebacker Kurt Gouveia, and kicker Lee Johnson—were still playing in 1996.

It was generally conceded that coach Chuck Stobart needed a win over the Cougars to keep his Utah job, even though his troops entered the game assured of a winning season. The Utes had lost four games by a total of eighteen points and had tied with San Diego State. A 6–4–1 team could beat BYU and finish 7–4–1, and with many returnees for 1985, the Stobart program seemed to be heading in the right direction. But it was his third year, and that was about as much security as Ute coaches could expect.

Although a close friend, Edwards didn't have Stobart's job status on his mind. His Cougars had spun off ten straight wins, but four of them had come by a total of just nineteen points. BYU was unranked at the start of the season, but the voters could hardly ignore an undefeated team; and after bouncing around the top ten from eighth to fourth for a month, only number-one Nebraska and number-two South Carolina were in front of BYU when the Cougs marched into Rice Stadium.

It was a bitter struggle that was tied 7–7 at the end of the first quarter. The same combo that had beaten number three Pitt in the opening game of the season teamed for the first BYU TD. Bosco hurled an eleven-yard pass to Adam Haysbert and Johnson added the point after for a 7–0 BYU lead. Utah got even on Molonai Hola's one-yard TD run and Andre Guardi's extra-point kick. The second-largest Rice Stadium crowd of all time, 36,110, could sense it was in for a tense afternoon.

Johnson's ten-yard field goal accounted for all the scoring in the second quarter, and when Kozlowski made a spectacular catch and scampered in for a nineteen-yard TD in the third quarter, Cougar fans were feeling a rout in the making. Utah quarterback Mark Stevens would have no part of it. He had scored a touchdown that was called back in the second quarter, but in the third, he hooked up with Thurman Beard for an eleven-yard scoring strike. Andre Guardi's extra point narrowed the Ute deficit to 17–14.

The play that ultimately kept BYU's record clean, propelled them to number one in the nation, and spelled the

end of Stobart's Ute coaching career came early in the fourth quarter. Bosco threw his third interception of the game, but at the tail end of the play, Utah's Tucker was flagged for a personal foul, and the Uteskis were moved from the BYU thirty-two yard line back to the forty-seven. Utah got close enough for a Guardi field goal attempt that was unsuccessful.

It was the sliver of light the Cougars had been looking for. After an afternoon of passing frustration, Bosco warmed up and drove BYU sixty yards, with the clinching score a four-yard pass to Kelly Smith. Johnson's PAT made it 24–14 and that was that.

By the time the Cougars were in the dressing room celebrating a perfect 8–0 WAC mark for their ninth straight league crown and luxuriating in the glow of an 11–0 record, they found out Oklahoma had upset number-one-ranked Nebraska and that number-two-ranked South Carolina had been stunned by Navy.

By Monday, the Cougars were ranked number one in the country. The bleeding hearts surfaced with NBC's Bryant Gumble claiming BYU had played a "Bo Diddley Tech" schedule. And of course, Oklahoma's Barry Switzer was crusading for his soon-to-be-scandal-ridden program to be number one in the country. And there was an unending whine from Ute partisans that BYU would be killed by any other school in the top ten.

But under fire, in the midst of a hostile Salt Lake City crowd that screamed its annual kindergarten-like alphabet lesson "B-Y-U Sucks!", BYU had kept its unbeaten record intact. The Cougars would finish the regular season with a home romp over Utah State and then rally to dump the University of Michigan in the Holiday Bowl.

Hail to the undefeated National Champs! Thousands of Uteski fans will go to their graves disputing the honor, many deriding it as more fiction than fact. But hundreds of thousands of Mormons will go to the celestial kingdom with their "We're No. 1" buttons. Imagine the reunion of the cousins on the other side.

Football's Greatest Day

Even if you don't actually remember them yourself, there are a lot of happy memories tucked away in the seventy-eight-game history of the Utah-BYU rivalry.

That may sound a little strange, but just imagine, for example, being a Ute fan during the first six years of the rivalry, 1922–1927. Those were the days of the Ruth and Gehrig Yankees, the Red Grange Bears, Bobby Jones winning golf tournaments.

You choose your sports heroes, I'll choose mine. And mine would be the Utah football team, which hammered the Cougars 49–0 in their first meeting. Salt Lake High, which had been on Utah's schedule just a decade or so earlier, put up a better fight than that. It went on the same way for five more years, with Utah smashing BYU by a cumulative score of 186–13, a margin not seen again until the Cougars' 1996–97 basketball season.

There have been a lot of those sort of Golden Eras in this series, like the identical 43–0 whippings the Utes inflicted in 1931 and 1934. Or, who wouldn't want seats on the fifty-yard-line in 1948 and '49, to watch back-to-back 30–0 and 38–0 routs? And here's to Cactus Jack Curtice, who coached the Utes for eight seasons and never lost to BYU; his last three seasons, Utah outscored the Y 109–15.

Let's hope the good old days have returned, too. Maybe the 1996 game will be just a blip in the middle of a decade or two of domination, one heralded by the sweet three-game winning streak of 1993–95.

There are so many wonderful memories, real and imagined, that one might believe it's difficult to pick out the best one, the one that stands out above it all. But it's not.

You can make a case for one of those early blowouts, I'm sure. I wasn't there, but they certainly sound like fun.

Perhaps you prefer 1978, the year Utah broke LaVell's hex when Randy Gomez quarterbacked Utah to a 23–22 come-from-behind win in Salt Lake. Or maybe your fondest memory was the first 34–31 win, the improbable one that shocked 65,000 in Cougar Stadium in 1993.

The next year was wonderful, too, the one that proved the first was no fluke, the one that ended up propelling Utah into AP's final top ten, the greatest home win for that fabulous Luther Elliss-Mike McCoy team. Choose that one if you like.

Or even 1995, the year Utah widened the gap between the two by manhandling the Cougars 34–17 in Provo. Tough to argue against that one.

But to me, the Greatest Football Game Ever Played will never be topped, probably never even approached. It's a day I still remember clearly, or think I do; truthfully, I probably was a little hazy on the details the very next day.

It's the November 19, 1988, spectacle in Rice Stadium, the game that to Ute fans will forever be known simply by its final score: 57–28.

It's a number I know better than my own phone number. It's a number that still makes me dance—and taunt the nearest person wearing blue. The next dog I own will be named 57–28 (we'll call him "Fifty" for short), and it doesn't strike me as a bad name for a kid, either. Certainly better than "Ty" or "Sark."

In short, it's the unapproachable day, the one moment in football history that makes up for all the unfathomable losses to cellar-dwellers or long afternoons in Provo. (As BYU proved the very next season by hammering Utah 70–31. Didn't matter.)

C'mon, a show of hands: Who still has that game on tape? Who pulls it out every November just to savor Scott Mitchell's passing or Garland Harris's pummeling sack once more? Who still has a chunk of goalpost, sliced up and sold as souvenirs by local Cub Scouts, in their den?

Thought so.

What made that day so special was that it was so unexpected. BYU had ripped the Utes fifteen of the previous sixteen years, the last nine in a row, and there was no reason to suspect 1988 would be any different.

BYU was 8–2 coming in, in the thick of the WAC race as usual, and even though they had nationally ranked Miami coming up two weeks later, there was no reason to

figure they would be overlooking their arch-rivals.

The Utes, meanwhile, were 5–5 and had won three straight. But their defense had allowed five different teams to run up five or more touchdowns on them (a precursor to having the nation's worst defense one year later). They were two-touchdown underdogs to the Cougars and seemed set for the usual frustrating day.

Like all of Jim Fassel's Utah teams, this one was built around the offense, particularly the passing game of Scott Mitchell. Just a sophomore, Mitchell was already establishing himself as the greatest quarterback in school history. Three times that season, Mitchell threw more than sixty passes in a game, and his 631 passing yards against Air Force set a new NCAA record that even the Provo media darlings couldn't touch. Okay, so they lost that game 56–49 because the Falcons set a new rushing record. Still, it was a dangerous offense, one that included Utah's all-time rushing leader Eddie Johnson, and had scored in the forties four times in five weeks.

But the unspoken fear that this game would be like all the rest hung over a lot of us Ute fans as we walked to the stadium that morning to wait for the gates to open. "Just the lead and the ball, that's all I ask," a friend begged. "Just one time and I'll be happy. The lead and the ball."

We asked for so little. The Utes delivered so much.

After all the usual rituals—heckling the BYU band as it piled off buses parked rather naively near the U student line, racing for prime seats in the student section, chanting insults at LaVell and the rest, singing Utah Man about five times—we settled into our seats.

Well, not exactly. I don't remember anybody in our section sitting down the entire day. Anyway, the game kicked off. And on the fourth play of the game, Mitchell was intercepted by Scott Peterson.

Same old Utes, we figured. Everyone did, probably including the Cougars.

Things changed in a hurry. BYU drove fifty yards, but Matt Bellini fumbled a handoff and Sean Knox recovered for Utah. A couple of quick passes later, Mitchell handed

to Johnson and it was 7–0.

That was only the start. BYU turned the ball over eight times that day, and never regained any momentum. Sean Covey, one of the more forgettable names in BYU's QB showcase, kept getting flattened or throwing interceptions, often both on the same play. On one memorable play,

Steve Griffin/THE SALT LAKE TRIBUNE

In a play that summed up the teams' 1988 matchup, Ute linebacker Garland Harris nails BYU QB Sean Covey to the Rice Stadium turf. Covey got the pass away, but it was intercepted.

Harris jackhammered Covey into the AstroTurf just as the quarterback lofted a popup that Greg Smith intercepted downfield. "That felt good," Harris said afterward, and the thousands of us in the stands could relate.

Meanwhile, the Utes scored touchdowns on six of their

nine possessions in the second and third quarters. And with the score 14–0, defensive tackle Sammy Tausinga found the ball in his gut, flung there by a panicked Covey, and rumbled (well, that's not the correct word; that makes the 300-pounder sound too fast) seventeen yards for the most comedic touchdown in the rivalry's history.

It was 27–7 at halftime, and Utah kept pouring it on in the second half. In fact, it could have been much worse. Carl Harry dropped a pass in the end zone once, and Mitchell underthrew him on a wide-open flea-flicker (yep, the Utes were trying everything). And a holding penalty called back Johnson's longest run of the day, a forty-yard breakaway.

The dominance was total, and mystifying. Johnson ran for 112 yards and four touchdowns on twenty-six carries. "I just love it. If I never play football again, I've got this memory. And it's the best," said Johnson, God love him.

And Mitchell was a spectacular leader, throwing for 384 yards against the hometown team that the Springville native spurned to attend the U. "It doesn't get any better than this," said the six-foot-six Golden Child.

The game ended with us chanting "Fassel, Fassel, Fassel . . ." an indication of how powerful the day's delirium was.

I lost my voice that day, but gained several new friends, since our section took up hugging total strangers in joy. (That's a tradition Ron McBride has adopted as his own after beating the Cougars.)

The one regret Ute fans may have about that glorious afternoon is that it ended about ten seconds too soon. Utah had the ball on the BYU eight as the clock expired.

Too bad. Sixty-four twenty-eight is an even better name for a dog.

Epilogue

Forget all their achievements, all the accolades, all the adoration that LaVell Edwards and Ron McBride receive. Suspend your admiration of their more immediate attainments for a moment, and take a step back.

Only by taking the long view can a football fan appreciate the phenomenal success the two coaches have pulled off. It's not so much all the victories, or the bowl games or the championships, not even the beatings they have given each other.

What Edwards and McBride have done is something many times more difficult: They've changed history.

The BYU-Utah rivalry historically resembles a pendulum rocking to and fro, rarely moved from its path but gradually heading for some sort of equilibrium. And the forces that have absorbed the pendulum's momentum and reversed its course are the forces of Edwards's and McBride's wills.

For nearly fifty seasons, Utah's supremacy was unchallenged by the Cougars, with only rare exceptions. The two programs were simply on different levels.

Then Edwards took over in Provo, and suddenly things changed. The pendulum moved the other way, with only two aberrations in the Cougars' success over nearly two decades.

McBride's arrival didn't alter the state of the rivalry quite so abruptly, at least not in the final score. But in some ways, the challenge he faced was bigger, since he took over a team in total disarray at a time when BYU was near the top of its game. Regardless of who did the better job, McBride clearly sent the pendulum back the other way, towards equilibrium—or parity.

Now, the BYU-Utah rivalry may have arrived at a moment nearly unprecedented in its history, a moment of uncertainty over who will dominate. The Utes have won three times in four years, but the Cougars believe their streak-stopping victory in 1996 could signal a return to the previous one-sided affairs.

Especially notable is the fact that both schools have raised their programs to levels undreamed of thirty years ago. Both get a level of respect nationally, both are able to recruit successfully and both seem able to remain contenders for conference titles even in so-called rebuilding years.

It's the first time both schools have achieved that level, a fact that has energized the fans on both sides and added even more meaning to their annual showdown, if that's possible. The players feel it too; historically, many of those in uniform are not native Utahns and don't feel the homegrown animosity that exists in the bleacher seats. When national acclaim and the WAC title are on the line, however, the game grows in stature, rivalry or not.

When Edwards upgraded BYU's program in the early 1970s, it appeared that such a parity was already near, and a natural rivalry with the Arizona schools, which normally competed for the WAC championship, was brewing.

But Utah's program was shortcircuited by a front-office mistake: the hiring of Tom Lovat to coach the Utes in 1974. Under his leadership, Utah's football team lost whatever national stature it owned, and fell far below the Cougars' rising standards. Lovat won just five games in three seasons, while BYU collected two conference crowns. In many ways, the Utes' rise under McBride has been a restoration of the program's former stature.

How is this relevant to today's BYU-Utah rivalry? We may be reaching similar mileposts again.

As the two schools drift toward a middle ground—meaning more competitive football games and nearly equal victories between the two teams—they still face the possibility of sudden upheaval.

The biggest factor can be summed up with one number: sixty-seven. That's how many birthdays Edwards will have had come October 11, and it's a number that soon will become more important to Brigham Young than his 228 wins or eighteen conference championships.

BYU has good reason to be concerned about the next decade, despite the fact that Edwards has signed a contract that extends into the new millennium. They've never had to replace a legend before, and few schools have a fresher understanding of how suddenly a program can sour than BYU. Its basketball team crashed from the heights of an NCAA tournament berth to a disastrous 1-25 season in just three years.

Edwards prefers to avoid them, but the questions linger around his football team: Who will coach the Cougars? Will BYU stay inside its longtime coaching staff, or conduct a nationwide search as the school did for the basketball program? And most importantly, how will the team and recruits respond to new leadership?

The Cougars have retained an aura of stability throughout Edwards's reign, and the Utes have more recently acquired that quality. It's one important factor in the two schools' recent successes, and a critical one if that success is to continue.

Edwards' staff has remained mostly intact throughout his tenure, a fact that would seem to argue for promoting one of his assistants, perhaps offensive coordinator Norm Chow. But the athletics department is now commanded by Rondo Fehlberg, a director without longtime ties to the coaches. He demonstrated that by hiring a non-university coach for the basketball team, picking Steve Cleveland, formerly the boss at a junior college in California. Could a similarly unknown future Cougar coach be toiling on a small-school staff thousands of miles from Utah?

Such a decision will impact BYU, and its bitter rival forty-five miles away, for years to come. The Cougars' relatively narrow recruiting base—Mormons and athletes willing to live by the school's honor-code requirements—makes this verdict crucial.

Still, despite the teams' unusual history, it seems unlikely that one school or the other could own its rival for decades at a time anymore. Even five consecutive victories could become a rarity. The pendulum may finally be settling down somewhere midway between the two combatants in one of sports' unique rivalries.

One thing unique about it is the fact that this matchup presents so few genuine upsets. The best team nearly always wins, to an extent that belies the emotion that normally infuses their games. All the great modern rivalries are pockmarked with occasional drop-dead shockers, but very few games fall into that category in the past three decades of BYU-Utah games. Utah's win in 1978, maybe, and perhaps the extent of the blowouts in 1980 and 1988. Other than that, BYU-Utah games are normally a pretty good barometer of the teams' relative strength.

The Cougars continue to aspire to greater heights, their appetite no doubt whetted by their national championship of 1984. Today, that yearning manifests itself in BYU's upgraded non-conference schedule, an attempt to compensate for the diluted WAC lineup.

Someday soon, however, it could mean leaving the Western Athletic Conference behind, in favor of a stronger, more competitive league. That decision, if made independently of the Utes, would forever alter their relationship, and could water it down just as separation has reduced Utah State's role to little more than an annual exhibition.

Or maybe, to the thousands of Utahns who loathe the Cougars and to their counterparts who can't stand the Utes, it wouldn't matter. The BYU-Utah game will always be the most important line on the schedule, the most anticipated afternoon of the fall. As long as they meet in late November with their fate and their faith on the line, Utah's Unholy War will continue to rage.

All–Unholy War Team

UTAH OFFENSE

Quarterback—Scott Mitchell
Running Back—Eddie Johnson
Running Back—Jamal Anderson
Wide Receiver—Frank Henry
Wide Receiver—Bryan Rowley
Tight End—Dennis Smith
H-Back—Henry Lusk
Center—Lance Scott
Guard—Tony Polychronis
Guard—Roy Ma'afala
Tackle—Anthony Brown
Tackle—Mike Vyfvinkel
Kicker—Chris Yergensen

UTAH DEFENSE

Lineman—Bronzell Miller
Lineman—Luther Elliss
Lineman—Sam Tausinga
Lineman—Henry Kaufusi
Linebacker—Guy Morrell
Linebacker—Mark Rexford
Linebacker—Garland Harris
Cornerback—Erroll Tucker
Cornerback—Ernest Boyd
Safety—Eric Jaconsen
Safety—Harold Lusk
Punter—Marv Bateman
Return Specialist—Erroll Tucker
(punts)
Return Specialist—Cal Beck
(kickoffs)

U of U Sports Information Office

Eddie Johnson holds Utah's career rushing record, but more importantly, he had his greatest game—112 yards and 4 touchdowns—in the Utes' 1988 blowout of BYU.

Tim Kelly/THE SALT LAKE TRIBUNE

Shay Muirbrook was a four-year starting linebacker at BYU. He was the defensive catalyst on the Cougars number-five-ranked 1996 team.

BYU OFFENSE

Quarterback—Ty Detmer
Running Back—Jamal Willis
Running Back—Todd Christensen
Wide Receiver—Glen Kozlowski
Wide Receiver—Eric Drage
Tight End—Gordon Hudson
H-Back—Itula Mili
Center—Bart Oates
Guard—Nick Eyre
Guard—Moe Elewonibi
Tackle—Louis Wong
Tackle—John Hunter
Kicker—David Lauder

BYU DEFENSE

Lineman—Mat Mendenhall
Lineman—Jason Buck
Lineman—Shawn Knight
Lineman—Glen Titensor
Linebacker—Todd Shell
Linebacker—Kurt Gouveia
Linebacker—Shay Muirbrook
Cornerback—Tom Holmoe
Cornerback—Brian Mitchell
Safety—Derwin Gray
Safety—Kyle Morrell
Punter—Lee Johnson
Return Specialist—Vai Sikahema
    (punts)
Return Specialist—James Dye
    (kickoffs)

A Century of Unholy War Crusades

1896—Utah 12, BY Adademy 4
1896—Utah 6, BY Academy 0
1896—BY Academy 8, Utah 6
1897—BY Academy 14, Utah 0
1897—BY Academy 22, Utah 0
1898—Utah 5, BYU 0
1922—Utah 49, BYU 0
1923—Utah 15, BYU 0
1924—Utah 35, BYU 6
1925—Utah 27, BYU 0
1926—Utah 40, BYU 7
1927—Utah 20, BYU 0
1928—Utah 0, BYU 0 (tie)
1929—Utah 45, BYU 13
1930—Utah 34, BYU 7
1931—Utah 43, BYU 0
1932—Utah 29, BYU 0
1933—Utah 21, BYU 6
1934—Utah 43, BYU 0
1935—Utah 32, BYU 0
1936—Utah 18, BYU 0
1937—Utah 14, BYU 0
1938—Utah 7, BYU 7 (tie)
1939—Utah 35, BYU 13
1940—Utah 12, BYU 6
1941—Utah 6, BYU 6 (tie)
1942—BYU 12, Utah 7
1946—Utah 35, BYU 6
1947—Utah 28, BYU 6
1948—Utah 30, BYU 0
1949—Utah 38, BYU 0
1950—Utah 28, BYU 28 (tie)
1951—Utah 7, BYU 6
1952—Utah 34, BYU 6
1953—Utah 33, BYU 32
1954—Utah 12, BYU 7
1955—Utah 41, BYU 9
1956—Utah 41, BYU 6
1957—Utah 27, BYU 0

1958—BYU 14, Utah 7
1959—Utah 20, BYU 8
1960—Utah 17, BYU 0
1961—Utah 21, BYU 20
1962—Utah 35, BYU 20
1963—Utah 15, BYU 6
1964—Utah 47, BYU 13
1965—BYU 25, Utah 20
1966—BYU 35, Utah 13
1967—BYU 17, Utah 13
1968—Utah 30, BYU 21
1969—Utah 16, BYU 6
1970—Utah 14, BYU 13
1971—Utah 17, BYU 15
1972—BYU 16, Utah 7
1973—BYU 46, Utah 22
1974—BYU 48, Utah 20
1975—BYU 51, Utah 20
1976—BYU 34, Utah 12
1977—BYU 38, Utah 8
1978—Utah 23, BYU 22
1979—BYU 27, Utah 0
1980—BYU 56, Utah 6
1981—BYU 56, Utah 28
1982—BYU 17, Utah 12
1983—BYU 55, Utah 7
1984—BYU 24, Utah 14
1985—BYU 38, Utah 28
1986—BYU 35, Utah 21
1987—BYU 21, Utah 18
1988—Utah 57, BYU 28
1989—BYU 70, Utah 31
1990—BYU 45, Utah 22
1991—BYU 48, Utah 17
1992—BYU 31, Utah 22
1993—Utah 34, BYU 31
1994—Utah 34, BYU 31
1995—Utah 34, BYU 17
1996—BYU 37, Utah 17